HAPTER 8

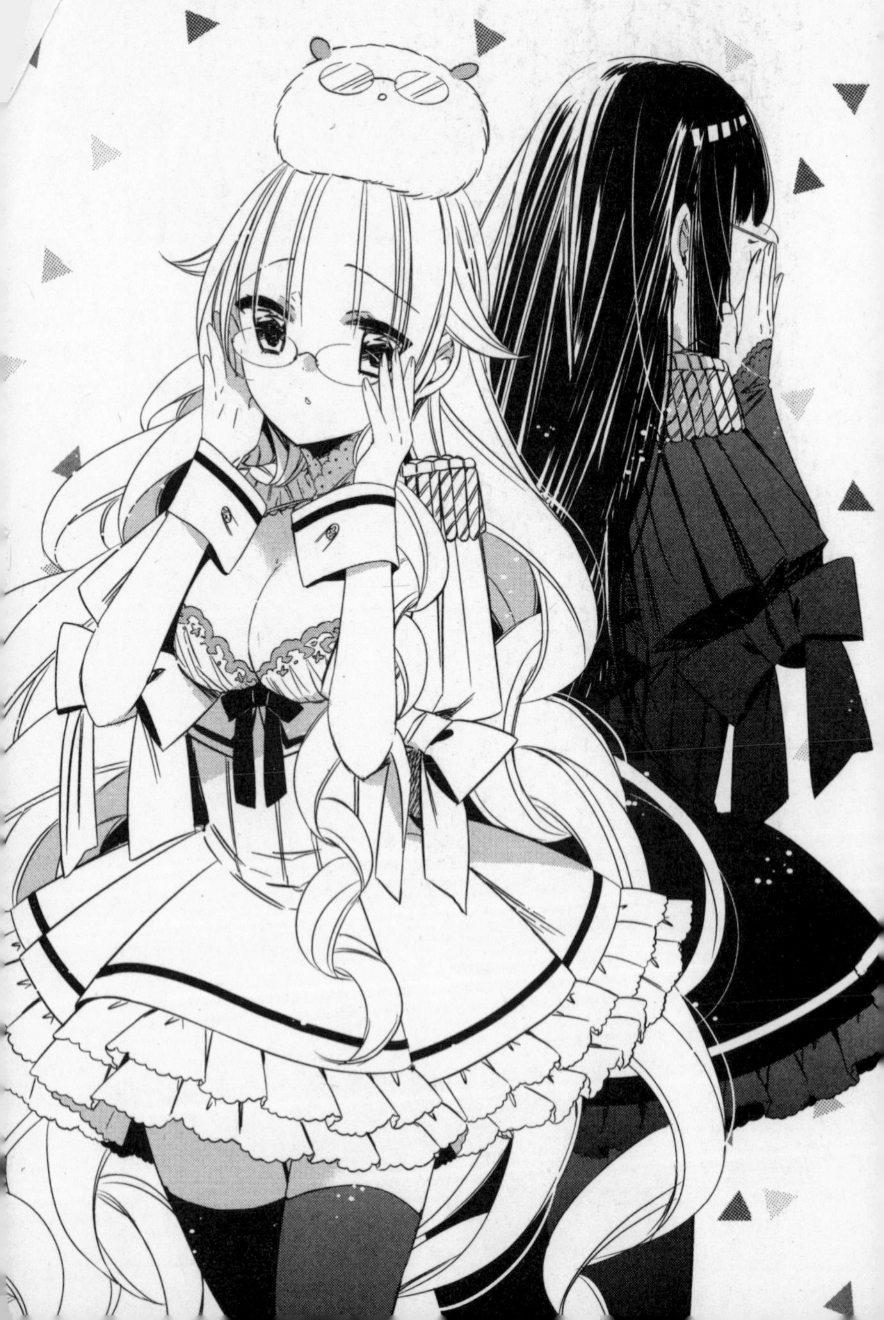

TRAINING

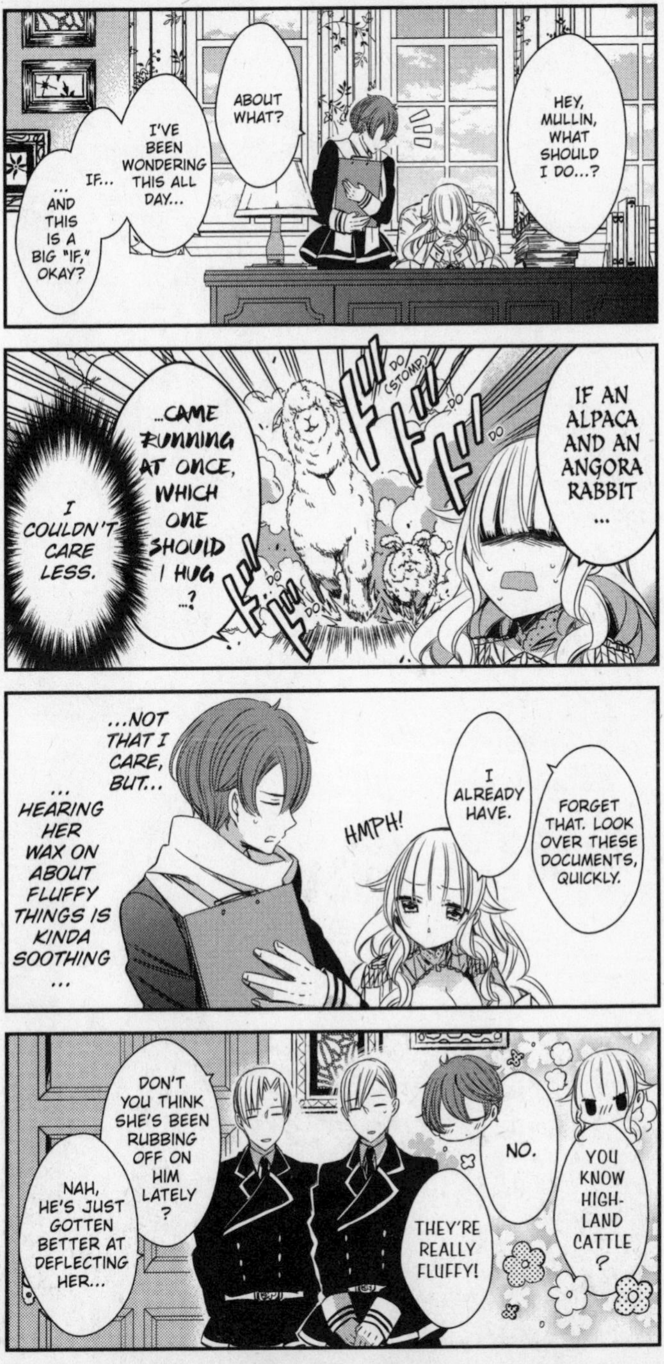
HEY, MULLIN, WHAT SHOULD I DO...?
ABOUT WHAT?
I'VE BEEN WONDERING THIS ALL DAY...
IF...
... AND THIS IS A BIG "IF," OKAY?
IF AN ALPACA AND AN ANGORA RABBIT ...
DO
DO (STOMP)
DO
...CAME RUNNING AT ONCE, WHICH ONE SHOULD I HUG ...?
DO DO
I COULDN'T CARE LESS.
FORGET THAT. LOOK OVER THESE DOCUMENTS, QUICKLY.
I ALREADY HAVE.
HMPH!
...NOT THAT I CARE, BUT...
... HEARING HER WAX ON ABOUT FLUFFY THINGS IS KINDA SOOTHING ...
YOU KNOW HIGH-LAND CATTLE ?
NO.
THEY'RE REALLY FLUFFY!
DON'T YOU THINK SHE'S BEEN RUBBING OFF ON HIM LATELY ?
NAH, HE'S JUST GOTTEN BETTER AT DEFLECTING HER...

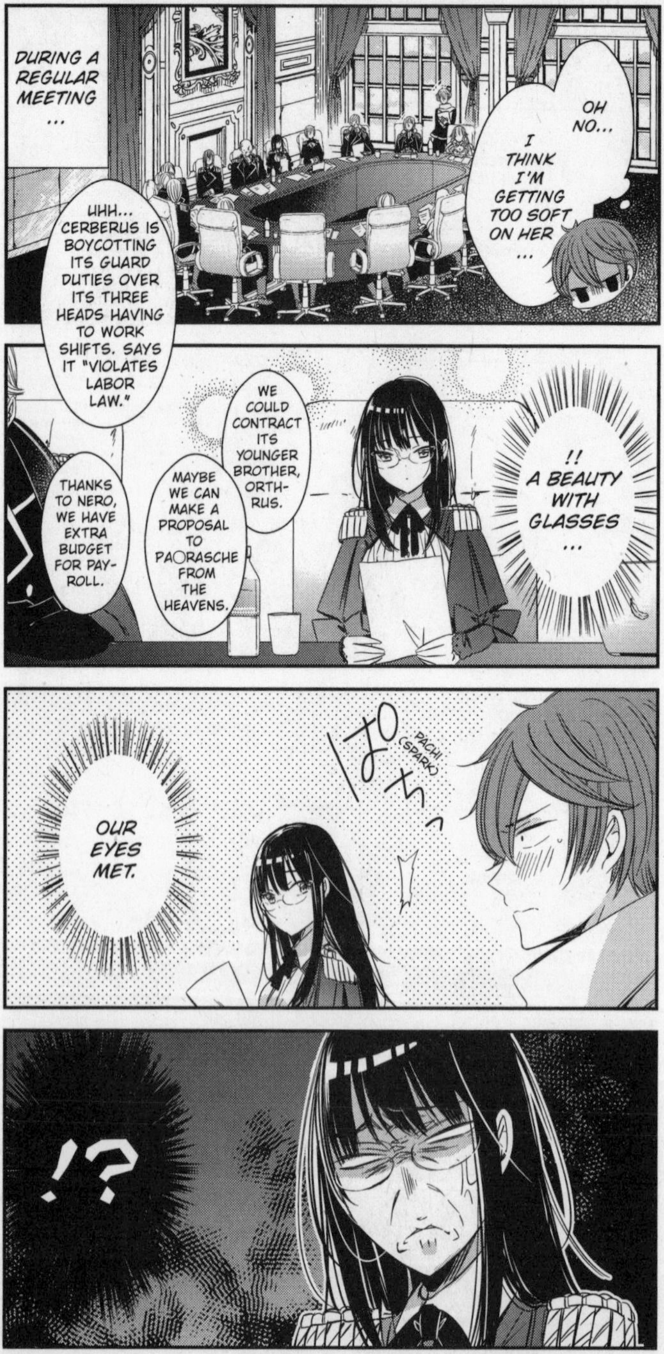
OH NO... I THINK I'M GETTING TOO SOFT ON HER...
DURING A REGULAR MEETING...
UHH... CERBERUS IS BOYCOTTING ITS GUARD DUTIES OVER ITS THREE HEADS HAVING TO WORK SHIFTS. SAYS IT "VIOLATES LABOR LAW."
!! A BEAUTY WITH GLASSES...
WE COULD CONTRACT ITS YOUNGER BROTHER, ORTH-RUS.
MAYBE WE CAN MAKE A PROPOSAL TO PA○RASCHE FROM THE HEAVENS.
THANKS TO NERO, WE HAVE EXTRA BUDGET FOR PAY-ROLL.
PACHI (SPARK)
OUR EYES MET.
!?

A GHASTLY EXPRESSION

A BEAUTY WITH A GHASTLY EXPRESSION

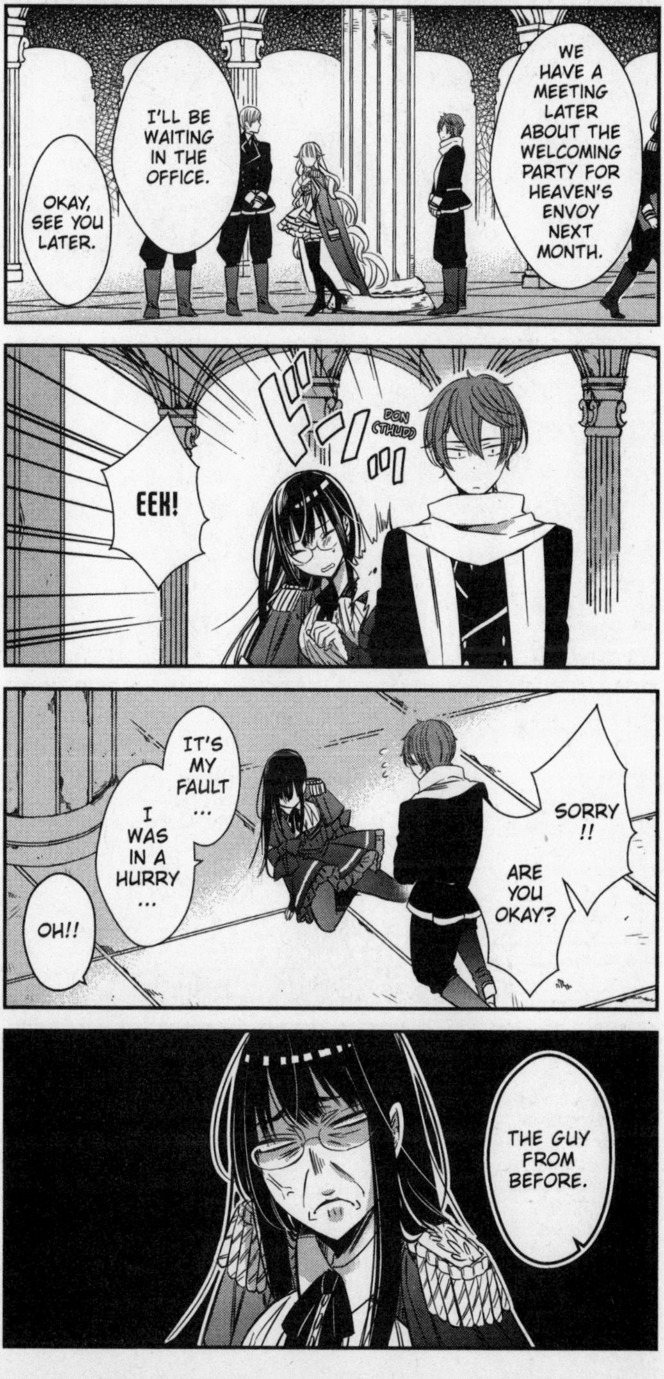
WE HAVE A MEETING LATER ABOUT THE WELCOMING PARTY FOR HEAVEN'S ENVOY NEXT MONTH.
I'LL BE WAITING IN THE OFFICE.
OKAY, SEE YOU LATER.
DON (THUD)
EEK!
SORRY!!
ARE YOU OKAY?
IT'S MY FAULT...
I WAS IN A HURRY...
OH!!
THE GUY FROM BEFORE.

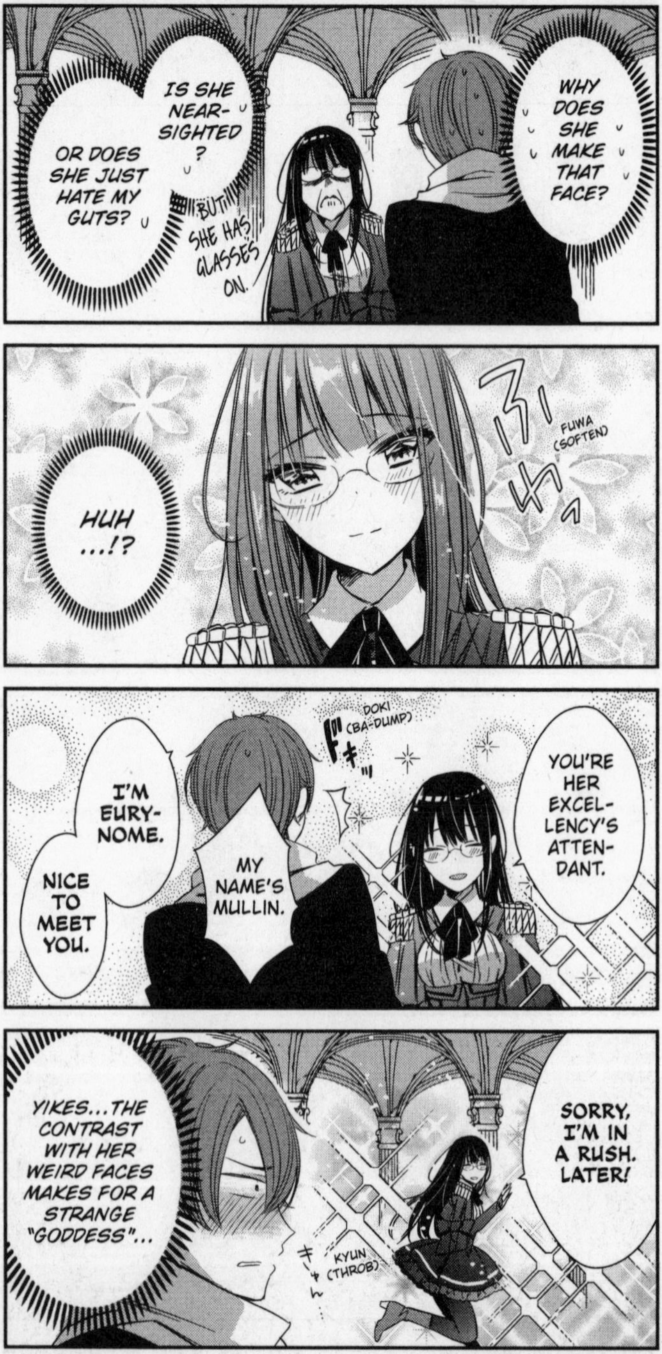
WHY DOES SHE MAKE THAT FACE?
IS SHE NEAR-SIGHTED?
BUT SHE HAS GLASSES ON.
OR DOES SHE JUST HATE MY GUTS?
ふわっ
FUWA (SOFTEN)
HUH...!?
YOU'RE HER EXCELLENCY'S ATTENDANT.
ドキッ
DOKI (BA-DUMP)
MY NAME'S MULLIN.
I'M EURYNOME.
NICE TO MEET YOU.
SORRY, I'M IN A RUSH. LATER!
キュん
KYUN (THROB)
YIKES...THE CONTRAST WITH HER WEIRD FACES MAKES FOR A STRANGE "GODDESS"...

TOO CLOSE!

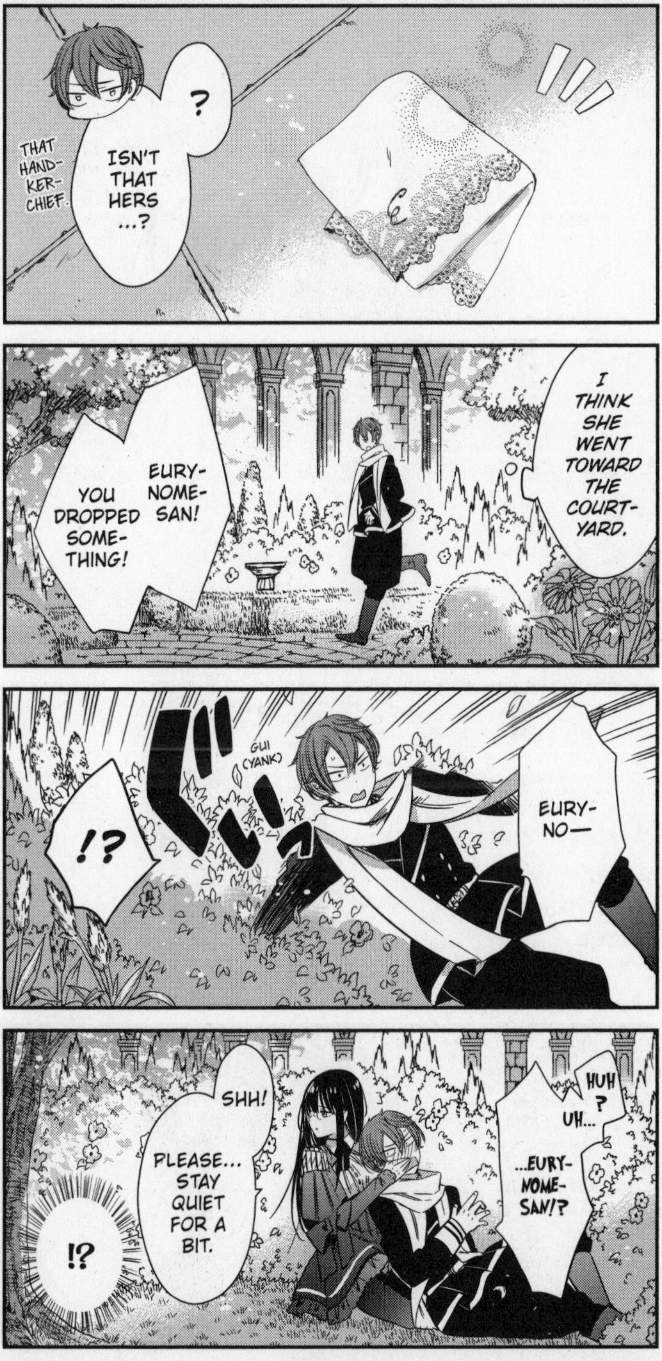
?
ISN'T THAT HERS ...?
THAT HANDKERCHIEF.
I THINK SHE WENT TOWARD THE COURTYARD.
EURYNOME-SAN!
YOU DROPPED SOMETHING!
EURY-NO—
GUI (YANK)
!?
HUH? UH...
...EURYNOME-SAN!?
SHH!
PLEASE... STAY QUIET FOR A BIT.
!?

BEAUTY WASTED

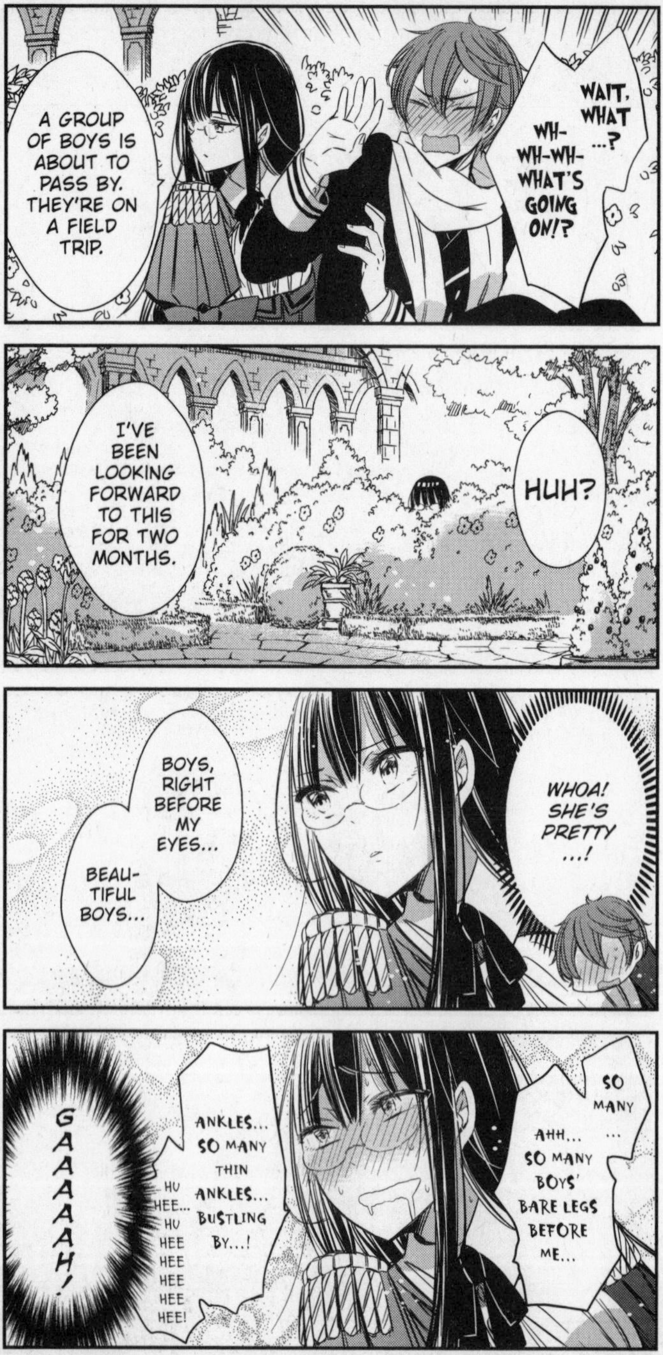
WAIT, WHAT ...?
WH-WH-WH-WHAT'S GOING ON!?
A GROUP OF BOYS IS ABOUT TO PASS BY. THEY'RE ON A FIELD TRIP.
HUH?
I'VE BEEN LOOKING FORWARD TO THIS FOR TWO MONTHS.
WHOA! SHE'S PRETTY ...!
BOYS, RIGHT BEFORE MY EYES...
BEAUTIFUL BOYS...
SO MANY ...
AHH... SO MANY BOYS' BARE LEGS BEFORE ME...
ANKLES... SO MANY THIN ANKLES... BUSTLING BY...!
HU HEE... HU HEE HEE HEE HEE HEE!
GAAAAAH!

TURNING TO SAND

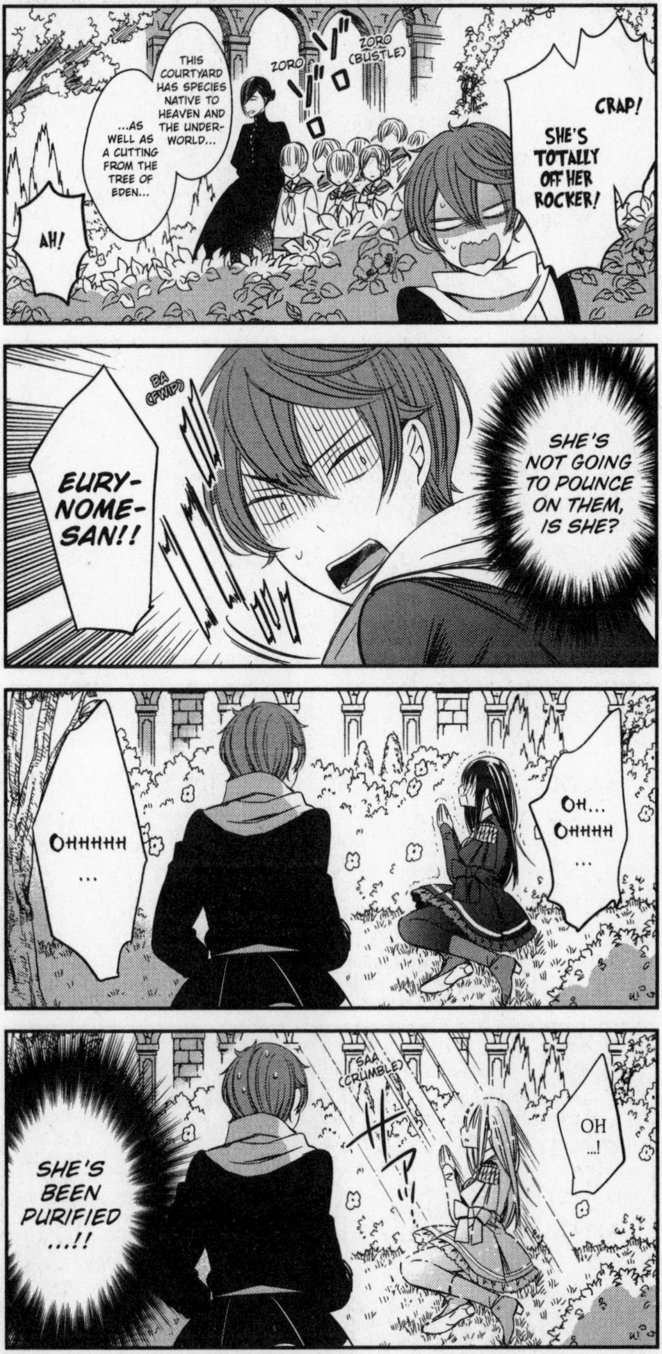
CRAP!
SHE'S TOTALLY OFF HER ROCKER!
ZORO (BUSTLE)
ZORO
THIS COURTYARD HAS SPECIES NATIVE TO HEAVEN AND THE UNDER-WORLD...
...AS WELL AS A CUTTING FROM THE TREE OF EDEN...
AH!
SHE'S NOT GOING TO POUNCE ON THEM, IS SHE?
BA (FWIP)
EURY-NOME-SAN!!
OH... OHHHH ...
OHHHHH ...
OH ...!
SAA (CRUMBLE)
SHE'S BEEN PURIFIED ...!!

DEFINITELY NOT HEALTHY

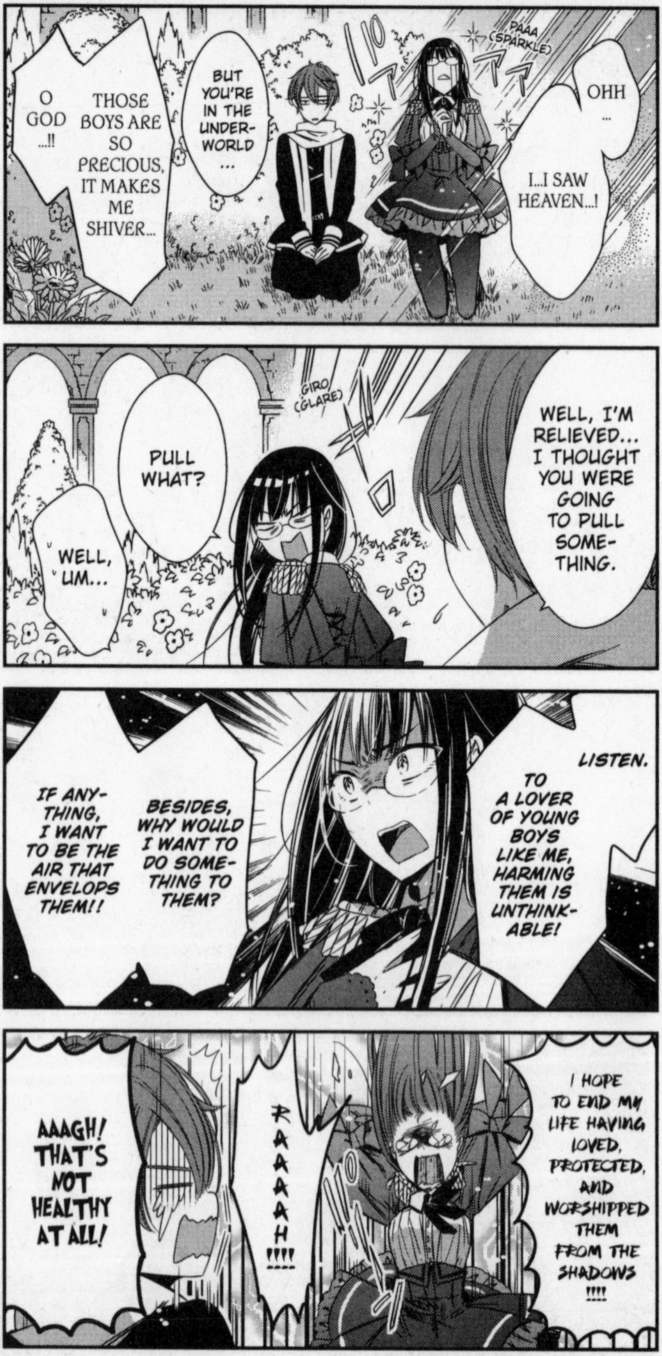
PAAA (SPARKLE)
OHH ...
I...I SAW HEAVEN...!
BUT YOU'RE IN THE UNDERWORLD ...
O GOD ...!!
THOSE BOYS ARE SO PRECIOUS, IT MAKES ME SHIVER...
WELL, I'M RELIEVED... I THOUGHT YOU WERE GOING TO PULL SOMETHING.
GIRO (GLARE)
PULL WHAT?
WELL, UM...
LISTEN.
TO A LOVER OF YOUNG BOYS LIKE ME, HARMING THEM IS UNTHINKABLE!
BESIDES, WHY WOULD I WANT TO DO SOMETHING TO THEM?
IF ANYTHING, I WANT TO BE THE AIR THAT ENVELOPS THEM!!
I HOPE TO END MY LIFE HAVING LOVED, PROTECTED, AND WORSHIPPED THEM FROM THE SHADOWS!!!!
RAAAAAAH!!!!
AAAGH! THAT'S NOT HEALTHY AT ALL!

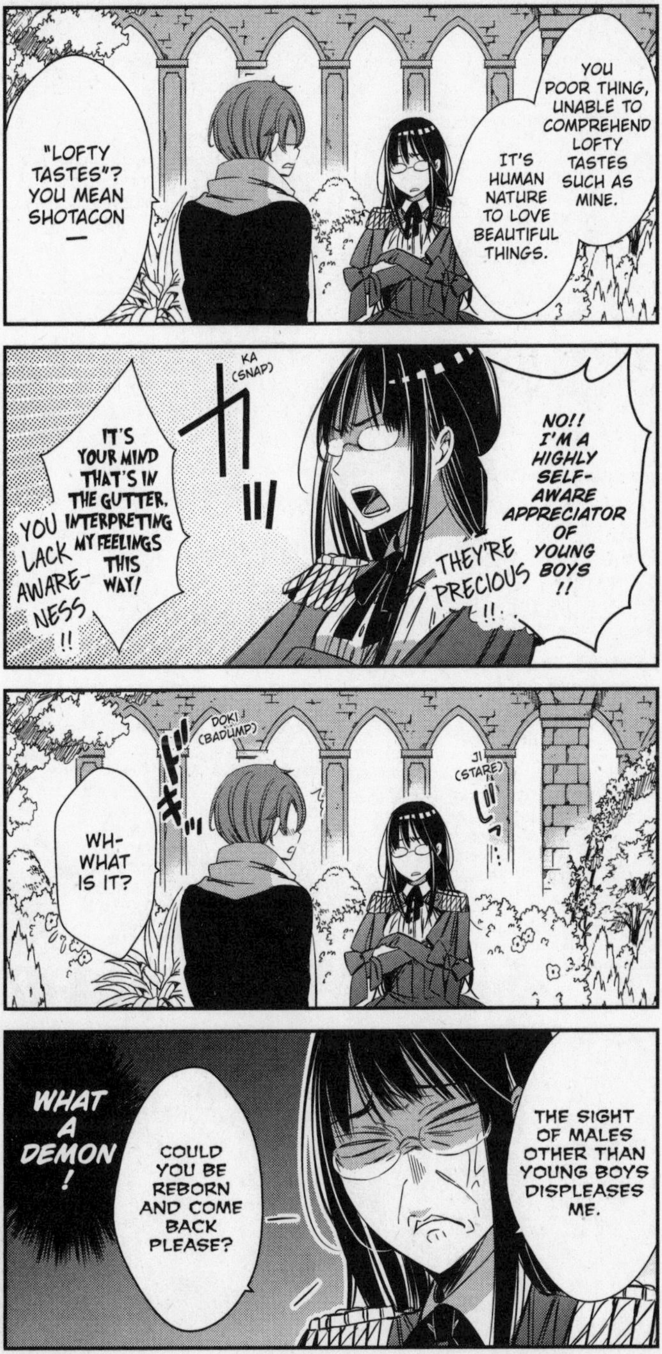
YOU POOR THING, UNABLE TO COMPREHEND LOFTY TASTES SUCH AS MINE.
IT'S HUMAN NATURE TO LOVE BEAUTIFUL THINGS.
"LOFTY TASTES"? YOU MEAN SHOTACON —
NO!! I'M A HIGHLY SELF-AWARE APPRECIATOR OF YOUNG BOYS !!
THEY'RE PRECIOUS !!
KA (SNAP)
IT'S YOUR MIND THAT'S IN THE GUTTER, INTERPRETING MY FEELINGS THIS WAY!
YOU LACK AWARENESS !!
JI (STARE)
DOKI (BADUMP)
WH-WHAT IS IT?
THE SIGHT OF MALES OTHER THAN YOUNG BOYS DISPLEASES ME.
COULD YOU BE REBORN AND COME BACK PLEASE?
WHAT A DEMON !

SO THAT'S WHAT HER EXPRESSION MEANS?

A FILTER CALLED "WINGS OF IMAGINATION"

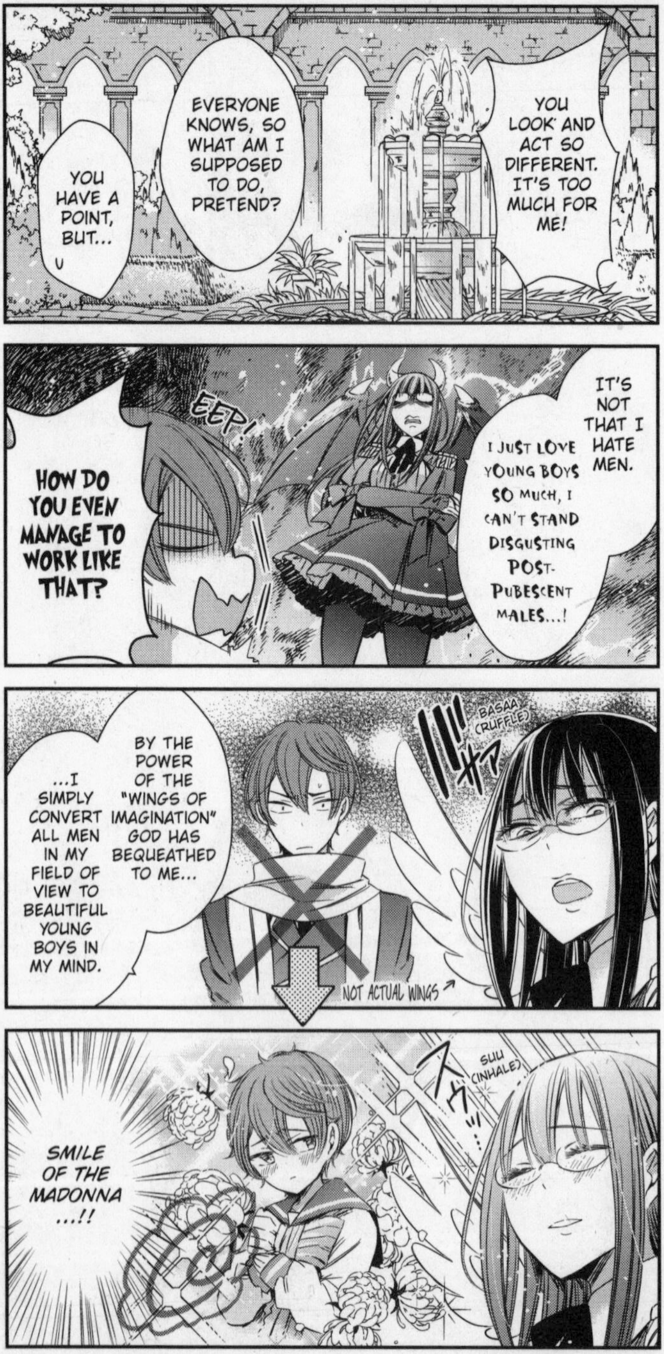
YOU LOOK AND ACT SO DIFFERENT. IT'S TOO MUCH FOR ME!
EVERYONE KNOWS, SO WHAT AM I SUPPOSED TO DO, PRETEND?
YOU HAVE A POINT, BUT...
IT'S NOT THAT I HATE MEN.
I JUST LOVE YOUNG BOYS SO MUCH, I CAN'T STAND DISGUSTING POST-PUBESCENT MALES...!
EEP!
HOW DO YOU EVEN MANAGE TO WORK LIKE THAT?
BASAA (RUFFLE)
BY THE POWER OF THE "WINGS OF IMAGINATION" GOD HAS BEQUEATHED TO ME...
...I SIMPLY CONVERT ALL MEN IN MY FIELD OF VIEW TO BEAUTIFUL YOUNG BOYS IN MY MIND.
NOT ACTUAL WINGS
SUU (INHALE)
SMILE OF THE MADONNA ...!!

THE PERSISTENT TYPE

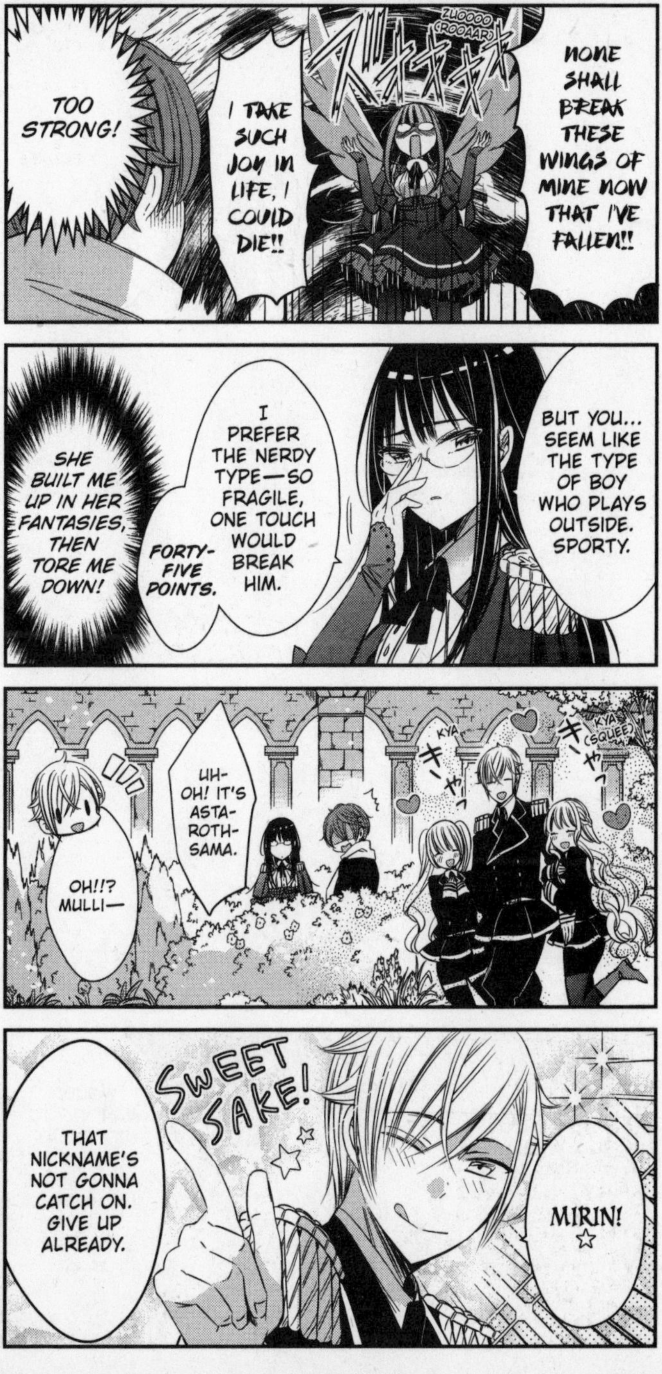
ZUOOOO (ROOAAR)
NONE SHALL BREAK THESE WINGS OF MINE NOW THAT I'VE FALLEN!!
I TAKE SUCH JOY IN LIFE, I COULD DIE!!
TOO STRONG!
BUT YOU... SEEM LIKE THE TYPE OF BOY WHO PLAYS OUTSIDE. SPORTY.
I PREFER THE NERDY TYPE—SO FRAGILE, ONE TOUCH WOULD BREAK HIM.
FORTY-FIVE POINTS.
SHE BUILT ME UP IN HER FANTASIES, THEN TORE ME DOWN!
KYA (SQUEE)
KYA
UH-OH! IT'S ASTAROTH-SAMA.
OH!!? MULLI—
MIRIN! ☆
SWEET SAKE!
THAT NICKNAME'S NOT GONNA CATCH ON. GIVE UP ALREADY.

BRUTAL

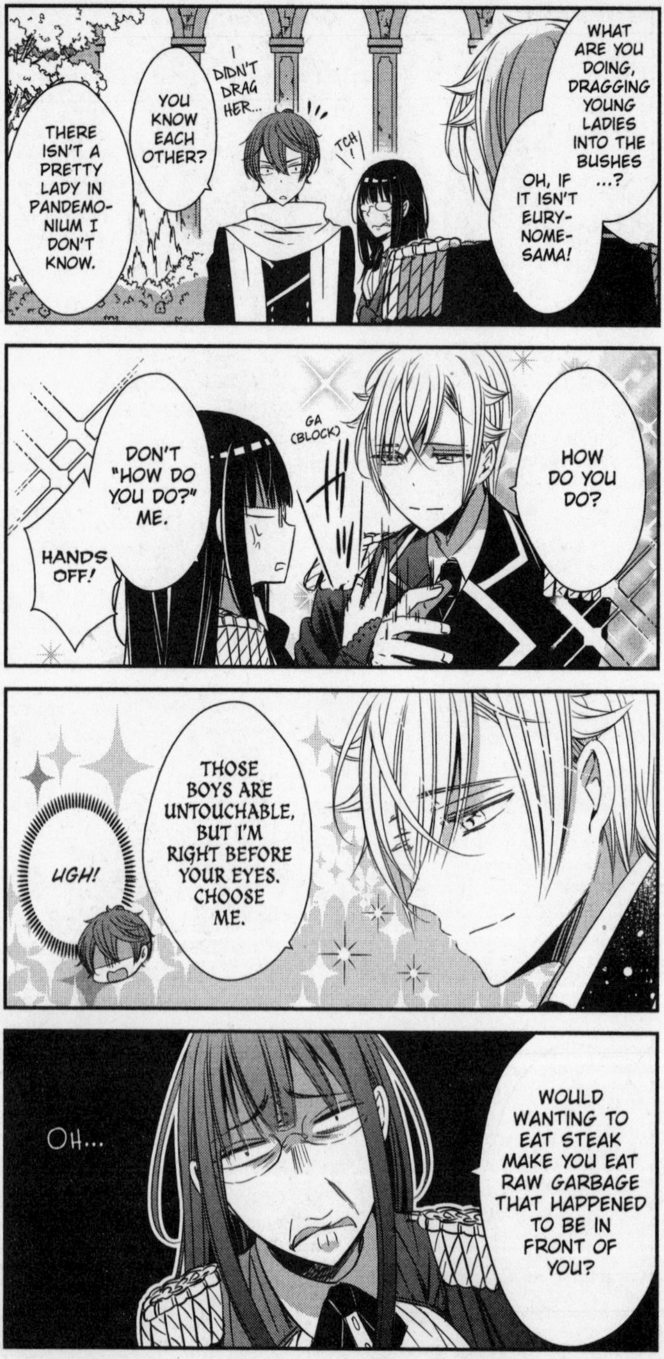
WHAT ARE YOU DOING, DRAGGING YOUNG LADIES INTO THE BUSHES ...?
OH, IF IT ISN'T EURYNOME-SAMA!
TCH!
I DIDN'T DRAG HER...
YOU KNOW EACH OTHER?
THERE ISN'T A PRETTY LADY IN PANDEMONIUM I DON'T KNOW.
HOW DO YOU DO?
GA (BLOCK)
DON'T "HOW DO YOU DO?" ME.
HANDS OFF!
THOSE BOYS ARE UNTOUCHABLE, BUT I'M RIGHT BEFORE YOUR EYES. CHOOSE ME.
UGH!
WOULD WANTING TO EAT STEAK MAKE YOU EAT RAW GARBAGE THAT HAPPENED TO BE IN FRONT OF YOU?
OH...

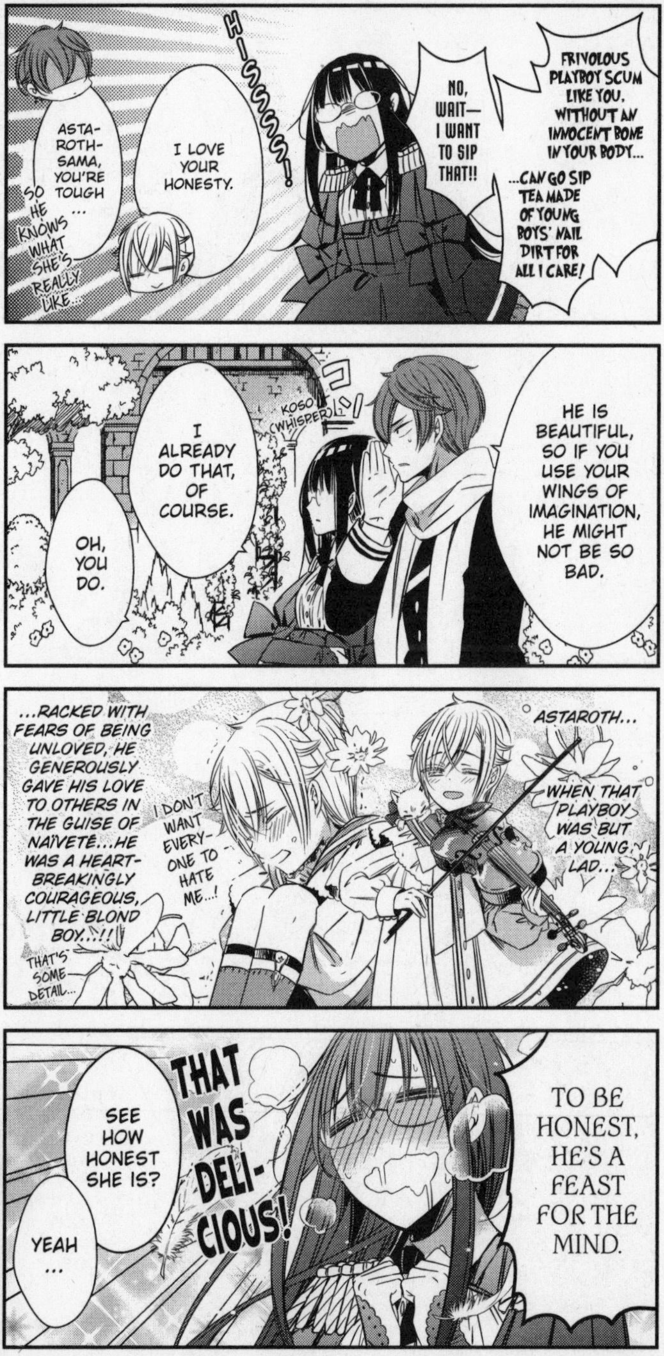
FRIVOLOUS PLAYBOY SCUM LIKE YOU, WITHOUT AN INNOCENT BONE IN YOUR BODY...
...CAN GO SIP TEA MADE OF YOUNG BOYS' NAIL DIRT FOR ALL I CARE!
NO, WAIT— I WANT TO SIP THAT!!
HISSSSS!
I LOVE YOUR HONESTY.
ASTAROTH-SAMA, YOU'RE TOUGH...
SO HE KNOWS WHAT SHE'S REALLY LIKE...
HE IS BEAUTIFUL, SO IF YOU USE YOUR WINGS OF IMAGINATION, HE MIGHT NOT BE SO BAD.
KOSO (WHISPER)
I ALREADY DO THAT, OF COURSE.
OH, YOU DO.
ASTAROTH...
WHEN THAT PLAYBOY WAS BUT A YOUNG LAD...
I DON'T WANT EVERYONE TO HATE ME...!
...RACKED WITH FEARS OF BEING UNLOVED, HE GENEROUSLY GAVE HIS LOVE TO OTHERS IN THE GUISE OF NAÏVETÉ...HE WAS A HEART-BREAKINGLY COURAGEOUS, LITTLE BLOND BOY...!!
THAT'S SOME DETAIL...
TO BE HONEST, HE'S A FEAST FOR THE MIND.
THAT WAS DELICIOUS!
SEE HOW HONEST SHE IS?
YEAH...

INNOCENT IN A WAY

HARD-CORE "PLAY"

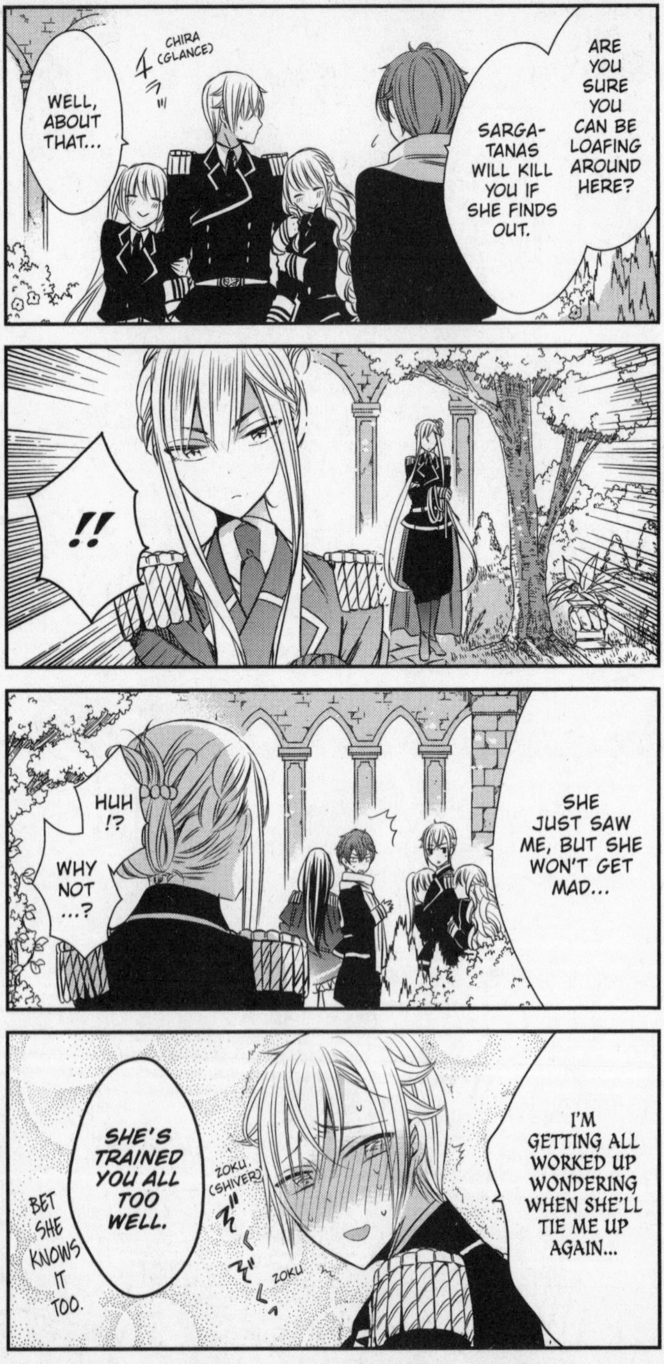
ARE YOU SURE YOU CAN BE LOAFING AROUND HERE?
SARGA-TANAS WILL KILL YOU IF SHE FINDS OUT.
CHIRA (GLANCE)
WELL, ABOUT THAT...
!!
SHE JUST SAW ME, BUT SHE WON'T GET MAD...
HUH!?
WHY NOT...?
I'M GETTING ALL WORKED UP WONDERING WHEN SHE'LL TIE ME UP AGAIN...
ZOKU (SHIVER)
ZOKU
SHE'S TRAINED YOU ALL TOO WELL.
BET SHE KNOWS IT TOO.

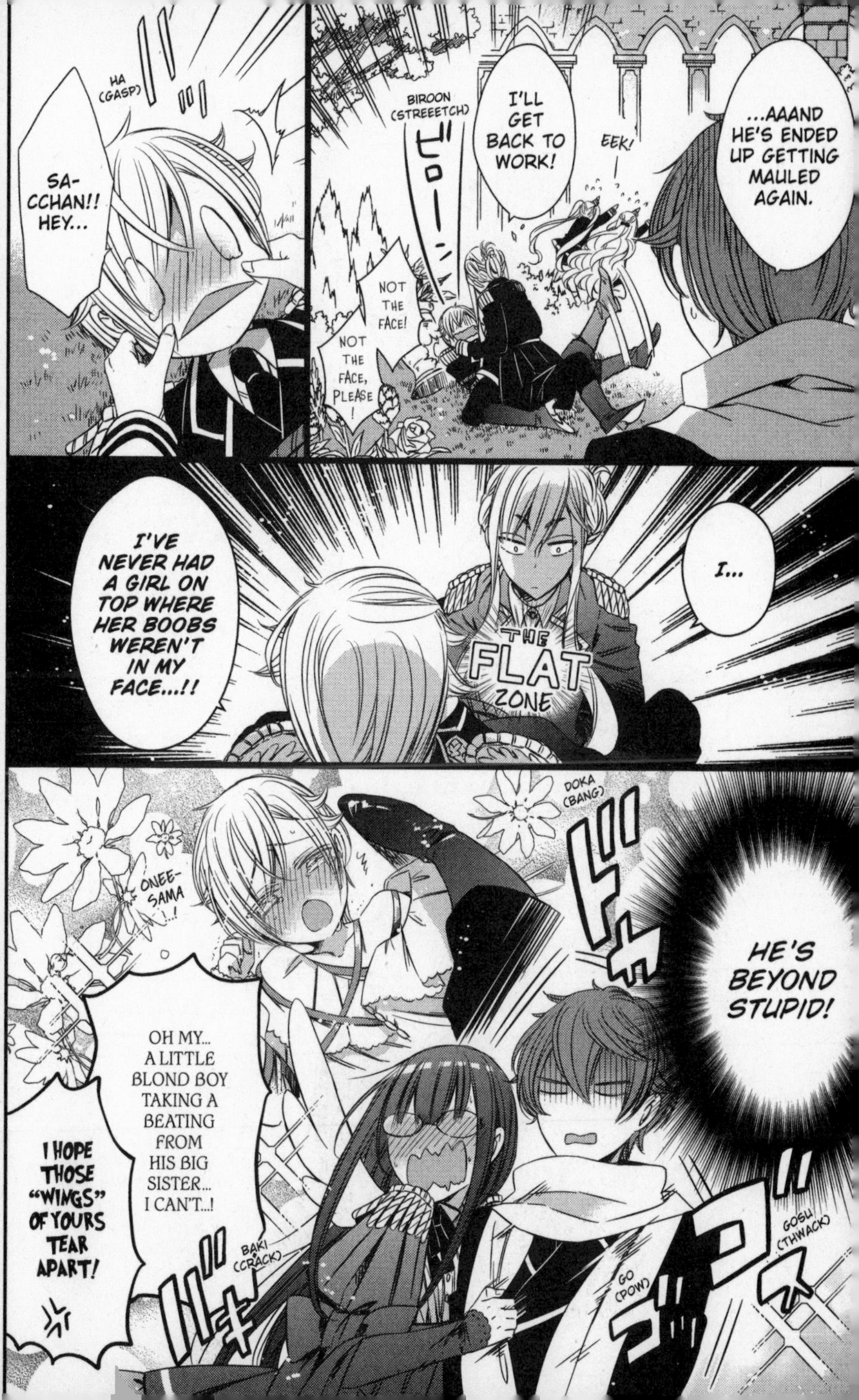
...AAAND HE'S ENDED UP GETTING MAULED AGAIN.
EEK!
I'LL GET BACK TO WORK!
BIROON (STREEETCH)
NOT THE FACE!
NOT THE FACE, PLEASE!
HA (GASP)
SA-CCHAN!! HEY...
I...
I'VE NEVER HAD A GIRL ON TOP WHERE HER BOOBS WEREN'T IN MY FACE...!!
THE FLAT ZONE
HE'S BEYOND STUPID!
DOKA (BANG)
GOSU (THWACK)
GO (POW)
ONEE-SAMA..!
OH MY... A LITTLE BLOND BOY TAKING A BEATING FROM HIS BIG SISTER... I CAN'T...!
BAKI (CRACK)
I HOPE THOSE "WINGS" OF YOURS TEAR APART!

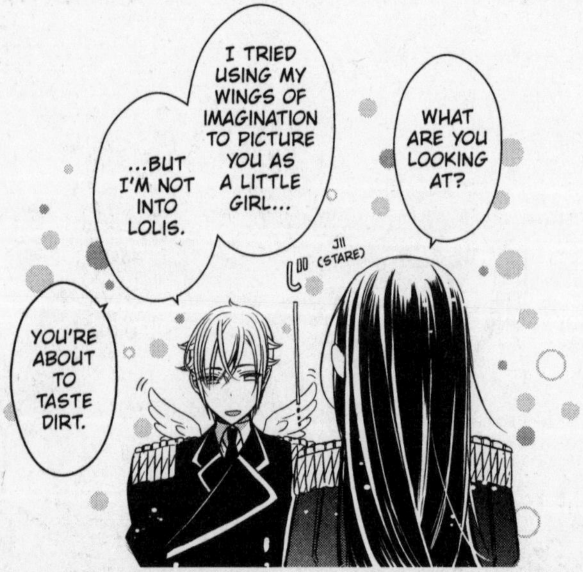
WHAT ARE YOU LOOKING AT?
JII (STARE)
I TRIED USING MY WINGS OF IMAGINATION TO PICTURE YOU AS A LITTLE GIRL...
...BUT I'M NOT INTO LOLIS.
YOU'RE ABOUT TO TASTE DIRT.

As Miss Beelzebub Likes

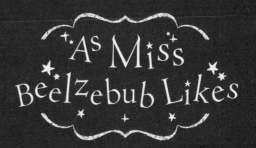

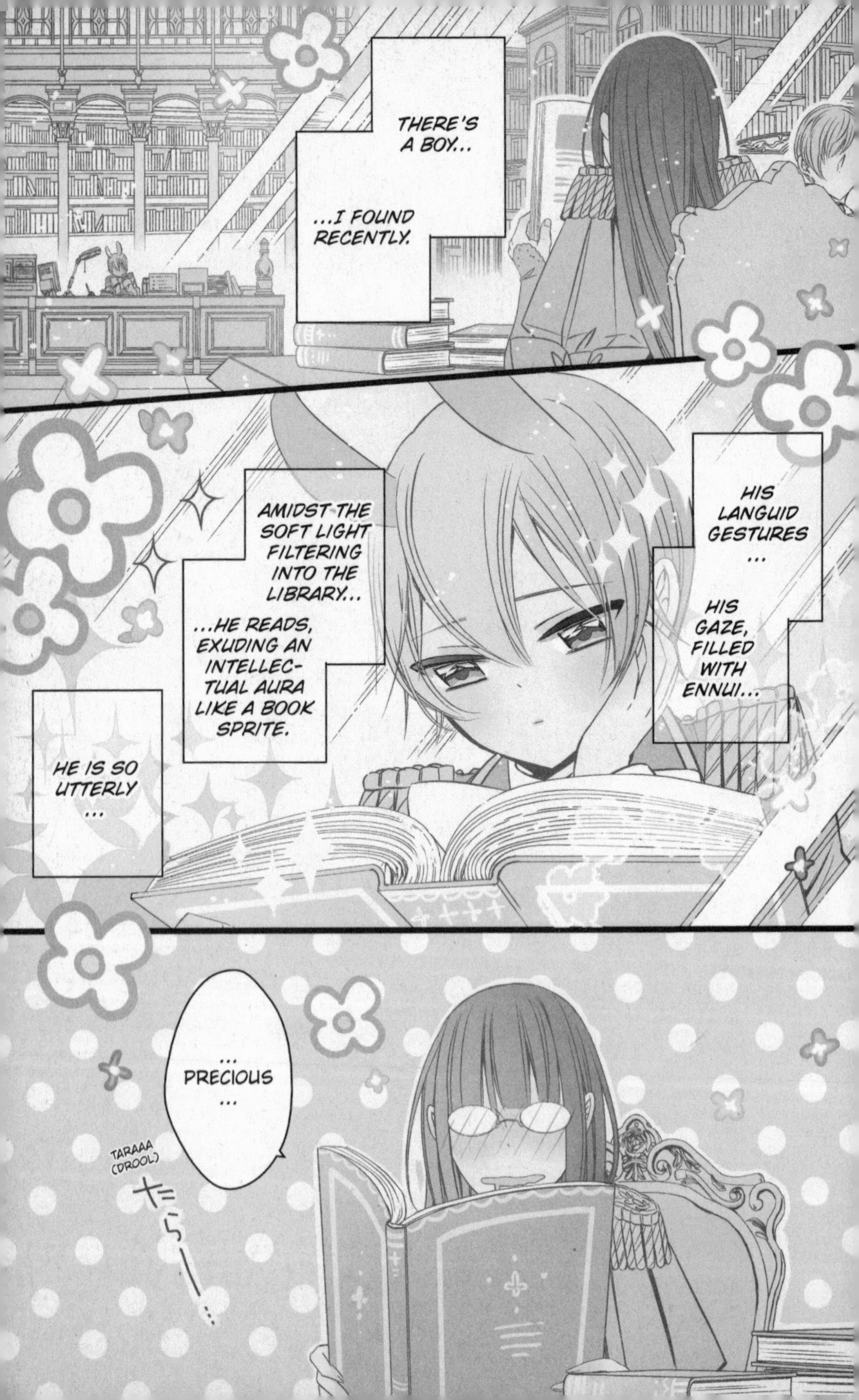
THERE'S A BOY...
...I FOUND RECENTLY.
HIS LANGUID GESTURES...
HIS GAZE, FILLED WITH ENNUI...
AMIDST THE SOFT LIGHT FILTERING INTO THE LIBRARY...
...HE READS, EXUDING AN INTELLECTUAL AURA LIKE A BOOK SPRITE.
HE IS SO UTTERLY...
...PRECIOUS...
TARAAA (DROOL)
たらー…

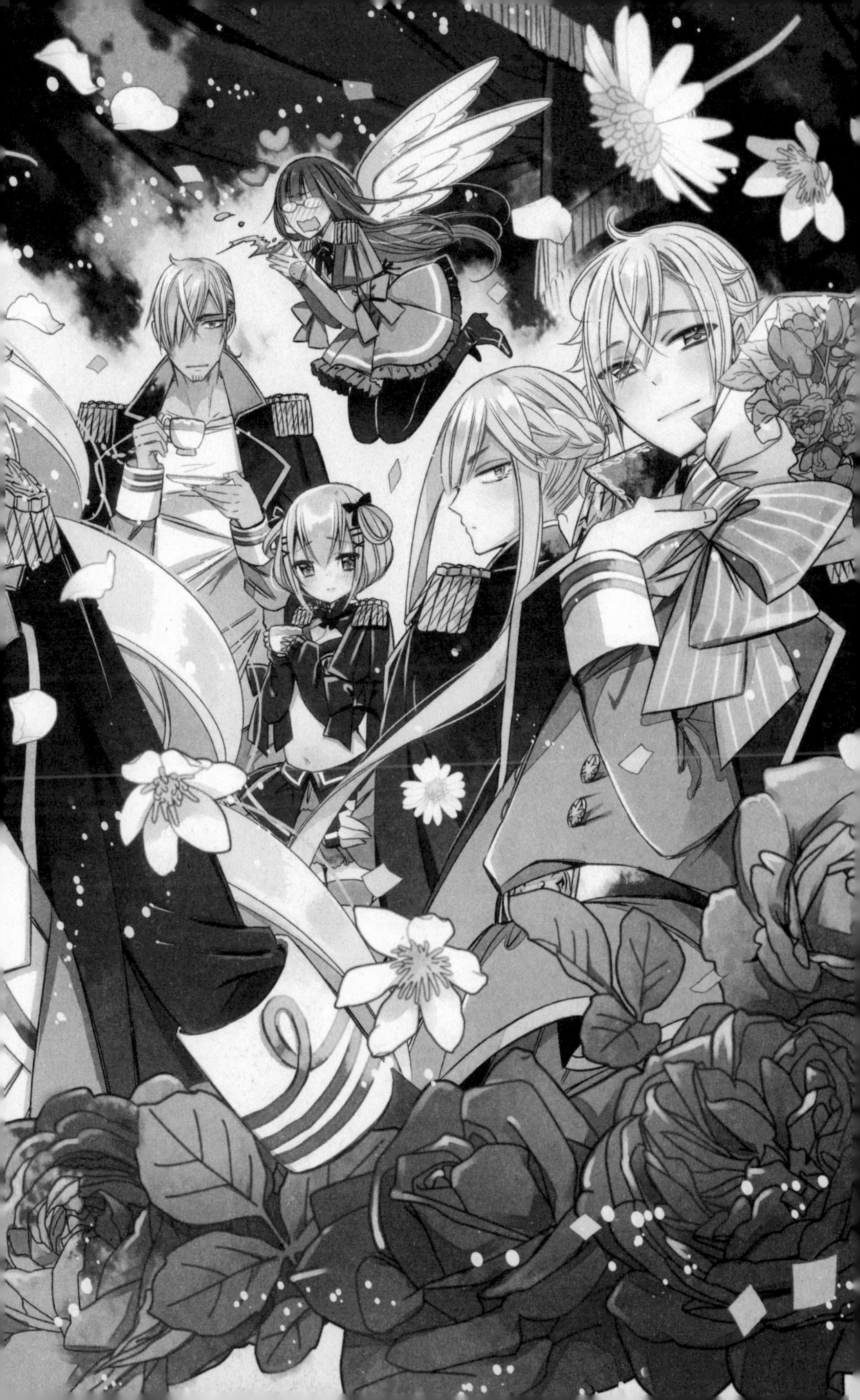

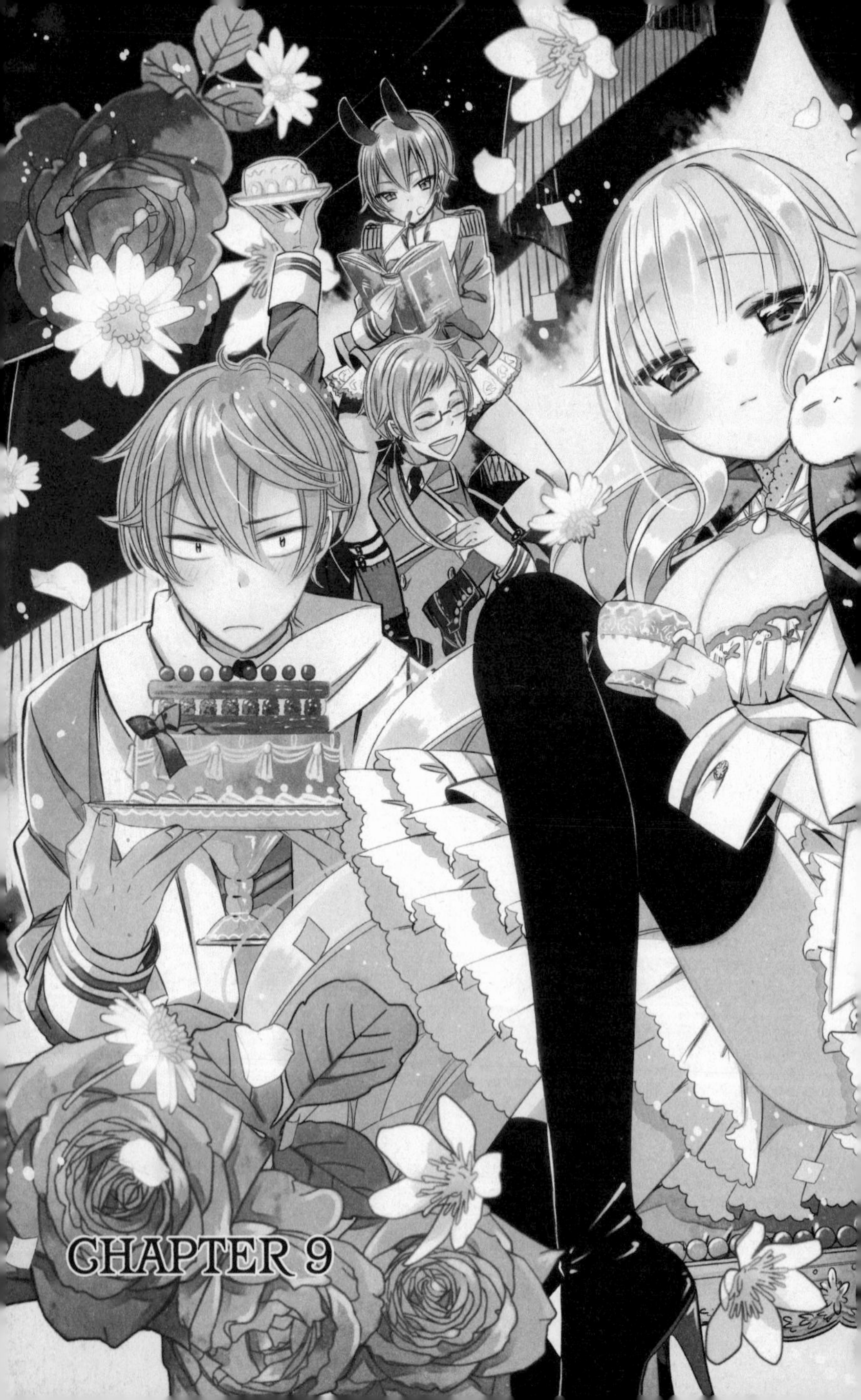
CHAPTER 9

As Miss Beelzebub Likes

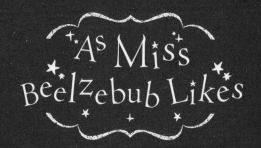

BRO: EVER TRUE TO HIMSELF

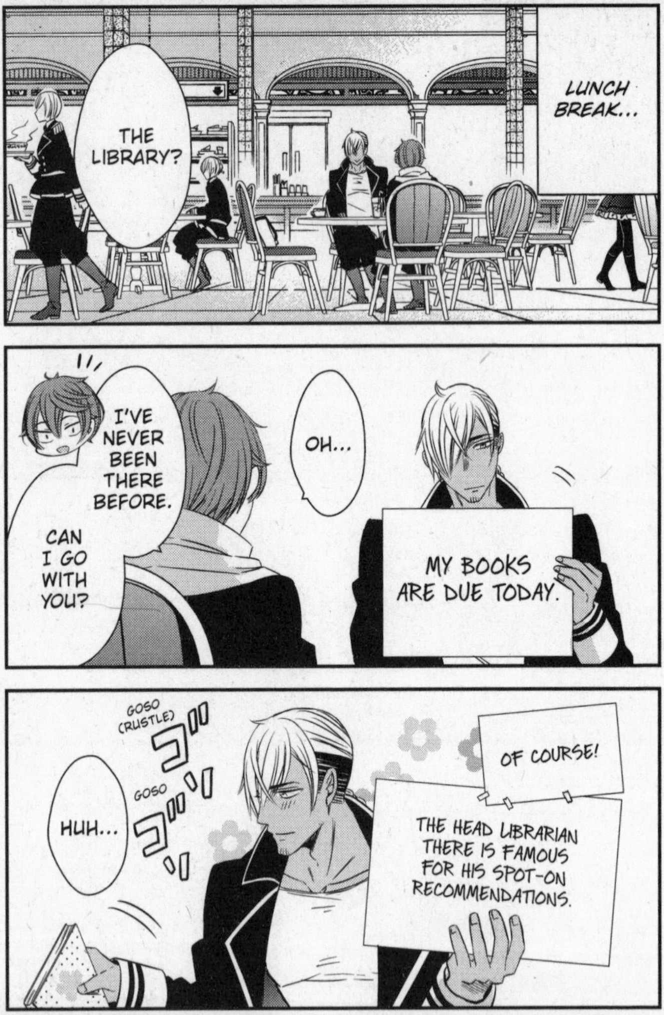

LUNCH BREAK...
THE LIBRARY?
MY BOOKS ARE DUE TODAY.
OH...
I'VE NEVER BEEN THERE BEFORE.
CAN I GO WITH YOU?
OF COURSE!
THE HEAD LIBRARIAN THERE IS FAMOUS FOR HIS SPOT-ON RECOMMENDATIONS.
GOSO (RUSTLE)
GOSO
HUH...

BOOKS: BEGINNERS' EMBROIDERY AND APPLIQUÉ / ASTROLOGICAL FORTUNE-TELLING FOR A HAPPY LIFE

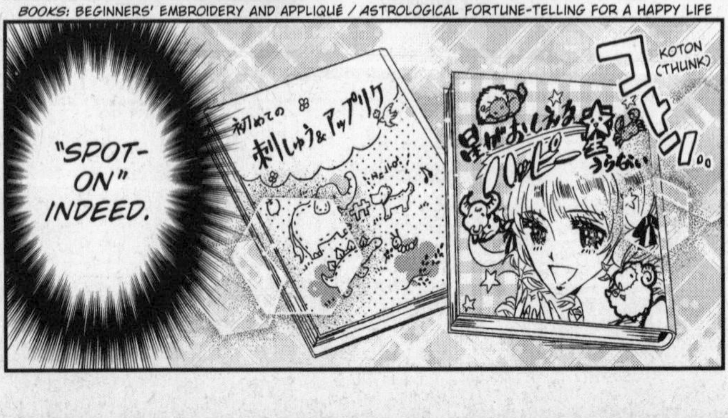

KOTON (THUNK)
星がおしえるハッピー占い
初めての刺しゅう&アップリケ
"SPOT-ON" INDEED.

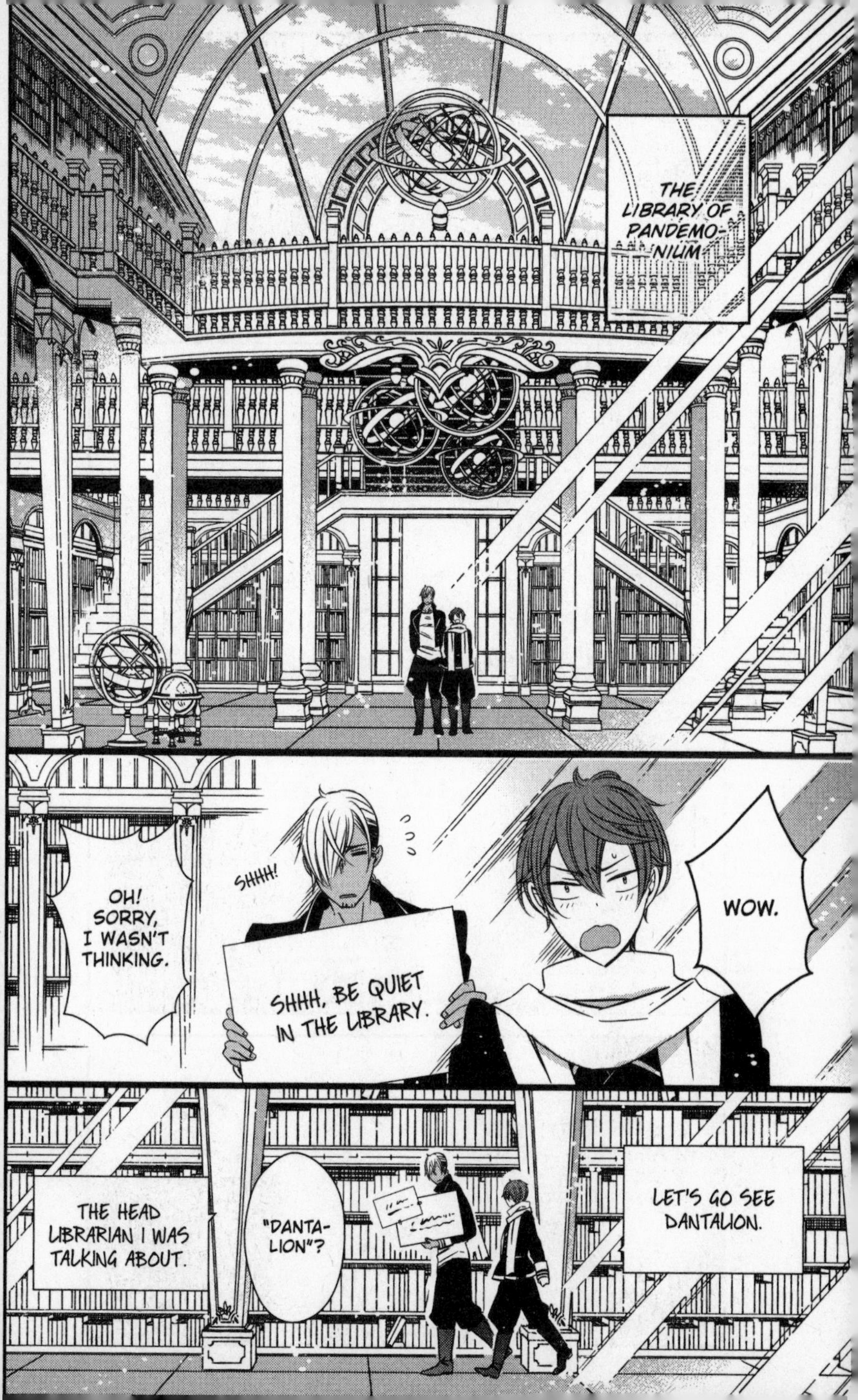
THE LIBRARY OF PANDEMONIUM
WOW.
SHHH!
SHHH, BE QUIET IN THE LIBRARY.
OH! SORRY, I WASN'T THINKING.
LET'S GO SEE DANTALION.
"DANTALION"?
THE HEAD LIBRARIAN I WAS TALKING ABOUT.

SECOND SNOOZE

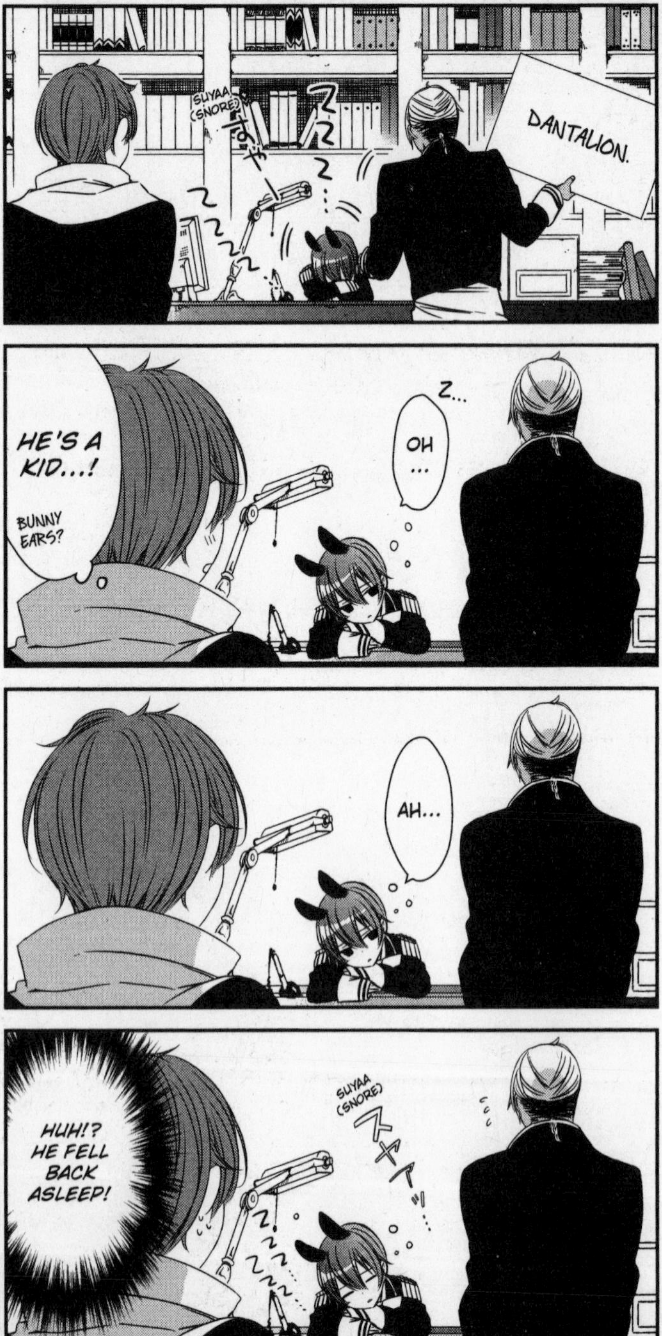
DANTALION.
SUYAA (SNORE)
Z...
OH ...
HE'S A KID...!
BUNNY EARS?
AH...
SUYAA (SNORE)
HUH!? HE FELL BACK ASLEEP!

HE SAYS IT LIKE IT'S OBVIOUS

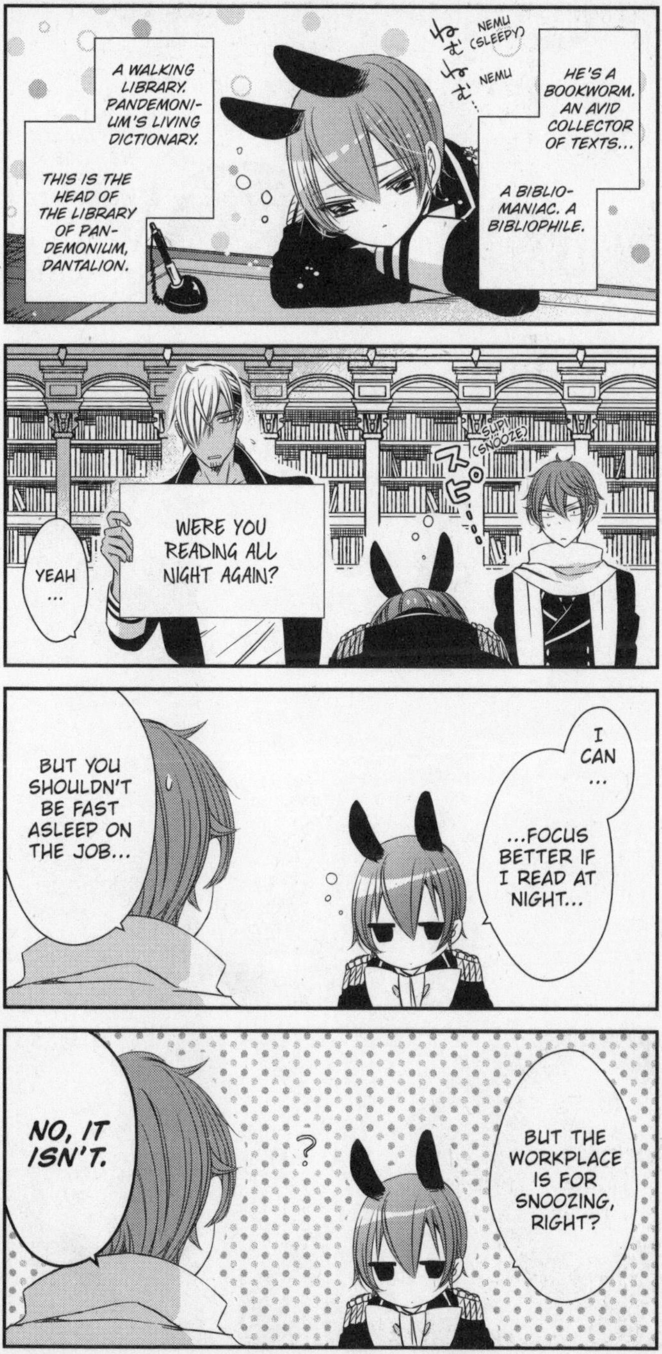
HE'S A BOOKWORM. AN AVID COLLECTOR OF TEXTS...
A BIBLIO-MANIAC. A BIBLIOPHILE.
ねむ NEMU (SLEEPY)
ねむ… NEMU
A WALKING LIBRARY. PANDEMONIUM'S LIVING DICTIONARY.
THIS IS THE HEAD OF THE LIBRARY OF PAN-DEMONIUM, DANTALION.
スピ… SUPI (SNOOZE)
WERE YOU READING ALL NIGHT AGAIN?
YEAH...
I CAN...
...FOCUS BETTER IF I READ AT NIGHT...
BUT YOU SHOULDN'T BE FAST ASLEEP ON THE JOB...
BUT THE WORKPLACE IS FOR SNOOZING, RIGHT?
?
NO, IT ISN'T.

HE SLEEPS LIKE OTHERS BREATHE

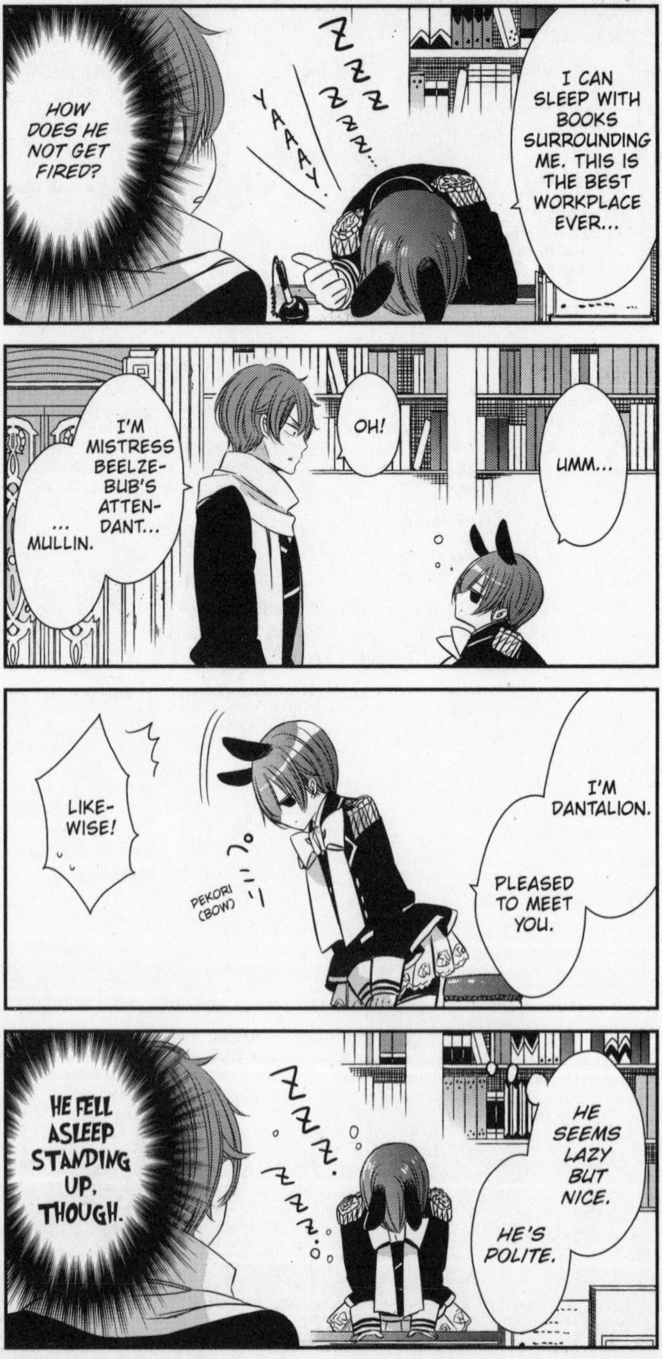
I CAN SLEEP WITH BOOKS SURROUNDING ME. THIS IS THE BEST WORKPLACE EVER...
ZZZ ZZZ...
YAAAY.
HOW DOES HE NOT GET FIRED?
UMM...
OH!
I'M MISTRESS BEELZE-BUB'S ATTEN-DANT...
... MULLIN.
I'M DANTALION.
PLEASED TO MEET YOU.
PEKORI (BOW)
LIKE-WISE!
HE SEEMS LAZY BUT NICE.
HE'S POLITE.
ZZZ.
ZZZ...
HE FELL ASLEEP STANDING UP, THOUGH.

HIS HEART IS FULL

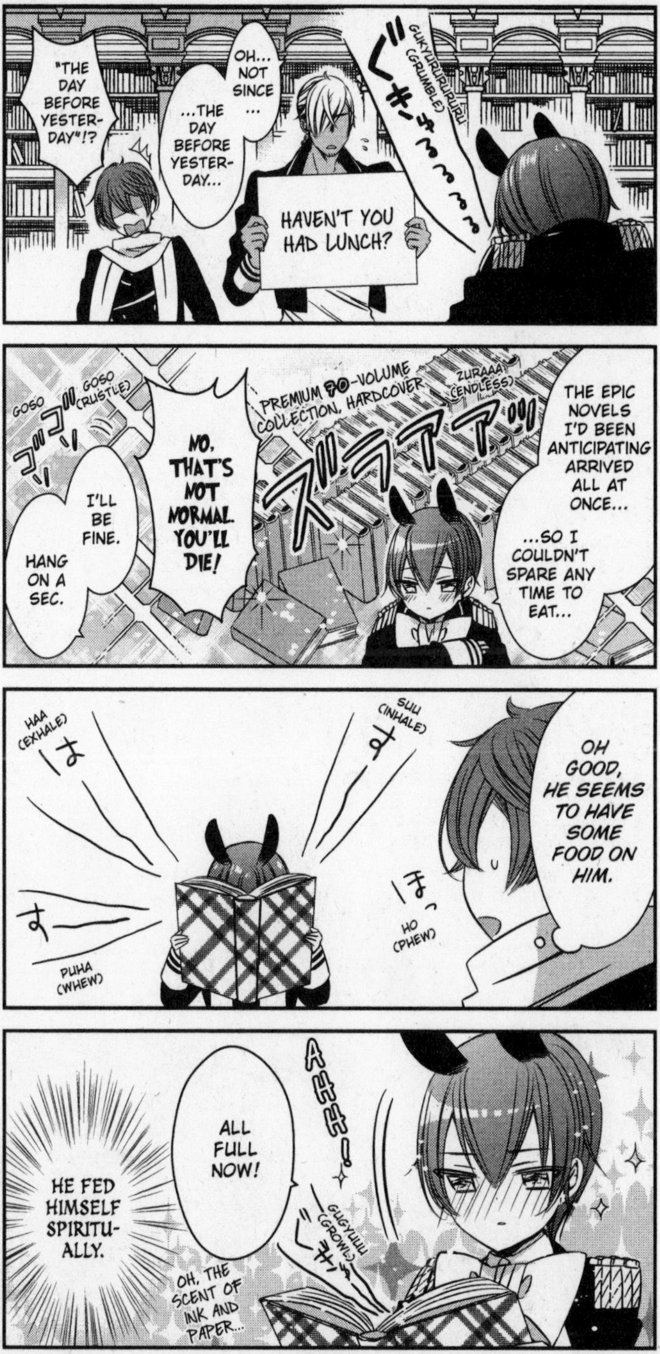
ぐきゅるるるるる
GUKYURURURURU (GRUMBLE)
OH... NOT SINCE ...
HAVEN'T YOU HAD LUNCH?
...THE DAY BEFORE YESTER-DAY...
"THE DAY BEFORE YESTER-DAY"!?
THE EPIC NOVELS I'D BEEN ANTICIPATING ARRIVED ALL AT ONCE...
...SO I COULDN'T SPARE ANY TIME TO EAT...
ZURAAA (ENDLESS)
ズラァア
PREMIUM 70-VOLUME COLLECTION, HARDCOVER
NO, THAT'S NOT NORMAL. YOU'LL DIE!
GOSO GOSO (RUSTLE)
ゴソゴソ
I'LL BE FINE.
HANG ON A SEC.
OH GOOD, HE SEEMS TO HAVE SOME FOOD ON HIM.
SUU (INHALE)
HO (PHEW)
HAA (EXHALE)
PUHA (WHEW)
AHHH!
ALL FULL NOW!
GUGYUUU (GROWL)
OH, THE SCENT OF INK AND PAPER...
HE FED HIMSELF SPIRITU-ALLY.

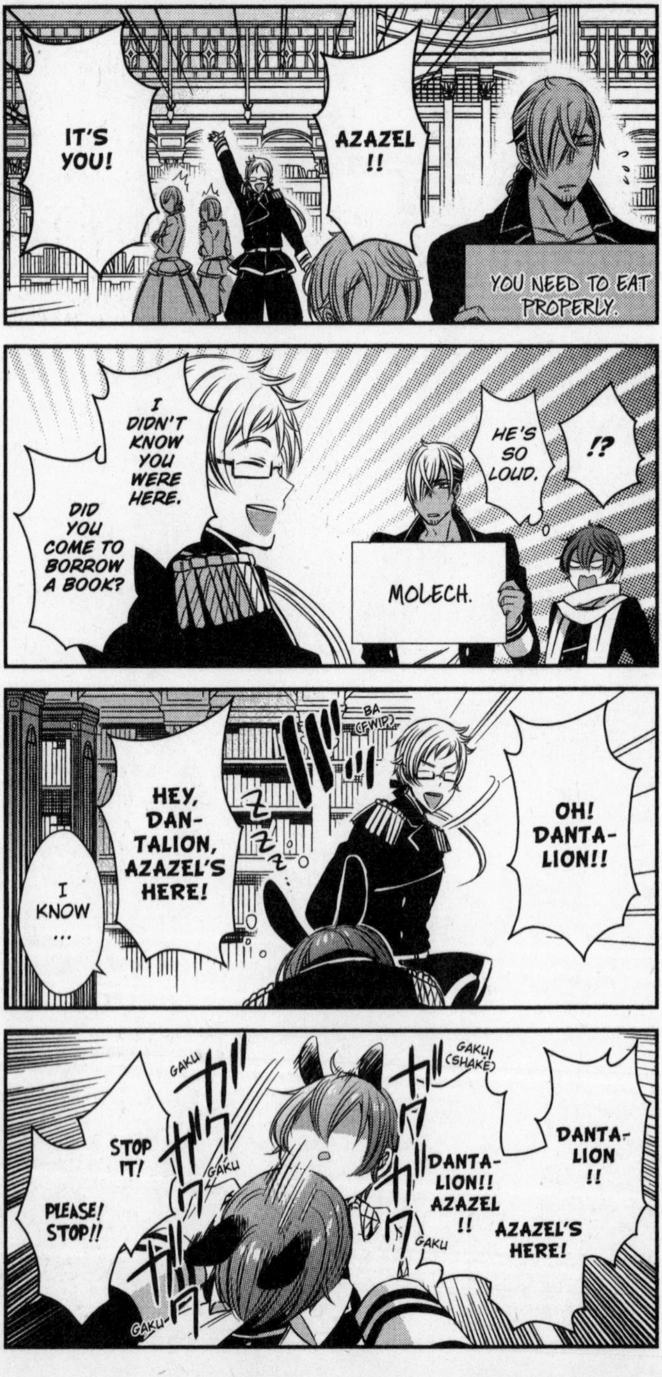
YOU NEED TO EAT PROPERLY.
AZAZEL !!
IT'S YOU!
!?
HE'S SO LOUD.
MOLECH.
I DIDN'T KNOW YOU WERE HERE.
DID YOU COME TO BORROW A BOOK?
OH! DANTA-LION!!
BA (FWIP)
HEY, DAN-TALION, AZAZEL'S HERE!
I KNOW ...
DANTA-LION !!
GAKU (SHAKE)
AZAZEL'S HERE!
DANTA-LION!! AZAZEL !!
GAKU
GAKU
STOP IT!
GAKU
PLEASE! STOP!!
GAKU-

HE'S AWAKE ALREADY!!

IN ONE EAR AND OUT THE OTHER

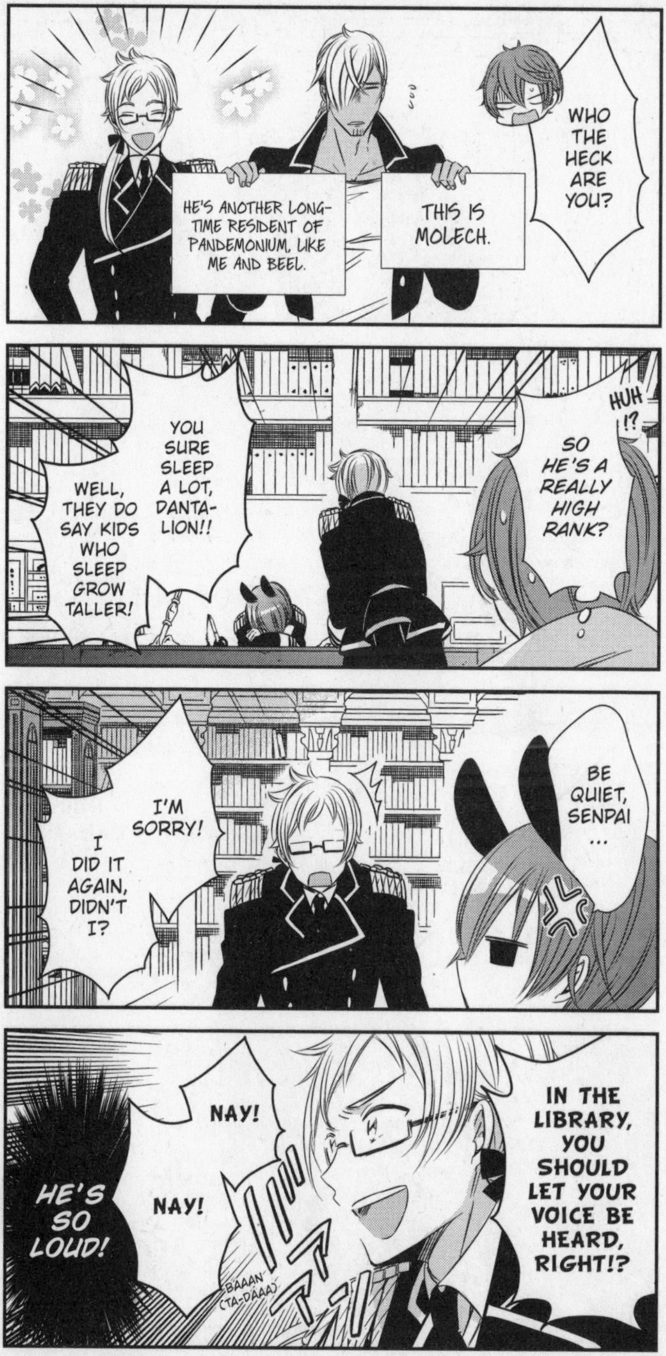

WHO THE HECK ARE YOU?
THIS IS MOLECH.
HE'S ANOTHER LONG-TIME RESIDENT OF PANDEMONIUM, LIKE ME AND BEEL.
HUH!?
SO HE'S A REALLY HIGH RANK?
YOU SURE SLEEP A LOT, DANTALION!!
WELL, THEY DO SAY KIDS WHO SLEEP GROW TALLER!
BE QUIET, SENPAI...
I'M SORRY!
I DID IT AGAIN, DIDN'T I?
IN THE LIBRARY, YOU SHOULD LET YOUR VOICE BE HEARD, RIGHT!?
BAAAN (TA-DAAA)
NAY!
NAY!
HE'S SO LOUD!

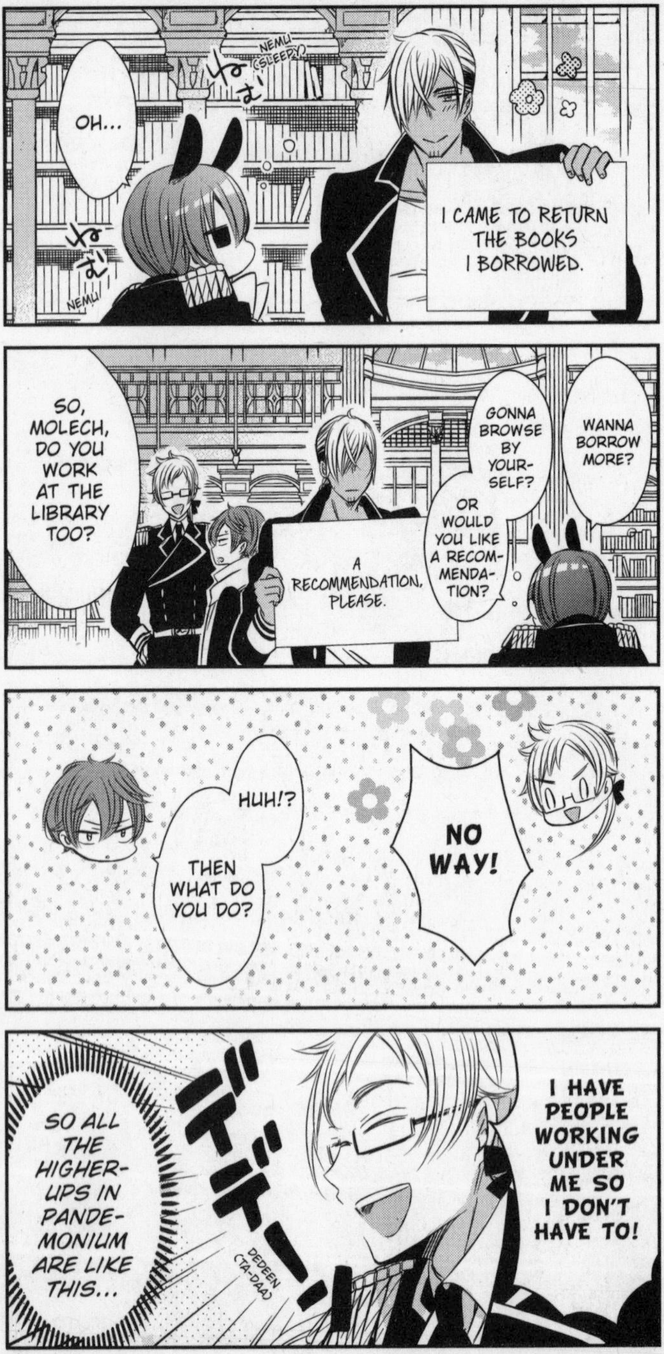
I CAME TO RETURN THE BOOKS I BORROWED.
NEMU (SLEEPY)
OH...
NEMU
WANNA BORROW MORE?
GONNA BROWSE BY YOURSELF?
OR WOULD YOU LIKE A RECOMMENDATION?
A RECOMMENDATION, PLEASE.
SO, MOLECH, DO YOU WORK AT THE LIBRARY TOO?
NO WAY!
HUH!?
THEN WHAT DO YOU DO?
I HAVE PEOPLE WORKING UNDER ME SO I DON'T HAVE TO!
DEDEEN (TA-DAA)
SO ALL THE HIGHER-UPS IN PANDEMONIUM ARE LIKE THIS...

A STEPLADDER

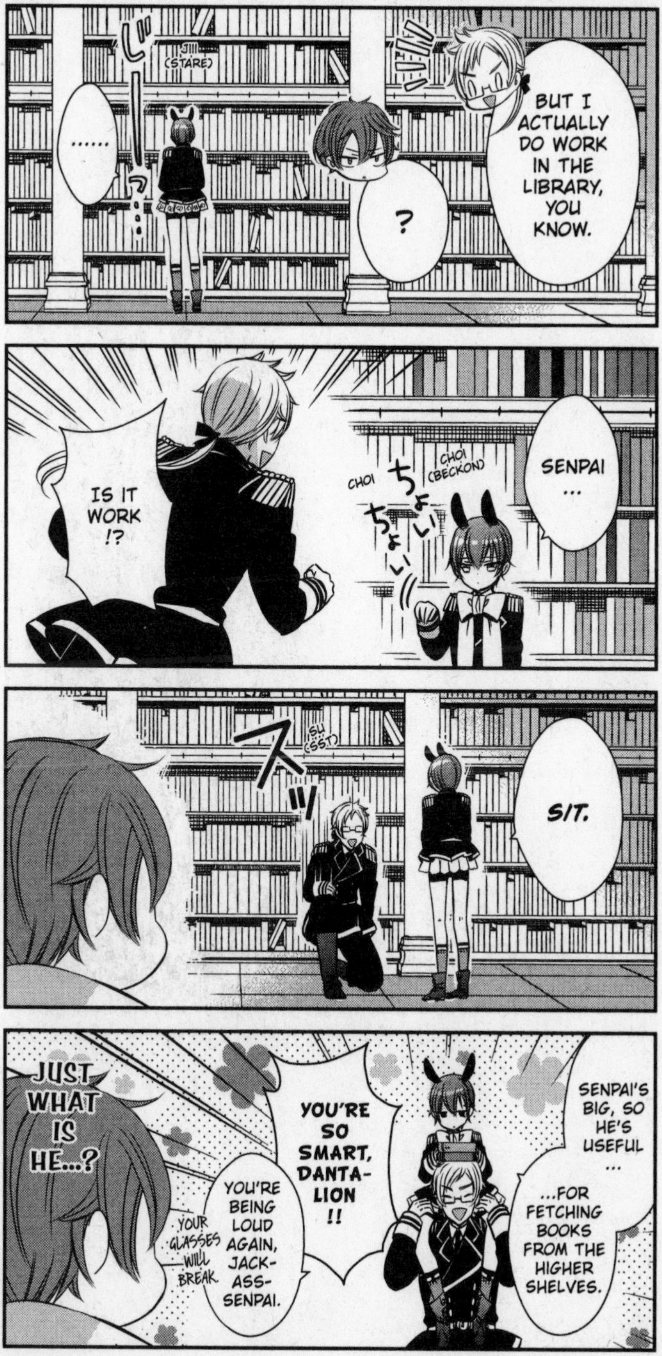
BUT I ACTUALLY DO WORK IN THE LIBRARY, YOU KNOW.
?
JIII (STARE)
......
SENPAI ...
CHOI (BECKON)
CHOI
IS IT WORK !?
SIT.
SU (SST)
SENPAI'S BIG, SO HE'S USEFUL ...
...FOR FETCHING BOOKS FROM THE HIGHER SHELVES.
YOU'RE SO SMART, DANTALION !!
YOU'RE BEING LOUD AGAIN, JACK-ASS-SENPAI.
YOUR GLASSES WILL BREAK.
JUST WHAT IS HE...?

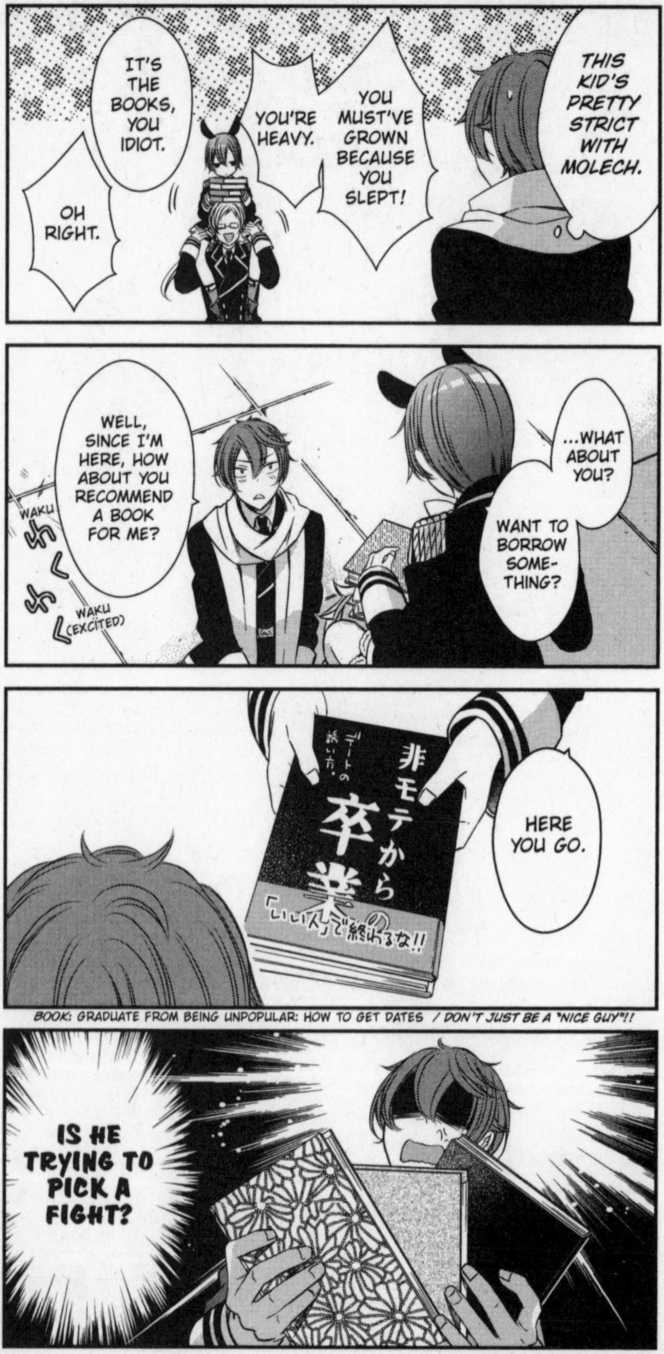
THIS KID'S PRETTY STRICT WITH MOLECH.
YOU MUST'VE GROWN BECAUSE YOU SLEPT!
YOU'RE HEAVY.
IT'S THE BOOKS, YOU IDIOT.
OH RIGHT.
...WHAT ABOUT YOU?
WANT TO BORROW SOME-THING?
WELL, SINCE I'M HERE, HOW ABOUT YOU RECOMMEND A BOOK FOR ME?
わく WAKU
わく WAKU (EXCITED)
HERE YOU GO.
非モテから卒業の
デートの誘い方
「いい人」で終わるな!!
BOOK: GRADUATE FROM BEING UNPOPULAR: HOW TO GET DATES / DON'T JUST BE A "NICE GUY"!!
IS HE TRYING TO PICK A FIGHT?

SPOT-ON

A BOOKWORM'S ULTIMATE REVENGE

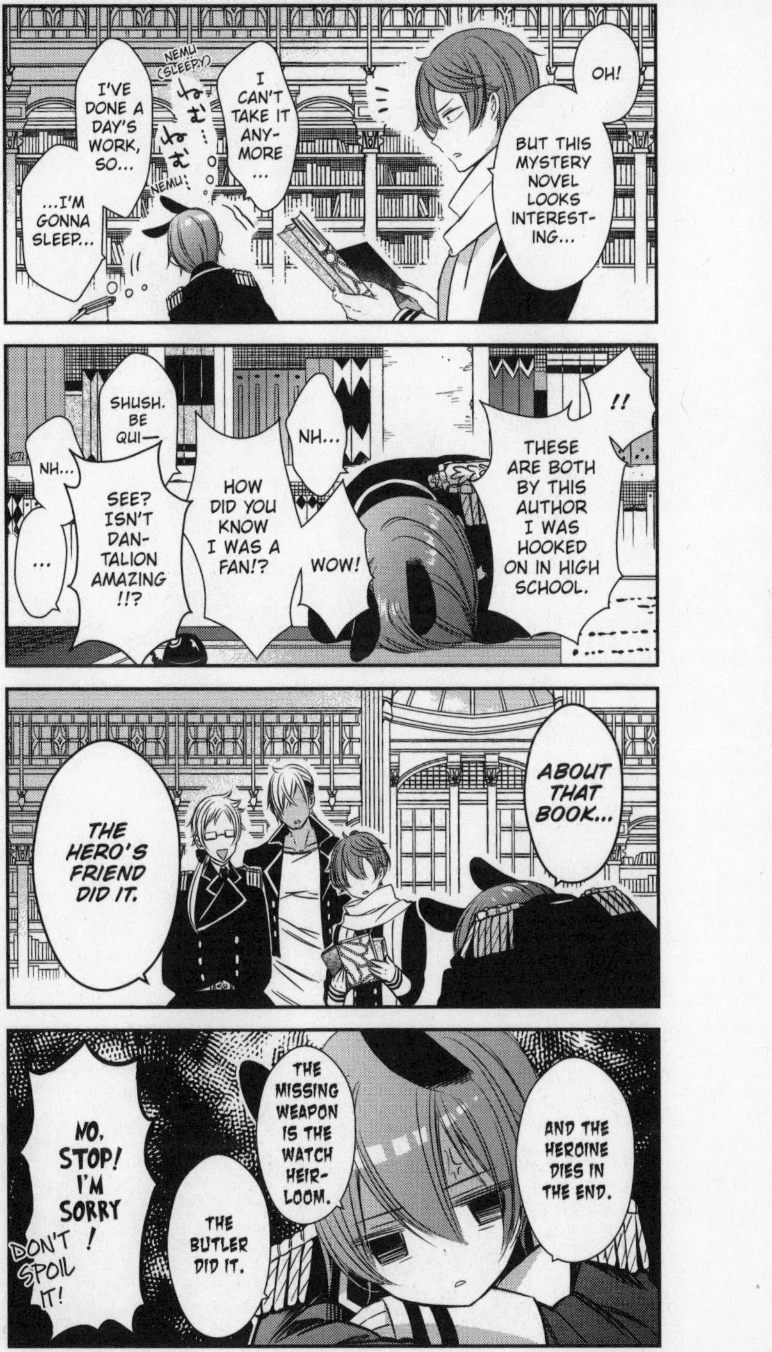
OH!
BUT THIS MYSTERY NOVEL LOOKS INTEREST-ING...
I CAN'T TAKE IT ANY-MORE...
NEMU (SLEEPY)
ねむ… ねむ…
NEMU
I'VE DONE A DAY'S WORK, SO...
...I'M GONNA SLEEP...
!!
THESE ARE BOTH BY THIS AUTHOR I WAS HOOKED ON IN HIGH SCHOOL.
NH...
WOW!
HOW DID YOU KNOW I WAS A FAN!?
SHUSH. BE QUI—
SEE? ISN'T DAN-TALION AMAZING !!?
NH...
...
ABOUT THAT BOOK...
THE HERO'S FRIEND DID IT.
AND THE HEROINE DIES IN THE END.
THE MISSING WEAPON IS THE WATCH HEIR-LOOM.
THE BUTLER DID IT.
NO, STOP! I'M SORRY!
DON'T SPOIL IT!

CLOSER, ONE METER AT A TIME

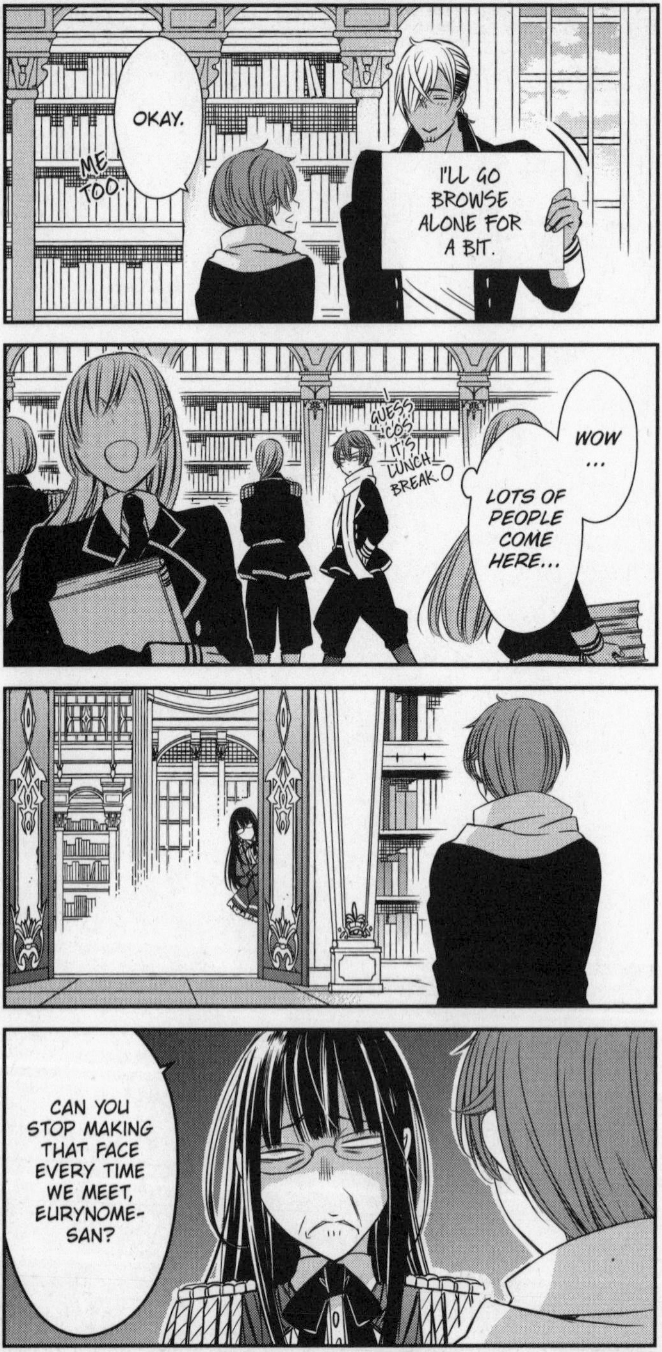

I'LL GO BROWSE ALONE FOR A BIT.
OKAY.
ME TOO.
WOW ... LOTS OF PEOPLE COME HERE...
I GUESS 'COS IT'S LUNCH BREAK.
CAN YOU STOP MAKING THAT FACE EVERY TIME WE MEET, EURYNOME-SAN?

LOST HER VOCABULARY (OTHER THAN "PRECIOUS")

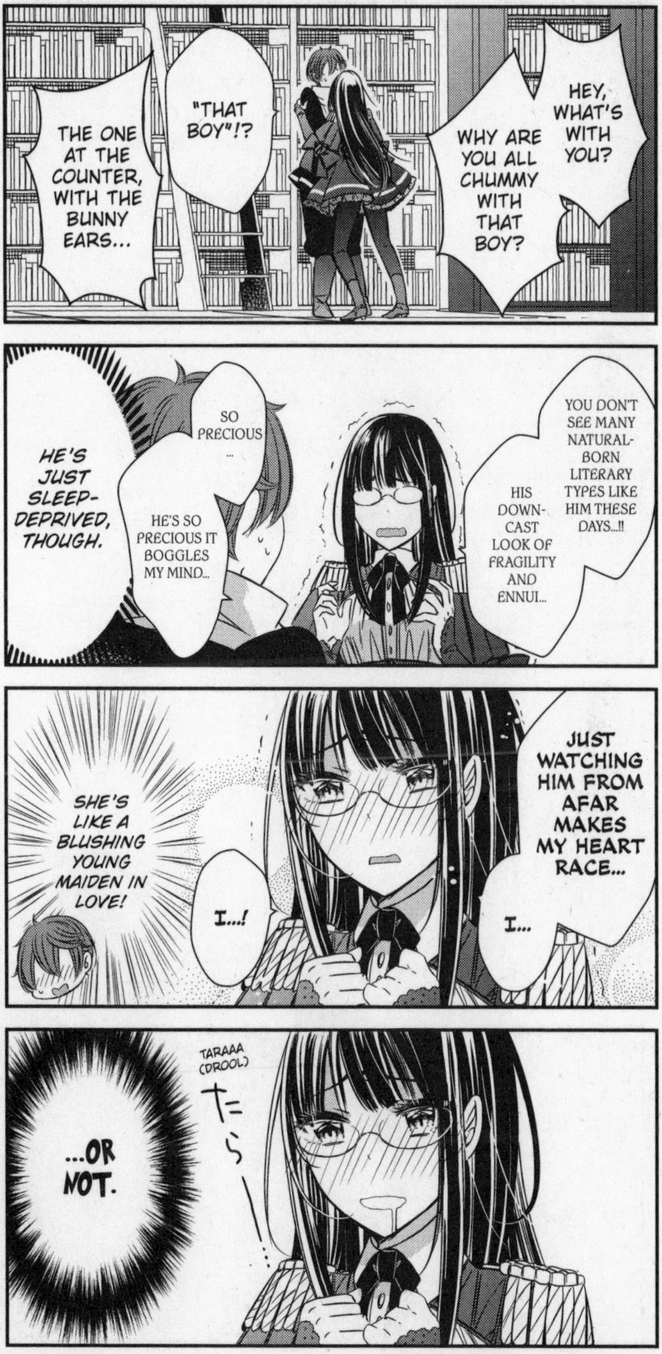
HEY, WHAT'S WITH YOU?
WHY ARE YOU ALL CHUMMY WITH THAT BOY?
"THAT BOY"!?
THE ONE AT THE COUNTER, WITH THE BUNNY EARS...
YOU DON'T SEE MANY NATURAL-BORN LITERARY TYPES LIKE HIM THESE DAYS...!!
HIS DOWN-CAST LOOK OF FRAGILITY AND ENNUI...
SO PRECIOUS ...
HE'S SO PRECIOUS IT BOGGLES MY MIND...
HE'S JUST SLEEP-DEPRIVED, THOUGH.
I...
JUST WATCHING HIM FROM AFAR MAKES MY HEART RACE...
I...!
SHE'S LIKE A BLUSHING YOUNG MAIDEN IN LOVE!
TARAAA (DROOL)
たら〜
...OR NOT.

CAN'T HELP BUT SMILE

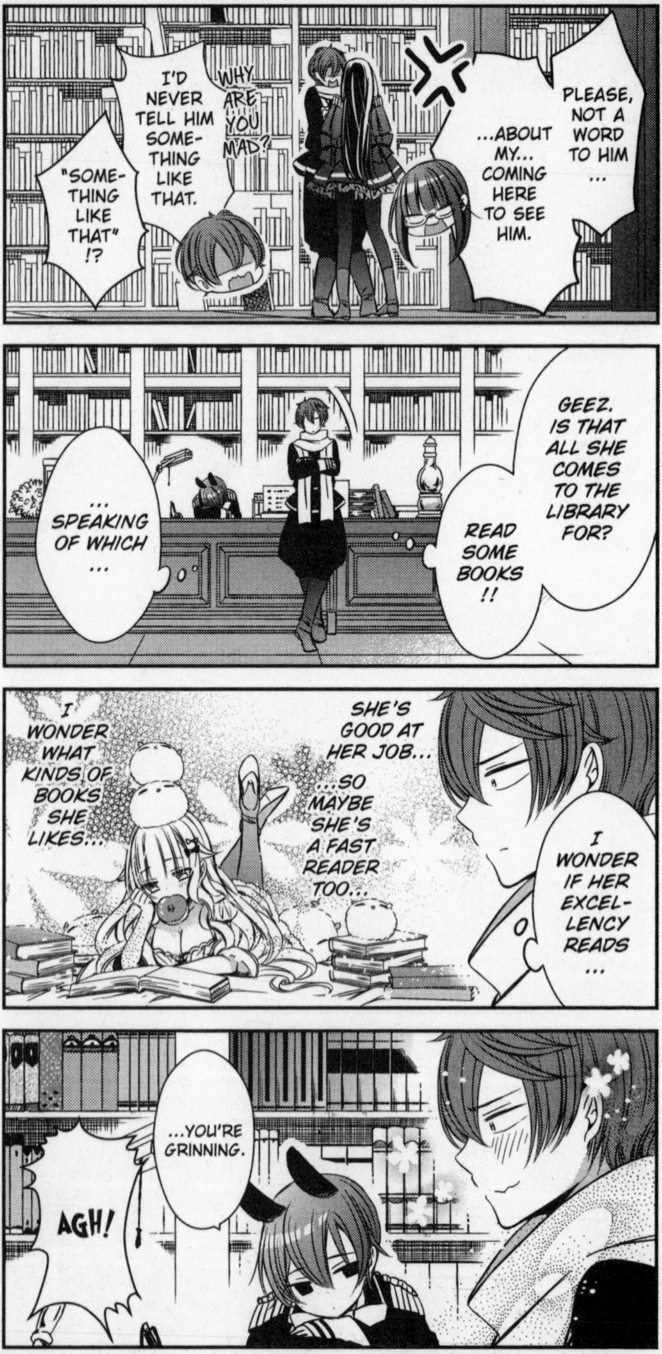
PLEASE, NOT A WORD TO HIM ...
...ABOUT MY... COMING HERE TO SEE HIM.
WHY ARE YOU MAD?
I'D NEVER TELL HIM SOME-THING LIKE THAT.
"SOME-THING LIKE THAT" !?
GEEZ. IS THAT ALL SHE COMES TO THE LIBRARY FOR?
READ SOME BOOKS !!
... SPEAKING OF WHICH ...
I WONDER IF HER EXCEL-LENCY READS ...
SHE'S GOOD AT HER JOB...
...SO MAYBE SHE'S A FAST READER TOO...
I WONDER WHAT KINDS OF BOOKS SHE LIKES...
...YOU'RE GRINNING.
AGH!

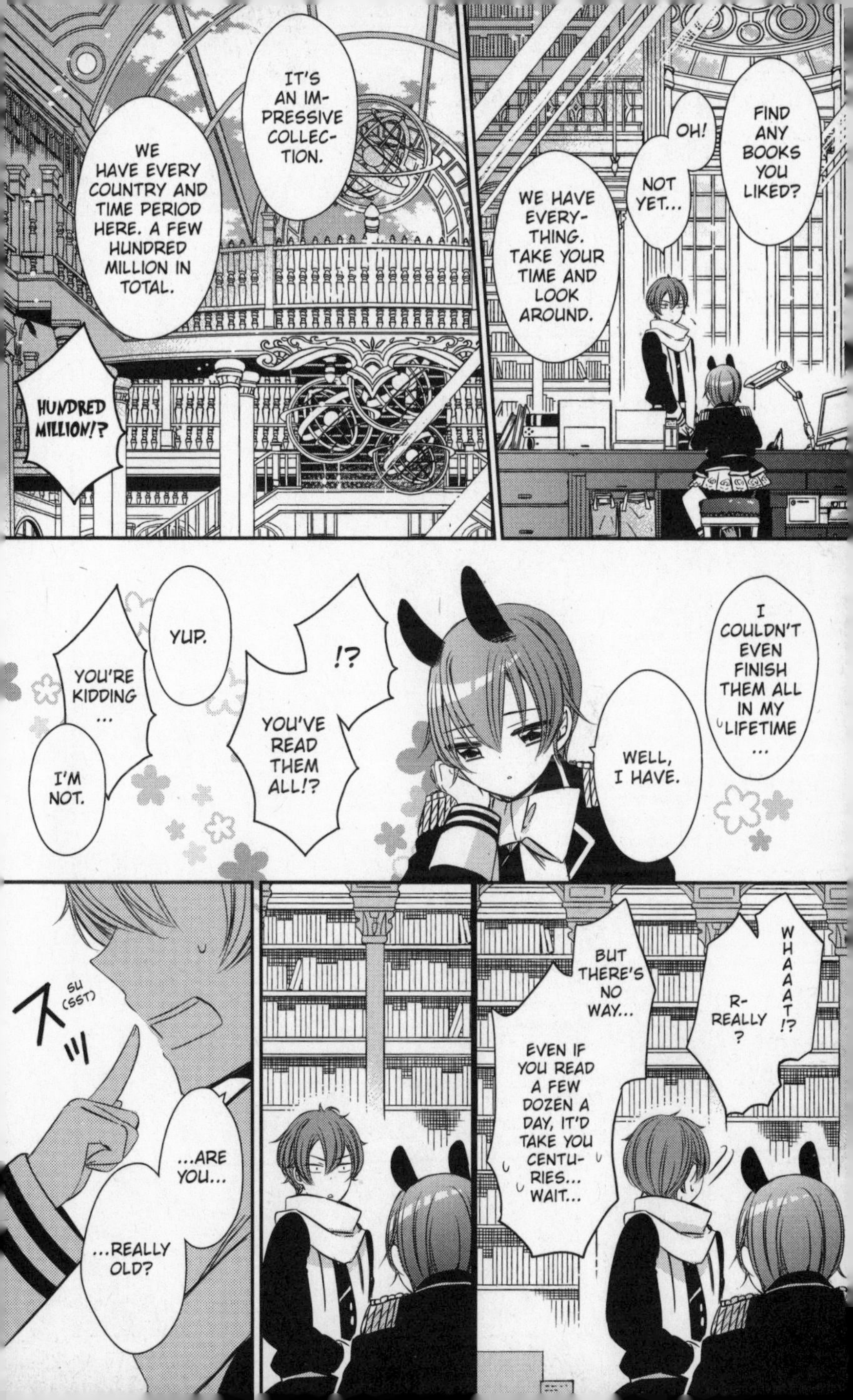
FIND ANY BOOKS YOU LIKED?
OH!
NOT YET...
WE HAVE EVERY-THING. TAKE YOUR TIME AND LOOK AROUND.
IT'S AN IM-PRESSIVE COLLEC-TION.
WE HAVE EVERY COUNTRY AND TIME PERIOD HERE. A FEW HUNDRED MILLION IN TOTAL.
HUNDRED MILLION!?
I COULDN'T EVEN FINISH THEM ALL IN MY LIFETIME...
WELL, I HAVE.
!?
YOU'VE READ THEM ALL!?
YUP.
YOU'RE KIDDING...
I'M NOT.
WHAAAAT!?
R-REALLY?
BUT THERE'S NO WAY...
EVEN IF YOU READ A FEW DOZEN A DAY, IT'D TAKE YOU CENTU-RIES... WAIT...
SU (SST)
...ARE YOU...
...REALLY OLD?

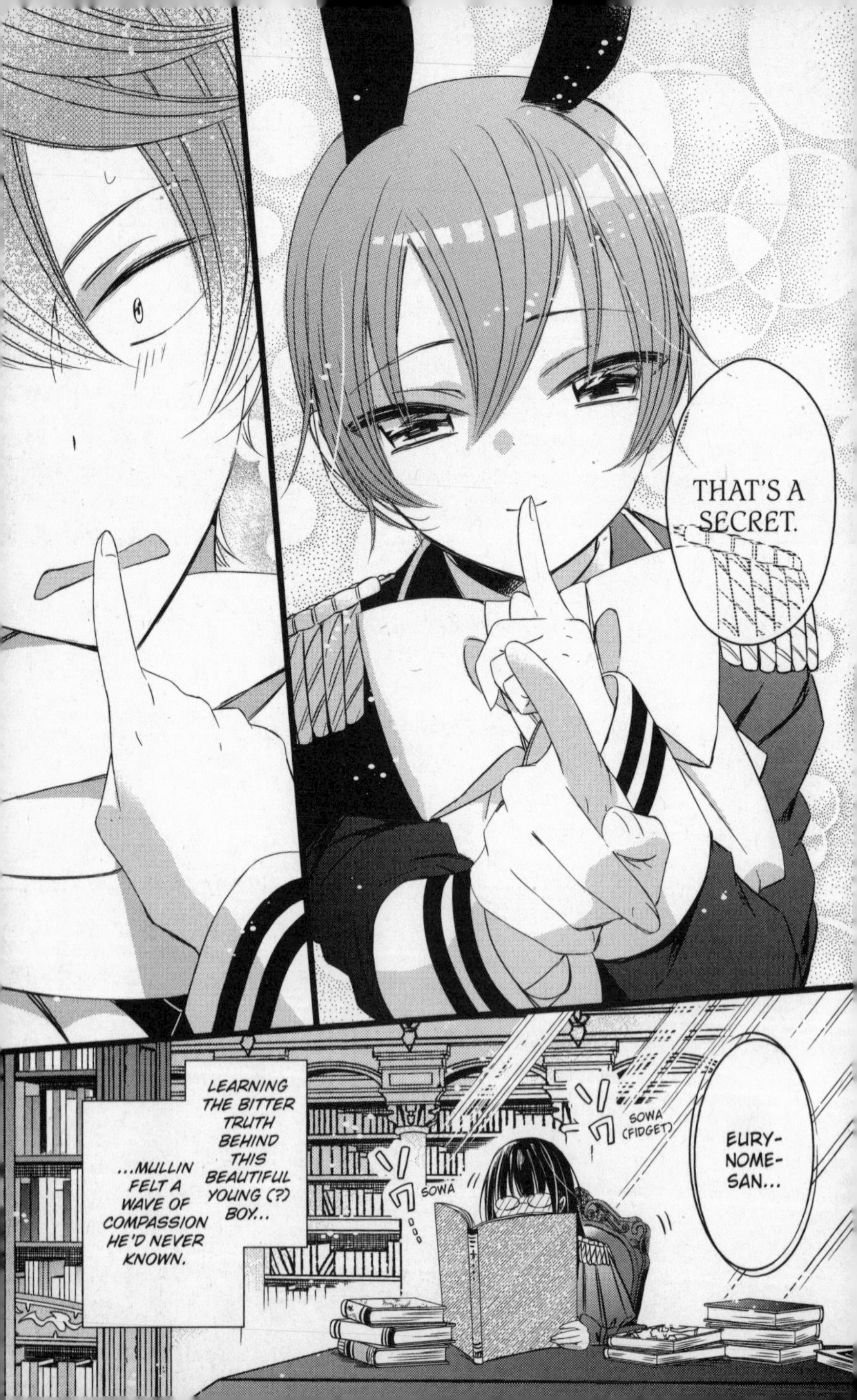
THAT'S A SECRET.
EURY-NOME-SAN...
SOWA (FIDGET)
SOWA
LEARNING THE BITTER TRUTH BEHIND THIS BEAUTIFUL YOUNG (?) BOY...
...MULLIN FELT A WAVE OF COMPASSION HE'D NEVER KNOWN.

As Miss Beelzebub Likes

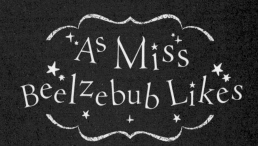

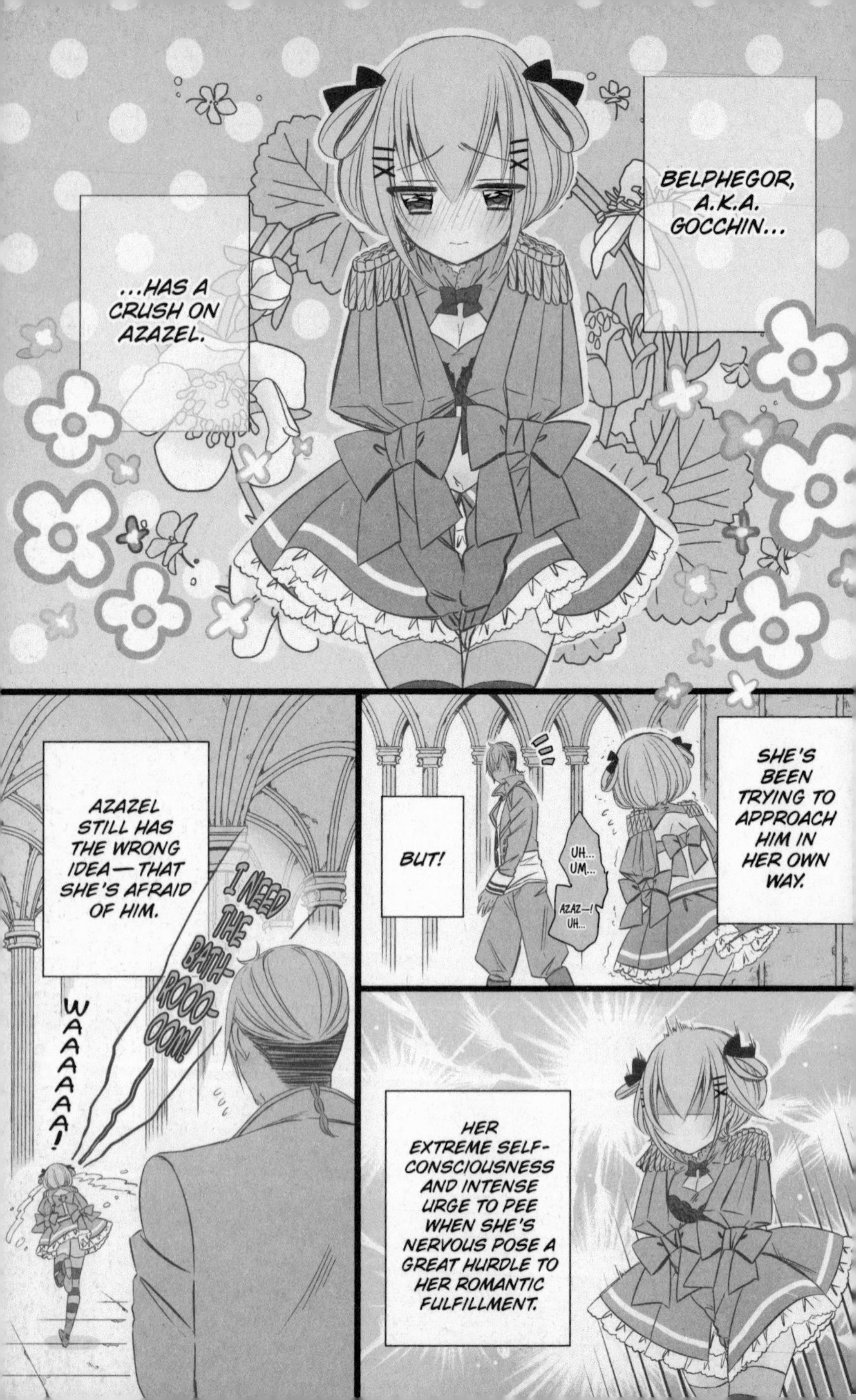
BELPHEGOR, A.K.A. GOCCHIN...
...HAS A CRUSH ON AZAZEL.
SHE'S BEEN TRYING TO APPROACH HIM IN HER OWN WAY.
UH... UM...
AZAZ—! UH...
BUT!
HER EXTREME SELF-CONSCIOUSNESS AND INTENSE URGE TO PEE WHEN SHE'S NERVOUS POSE A GREAT HURDLE TO HER ROMANTIC FULFILLMENT.
AZAZEL STILL HAS THE WRONG IDEA—THAT SHE'S AFRAID OF HIM.
I NEED THE BATH-ROOO-OOM!
WAAAAAAA!

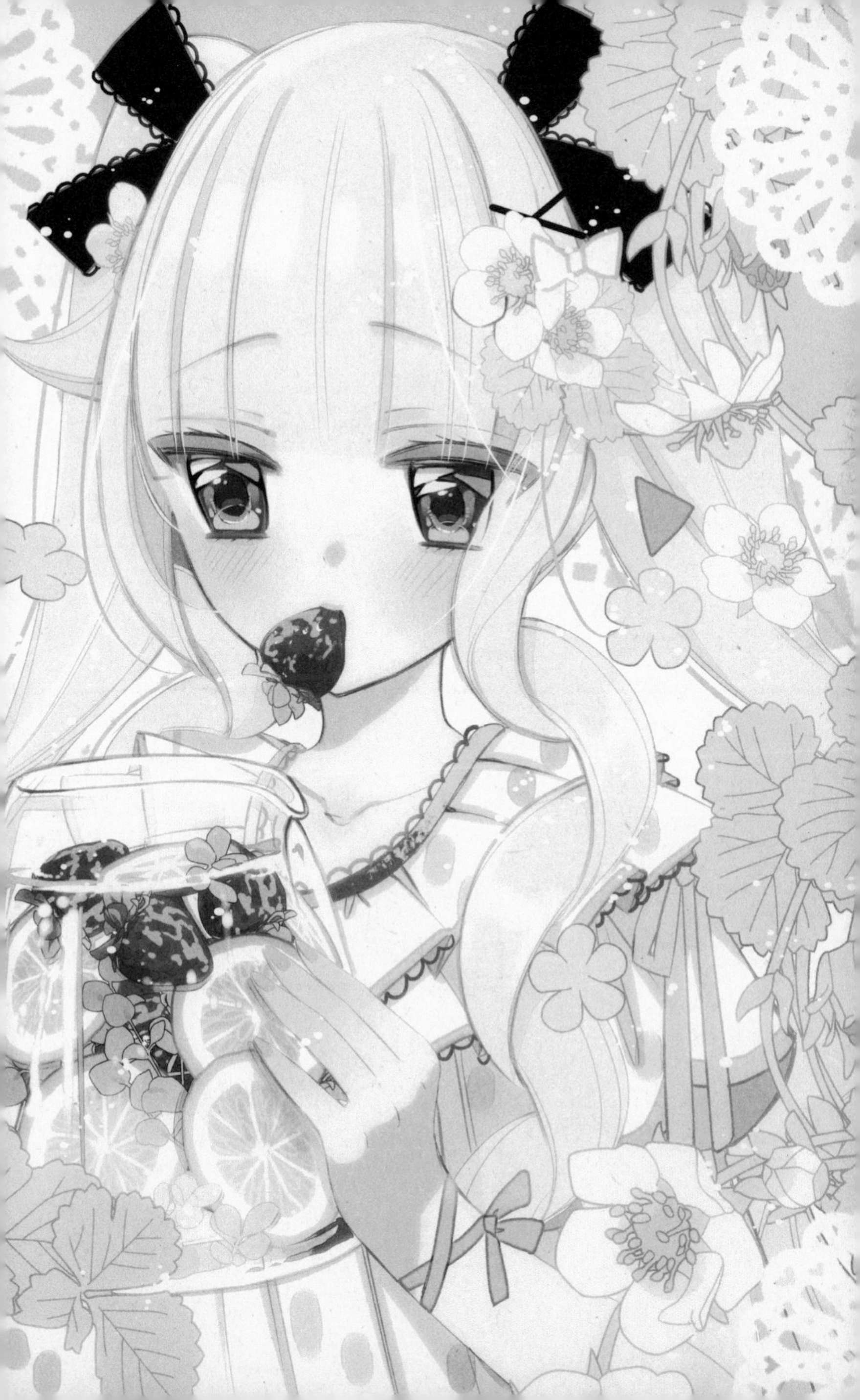

CHAPTER 10

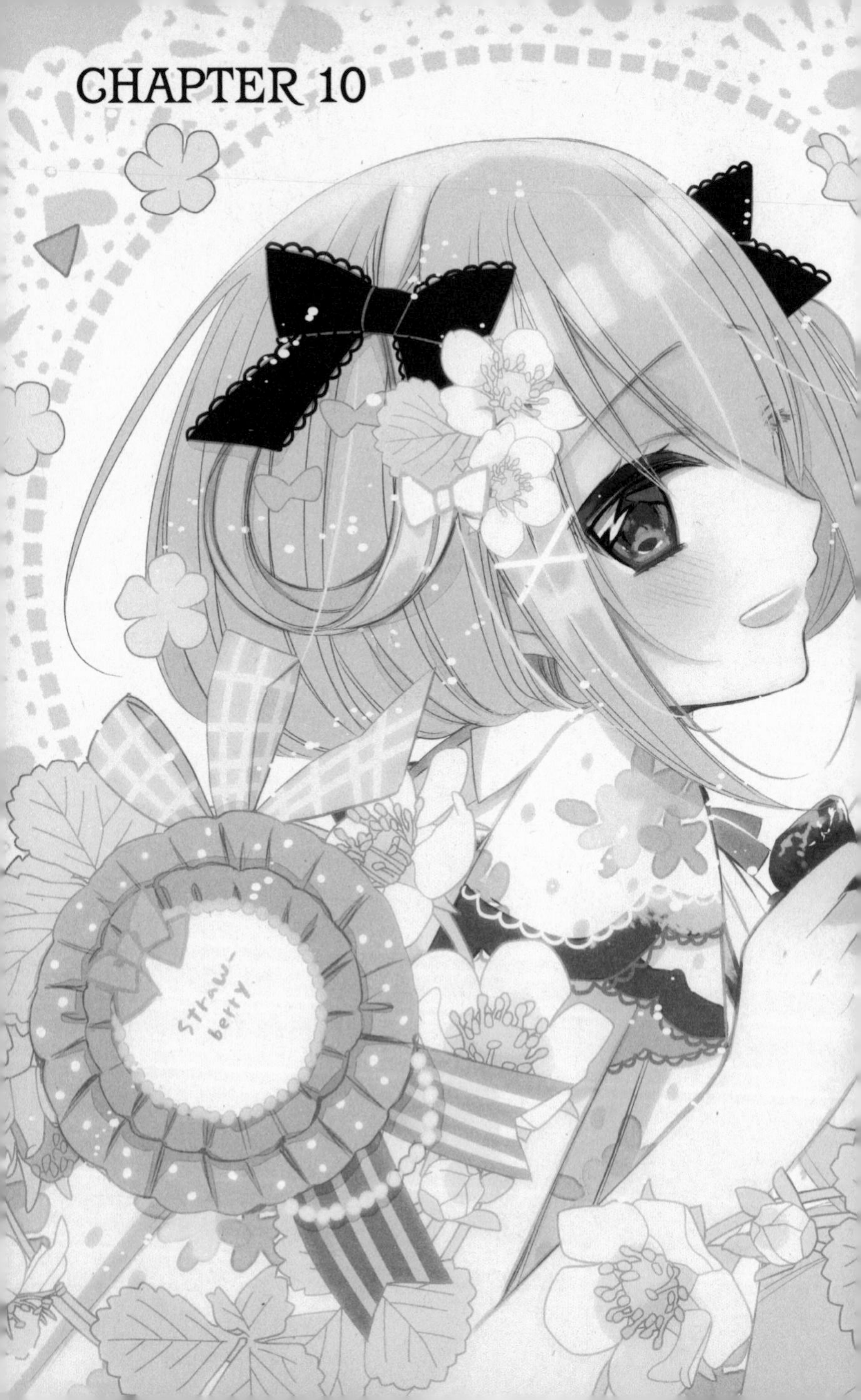
straw-
berry

As Miss Beelzebub Likes

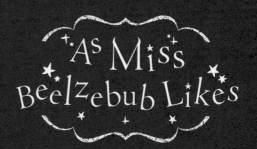

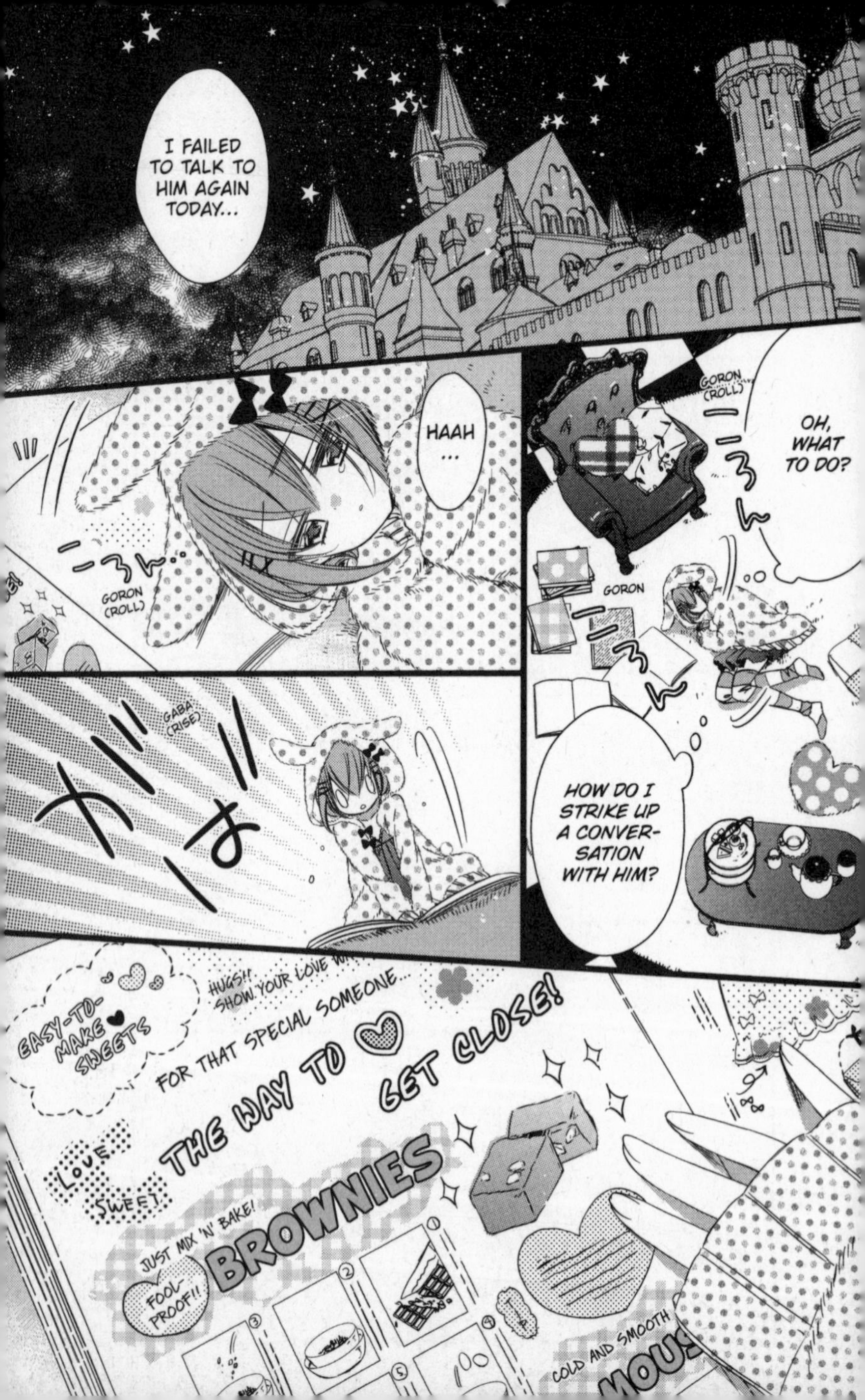
I FAILED TO TALK TO HIM AGAIN TODAY...
GORON (ROLL)
OH, WHAT TO DO?
GORON
HOW DO I STRIKE UP A CONVERSATION WITH HIM?
HAAH...
GORON (ROLL)
GABA (RISE)
HUGS!! SHOW YOUR LOVE
EASY-TO-MAKE SWEETS
FOR THAT SPECIAL SOMEONE...
THE WAY TO ♥ GET CLOSE!
LOVE
SWEET
BROWNIES
JUST MIX 'N' BAKE!
FOOL-PROOF!!
COLD AND SMOOTH
MOUS

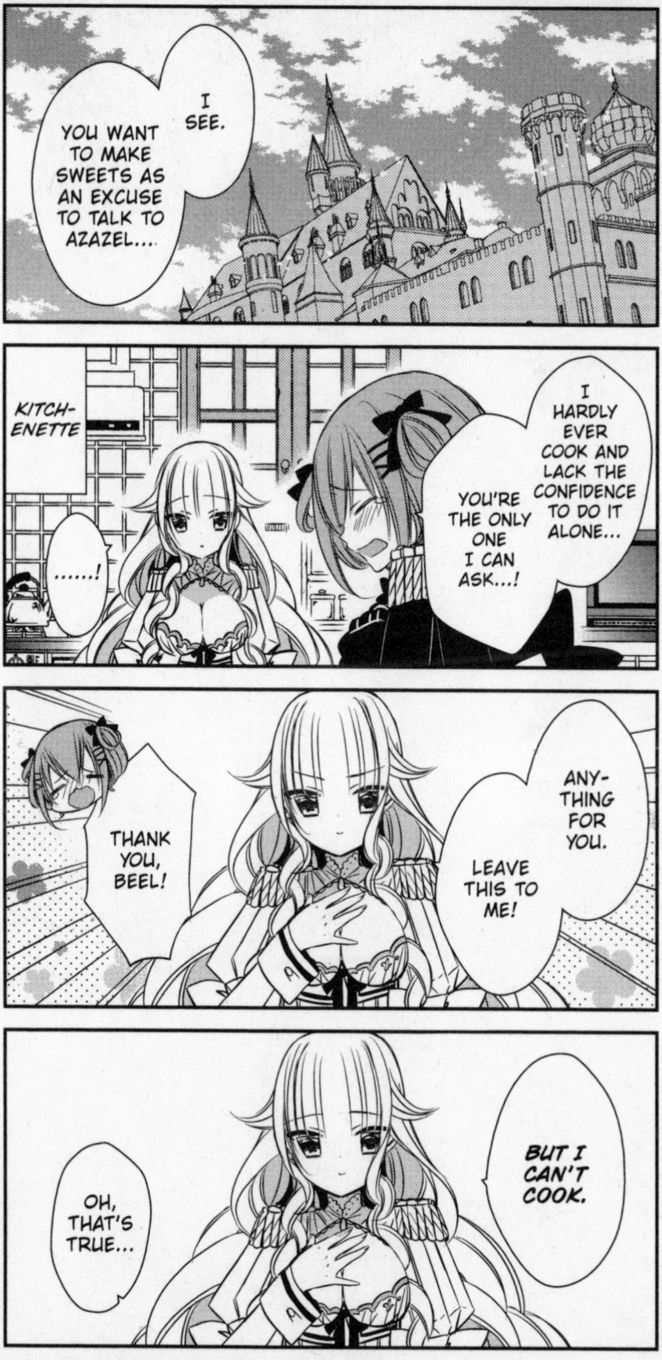
I SEE.
YOU WANT TO MAKE SWEETS AS AN EXCUSE TO TALK TO AZAZEL....
I HARDLY EVER COOK AND LACK THE CONFIDENCE TO DO IT ALONE...
YOU'RE THE ONLY ONE I CAN ASK...!
KITCH-ENETTE
......!
ANY-THING FOR YOU.
LEAVE THIS TO ME!
THANK YOU, BEEL!
BUT I CAN'T COOK.
OH, THAT'S TRUE...

DEFEATS THE PURPOSE

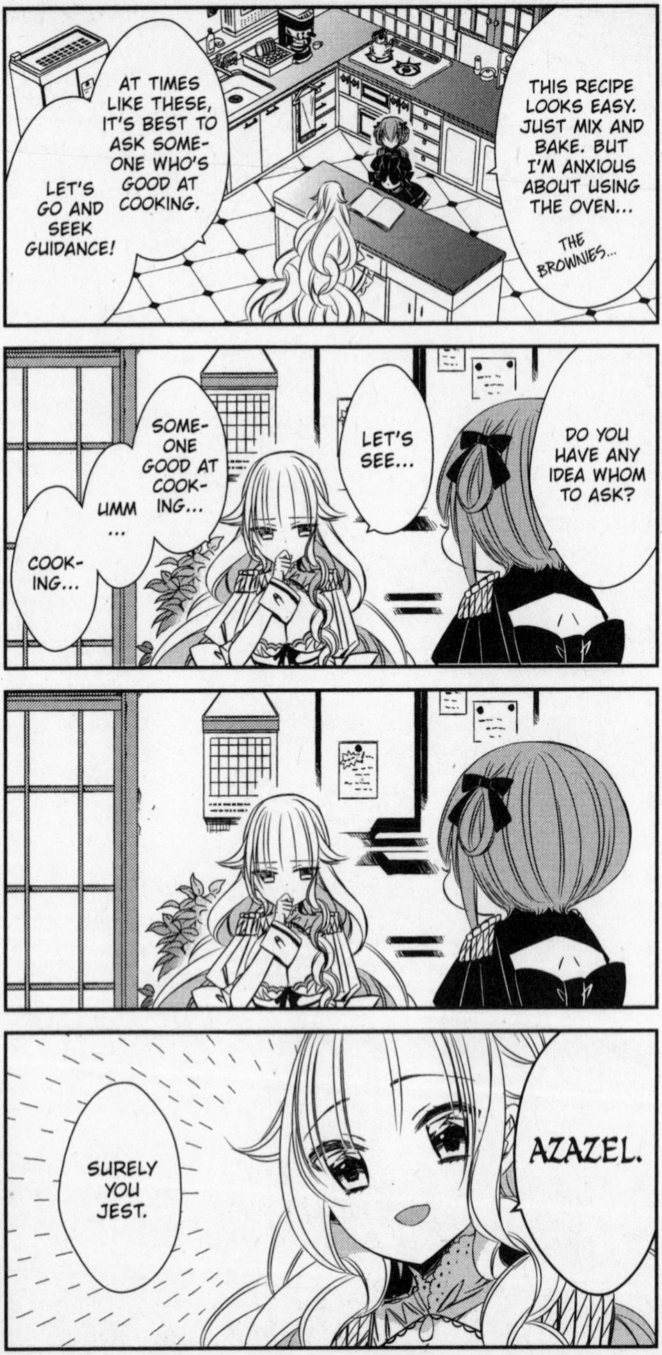
THIS RECIPE LOOKS EASY. JUST MIX AND BAKE. BUT I'M ANXIOUS ABOUT USING THE OVEN...
THE BROWNIES...
AT TIMES LIKE THESE, IT'S BEST TO ASK SOME-ONE WHO'S GOOD AT COOKING.
LET'S GO AND SEEK GUIDANCE!
DO YOU HAVE ANY IDEA WHOM TO ASK?
LET'S SEE...
SOME-ONE GOOD AT COOK-ING...
UMM ...
COOK-ING...
AZAZEL.
SURELY YOU JEST.

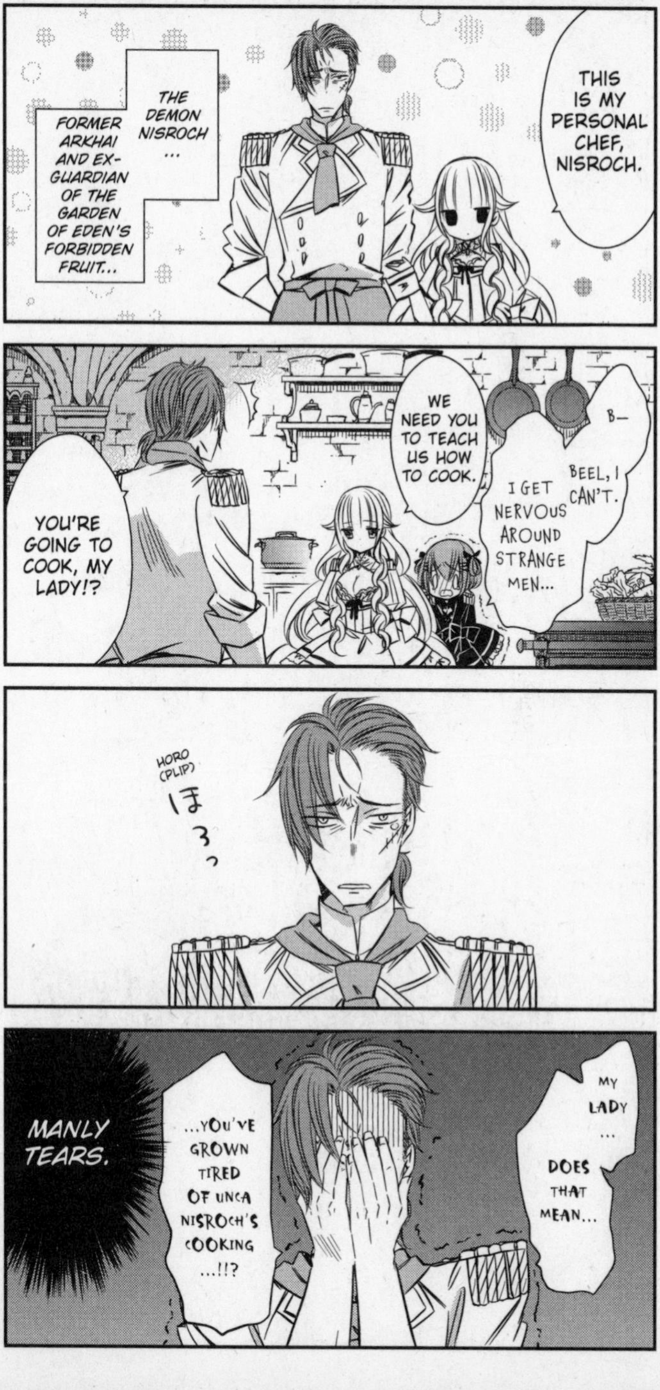
THIS IS MY PERSONAL CHEF, NISROCH.
THE DEMON NISROCH...
FORMER ARKHAI AND EX-GUARDIAN OF THE GARDEN OF EDEN'S FORBIDDEN FRUIT...
B—
BEEL, I CAN'T.
I GET NERVOUS AROUND STRANGE MEN...
WE NEED YOU TO TEACH US HOW TO COOK.
YOU'RE GOING TO COOK, MY LADY!?
HORO (PLIP)
ほろっ
MY LADY... DOES THAT MEAN...
...YOU'VE GROWN TIRED OF UNCA NISROCH'S COOKING...!!?
MANLY TEARS.

UNCA NISROCH

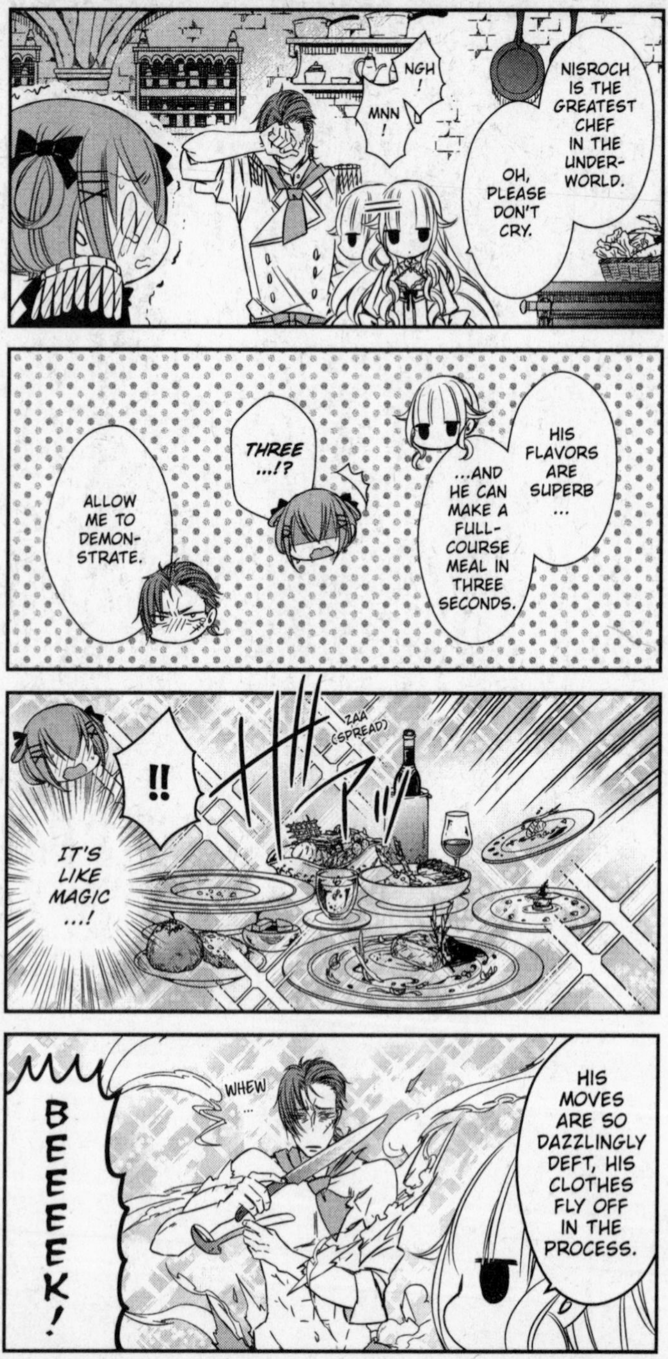
NISROCH IS THE GREATEST CHEF IN THE UNDERWORLD.
OH, PLEASE DON'T CRY.
NGH!
MNN!
HIS FLAVORS ARE SUPERB...
...AND HE CAN MAKE A FULL-COURSE MEAL IN THREE SECONDS.
THREE...!?
ALLOW ME TO DEMONSTRATE.
ZAA (SPREAD)
!!
IT'S LIKE MAGIC...!
HIS MOVES ARE SO DAZZLINGLY DEFT, HIS CLOTHES FLY OFF IN THE PROCESS.
WHEW...
BEEEEK!

A GORGEOUS PERFORMANCE

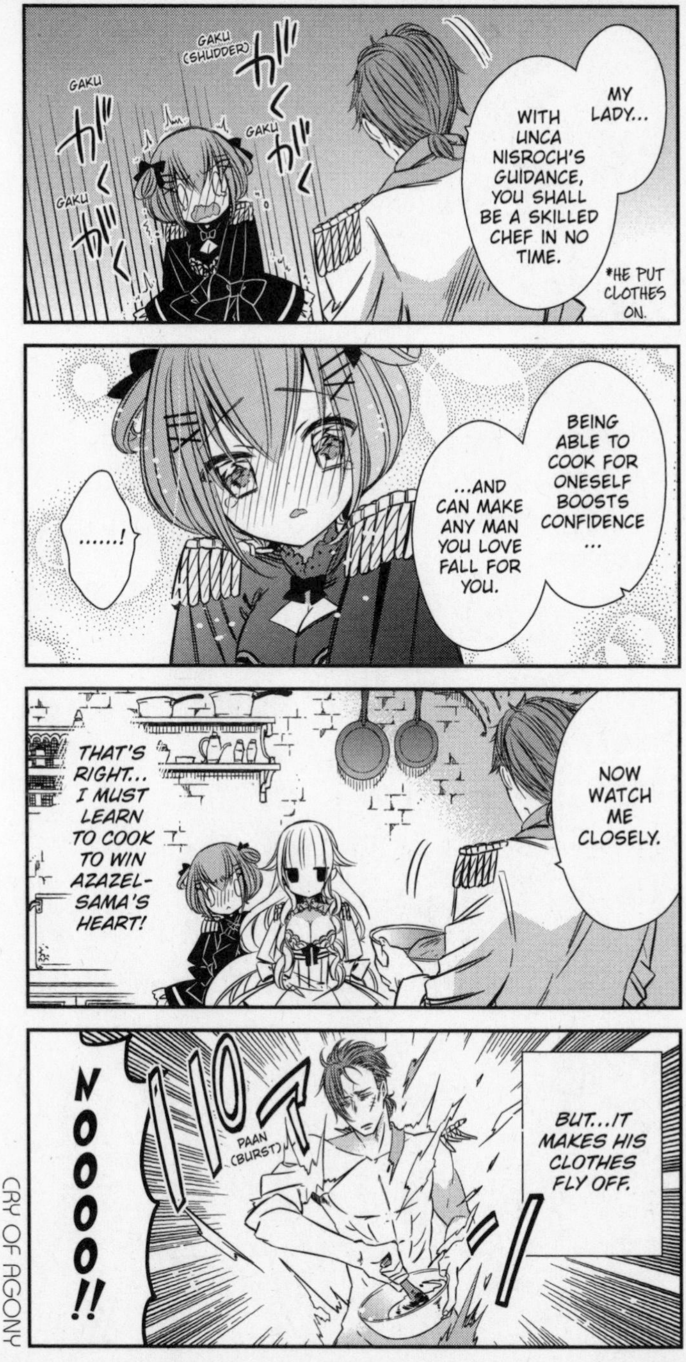
MY LADY... WITH UNCA NISROCH'S GUIDANCE, YOU SHALL BE A SKILLED CHEF IN NO TIME.
*HE PUT CLOTHES ON.
GAKU (SHUDDER)
GAKU
GAKU
GAKU
BEING ABLE TO COOK FOR ONESELF BOOSTS CONFIDENCE...
...AND CAN MAKE ANY MAN YOU LOVE FALL FOR YOU.
......!
NOW WATCH ME CLOSELY.
THAT'S RIGHT... I MUST LEARN TO COOK TO WIN AZAZEL-SAMA'S HEART!
BUT...IT MAKES HIS CLOTHES FLY OFF.
PAAN (BURST)
NOOOOO!!
CRY OF AGONY

POSITIVE

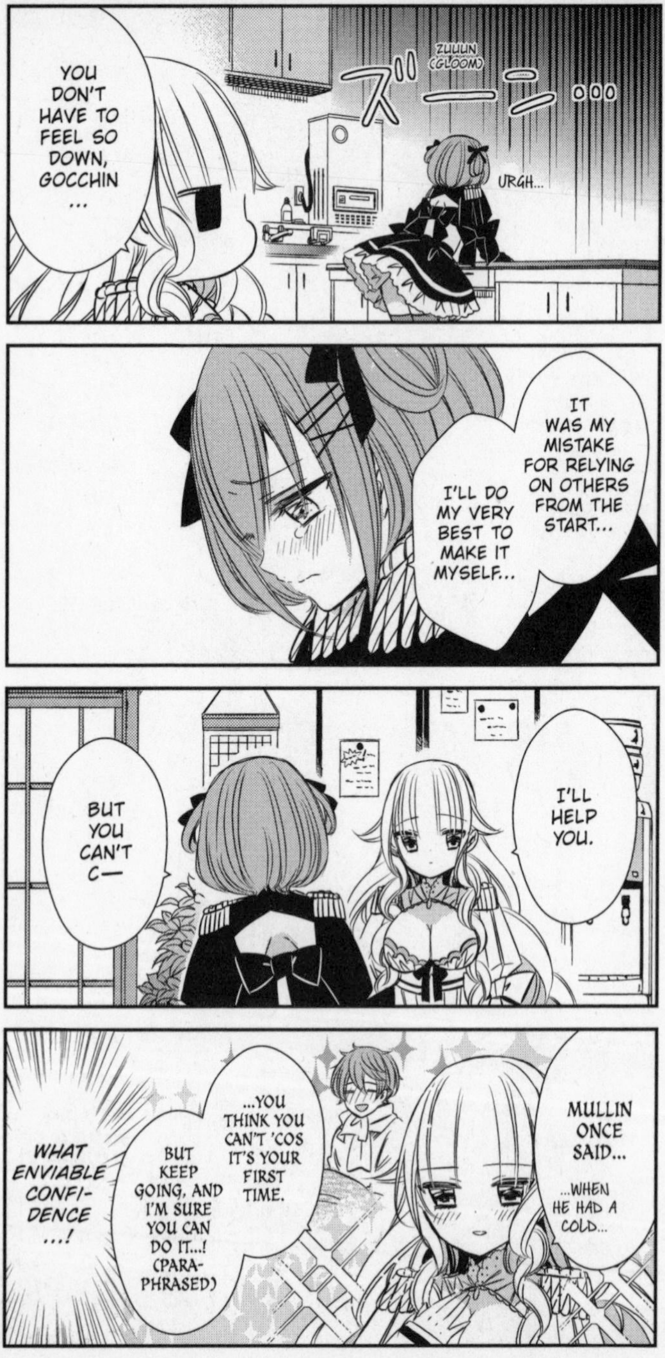
ZUUUN (GLOOM)
ズーン...
URGH...
YOU DON'T HAVE TO FEEL SO DOWN, GOCCHIN...
IT WAS MY MISTAKE FOR RELYING ON OTHERS FROM THE START...
I'LL DO MY VERY BEST TO MAKE IT MYSELF...
I'LL HELP YOU.
BUT YOU CAN'T C—
MULLIN ONCE SAID...
...WHEN HE HAD A COLD...
...YOU THINK YOU CAN'T 'COS IT'S YOUR FIRST TIME.
BUT KEEP GOING, AND I'M SURE YOU CAN DO IT...! (PARAPHRASED)
WHAT ENVIABLE CONFIDENCE...!

GORILLA GIRL

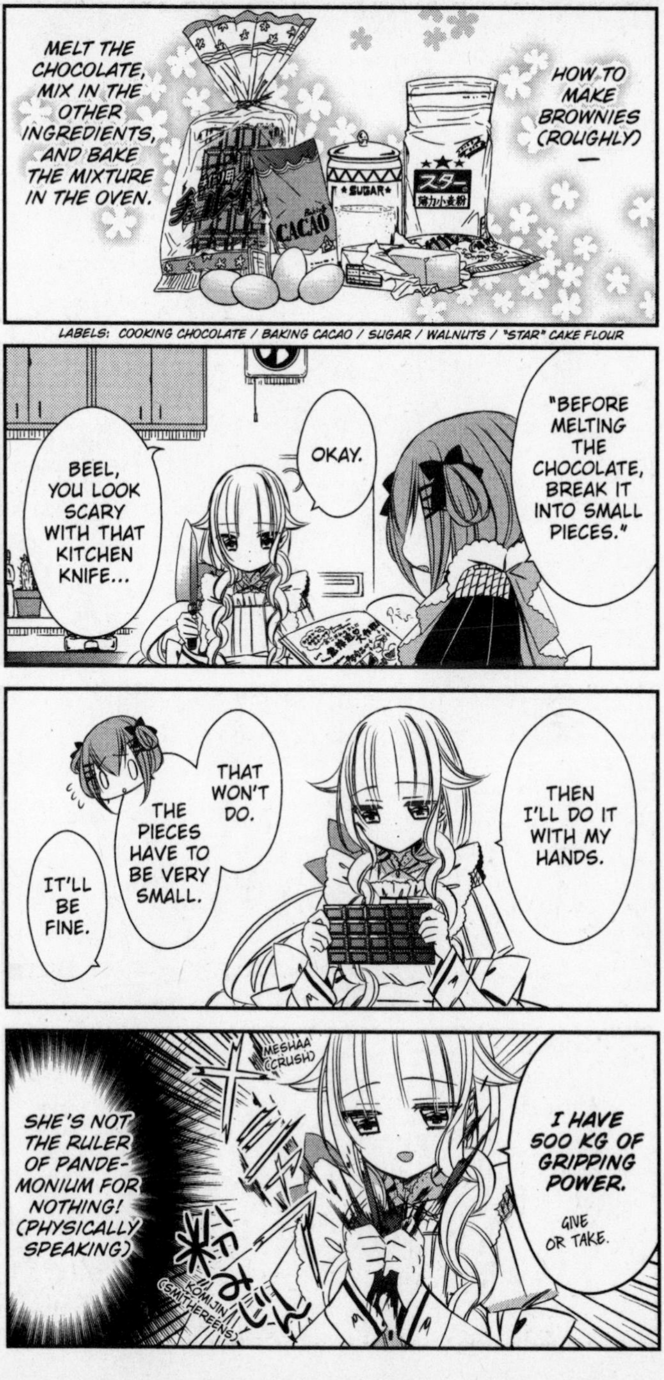
HOW TO MAKE BROWNIES (ROUGHLY) —
MELT THE CHOCOLATE, MIX IN THE OTHER INGREDIENTS, AND BAKE THE MIXTURE IN THE OVEN.
CACAO
SUGAR
LABELS: COOKING CHOCOLATE / BAKING CACAO / SUGAR / WALNUTS / "STAR" CAKE FLOUR
"BEFORE MELTING THE CHOCOLATE, BREAK IT INTO SMALL PIECES."
OKAY.
BEEL, YOU LOOK SCARY WITH THAT KITCHEN KNIFE...
THEN I'LL DO IT WITH MY HANDS.
THAT WON'T DO.
THE PIECES HAVE TO BE VERY SMALL.
IT'LL BE FINE.
I HAVE 500 KG OF GRIPPING POWER.
GIVE OR TAKE.
MESHAA (CRUSH)
KOMIJIN (SMITHEREENS)
SHE'S NOT THE RULER OF PANDE-MONIUM FOR NOTHING! (PHYSICALLY SPEAKING)

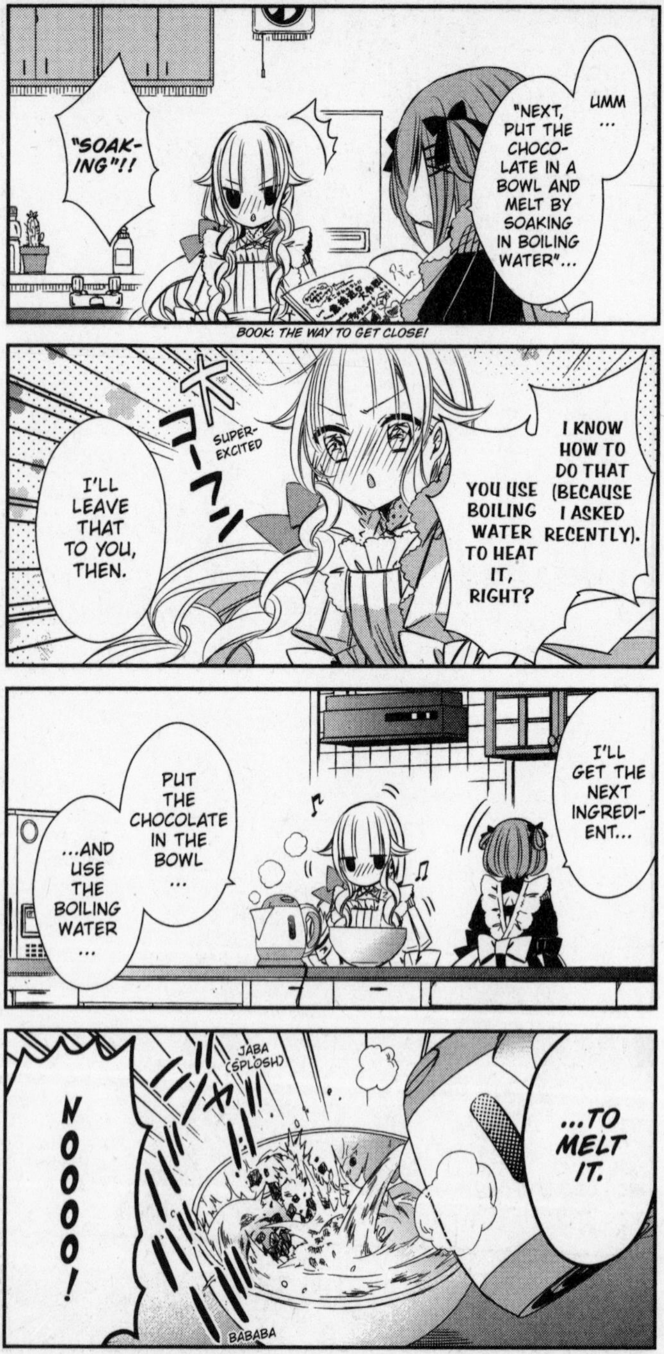
UMM ...
"NEXT, PUT THE CHOCOLATE IN A BOWL AND MELT BY SOAKING IN BOILING WATER"...
"SOAKING"!!
BOOK: THE WAY TO GET CLOSE!
I KNOW HOW TO DO THAT (BECAUSE I ASKED RECENTLY).
YOU USE BOILING WATER TO HEAT IT, RIGHT?
SUPER-EXCITED
I'LL LEAVE THAT TO YOU, THEN.
I'LL GET THE NEXT INGREDIENT...
PUT THE CHOCOLATE IN THE BOWL ...
...AND USE THE BOILING WATER ...
...TO MELT IT.
JABA (SPLOSH)
NOOOOO!
BABABA

DIRECTLY IN

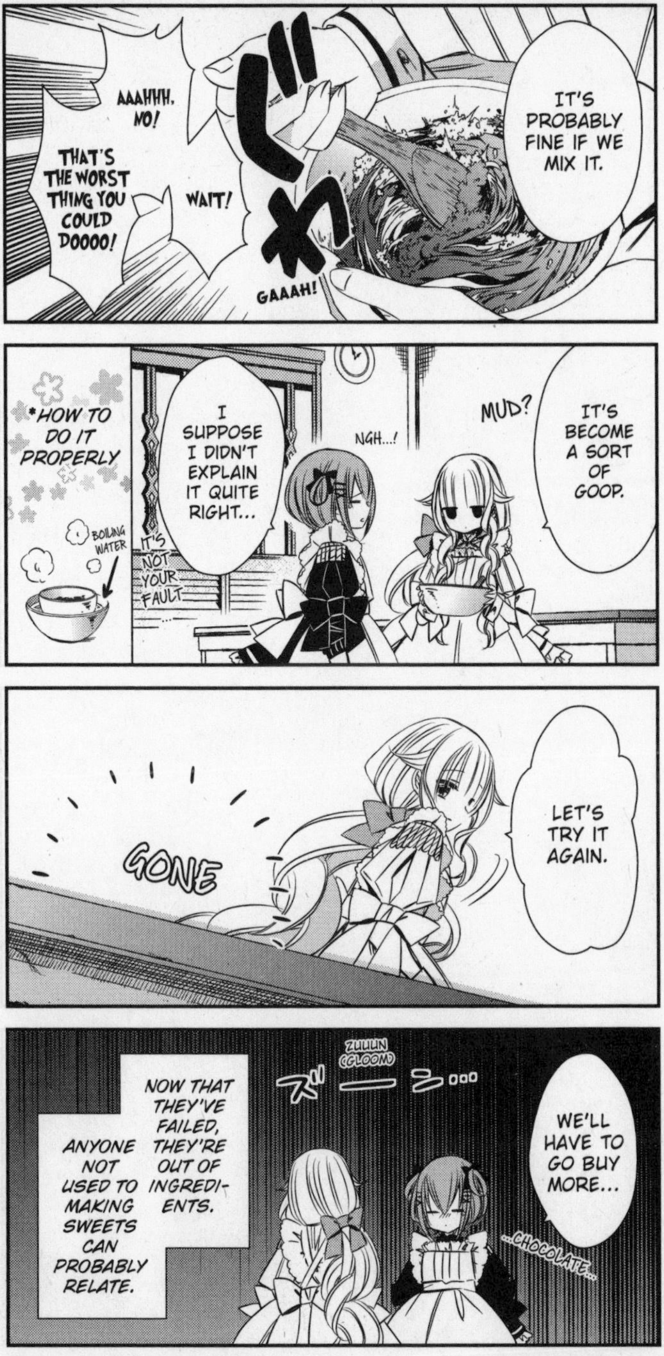
IT'S PROBABLY FINE IF WE MIX IT.
GAAAH!
WAIT!
AAAHHH, NO!
THAT'S THE WORST THING YOU COULD DOOOO!
IT'S BECOME A SORT OF GOOP.
MUD?
NGH...!
I SUPPOSE I DIDN'T EXPLAIN IT QUITE RIGHT...
IT'S NOT YOUR FAULT...
*HOW TO DO IT PROPERLY
BOILING WATER
LET'S TRY IT AGAIN.
GONE
WE'LL HAVE TO GO BUY MORE...
ズーン...
ZUUUN (GLOOM)
...CHOCOLATE...
NOW THAT THEY'VE FAILED, THEY'RE OUT OF INGREDI- ENTS.
ANYONE NOT USED TO MAKING SWEETS CAN PROBABLY RELATE.

NO MORE CHOCOLATE

BFFs

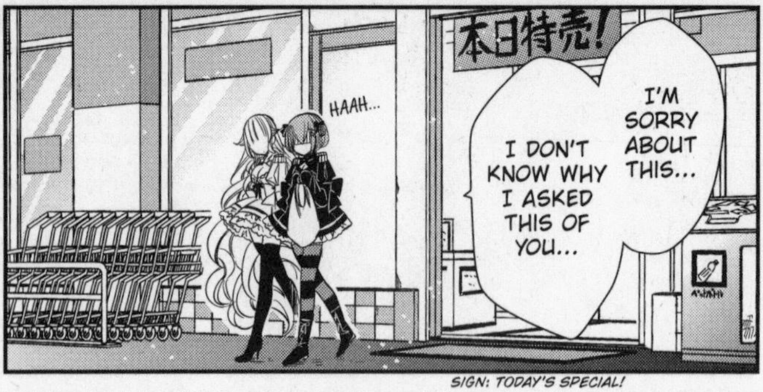
本日特売!
I'M SORRY ABOUT THIS...
I DON'T KNOW WHY I ASKED THIS OF YOU...
HAAH...
SIGN: TODAY'S SPECIAL!

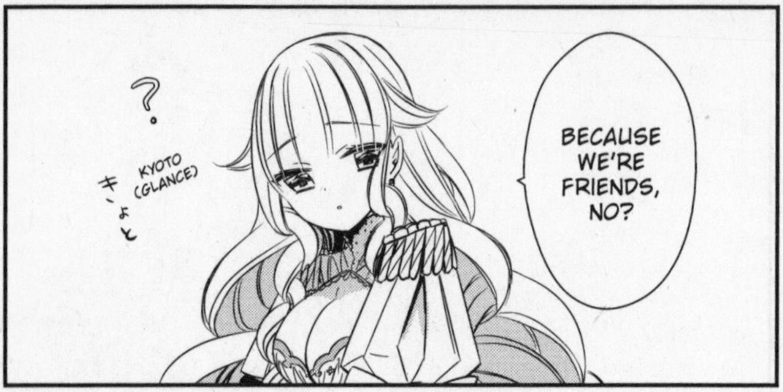
BECAUSE WE'RE FRIENDS, NO?
?
KYOTO (GLANCE)

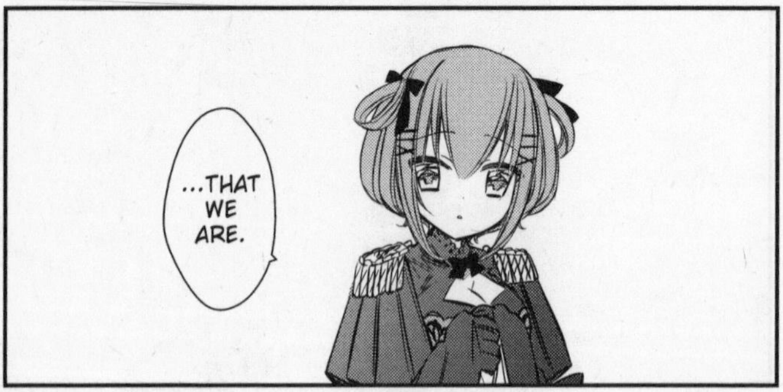
...THAT WE ARE.

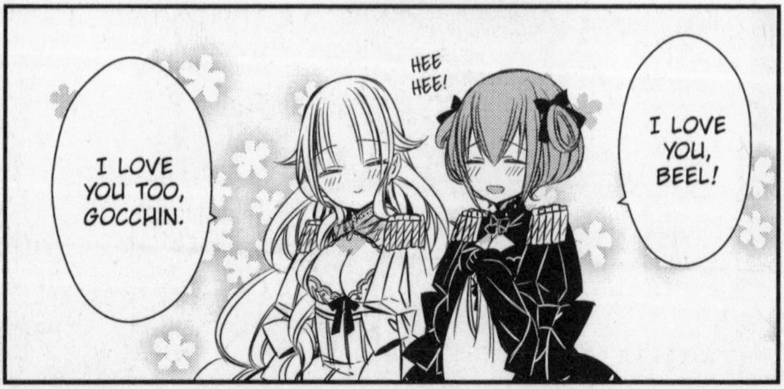
I LOVE YOU, BEEL!
HEE HEE!
I LOVE YOU TOO, GOCCHIN.

FLUFFY...

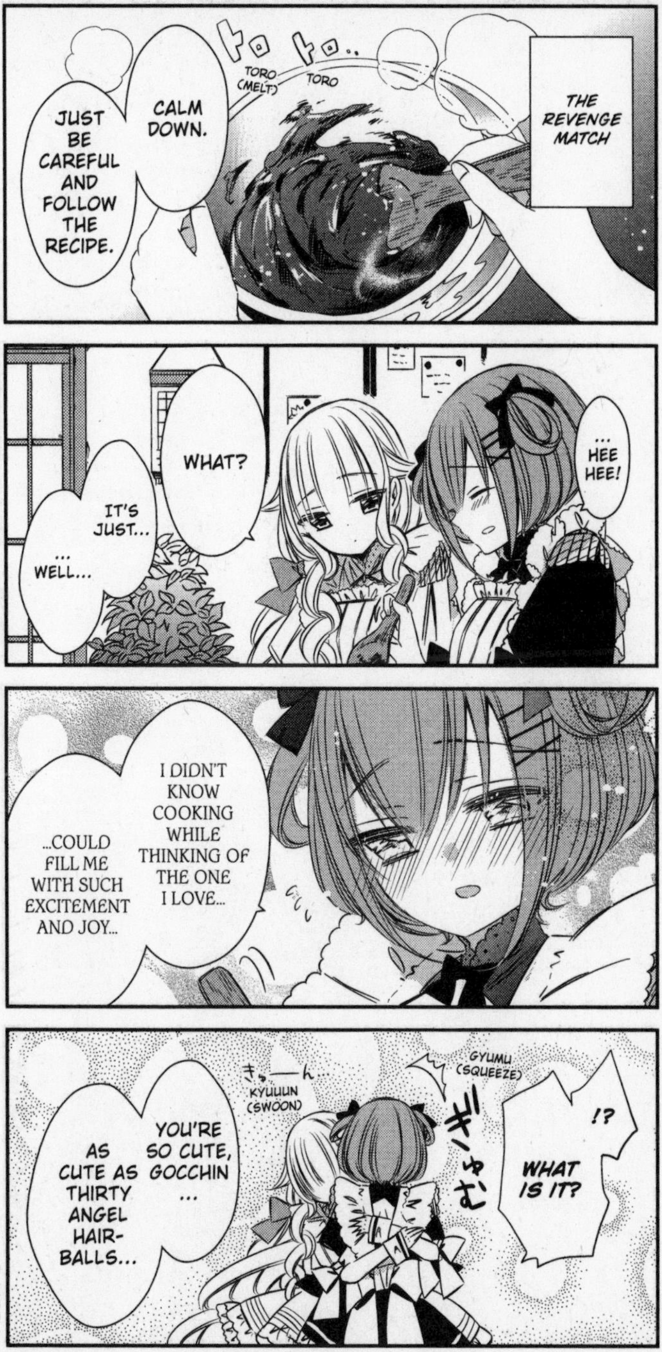
THE REVENGE MATCH
トロ トロ..
TORO (MELT) TORO
CALM DOWN.
JUST BE CAREFUL AND FOLLOW THE RECIPE.
... HEE HEE!
WHAT?
IT'S JUST... ... WELL...
I DIDN'T KNOW COOKING WHILE THINKING OF THE ONE I LOVE...
...COULD FILL ME WITH SUCH EXCITEMENT AND JOY...
!?
WHAT IS IT?
ぎゅむ
GYUMU (SQUEEZE)
きゅーん...
KYUUUN (SWOON)
YOU'RE SO CUTE, GOCCHIN...
AS CUTE AS THIRTY ANGEL HAIR-BALLS...

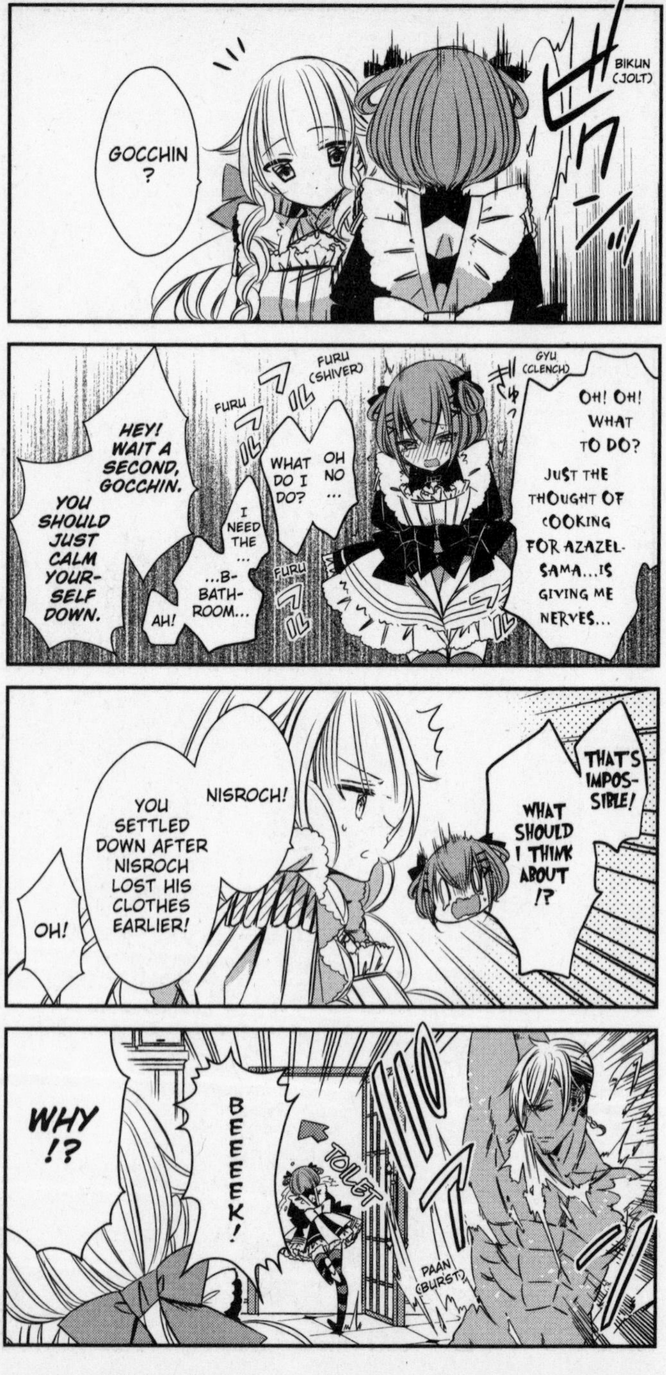
BIKUN (JOLT)
GOCCHIN ?
GYU (CLENCH)
OH! OH! WHAT TO DO?
JUST THE THOUGHT OF COOKING FOR AZAZEL-SAMA...IS GIVING ME NERVES...
FURU (SHIVER)
FURU
OH NO ...
WHAT DO I DO?
FURU
I NEED THE ...
...B-BATH-ROOM...
AH!
HEY! WAIT A SECOND, GOCCHIN.
YOU SHOULD JUST CALM YOUR-SELF DOWN.
THAT'S IMPOS-SIBLE!
WHAT SHOULD I THINK ABOUT !?
NISROCH!
YOU SETTLED DOWN AFTER NISROCH LOST HIS CLOTHES EARLIER!
OH!
PAAN (BURST)
TOILET
BEEEEK!
WHY !?

ALL MIXED-UP

SHE COOLED OFF

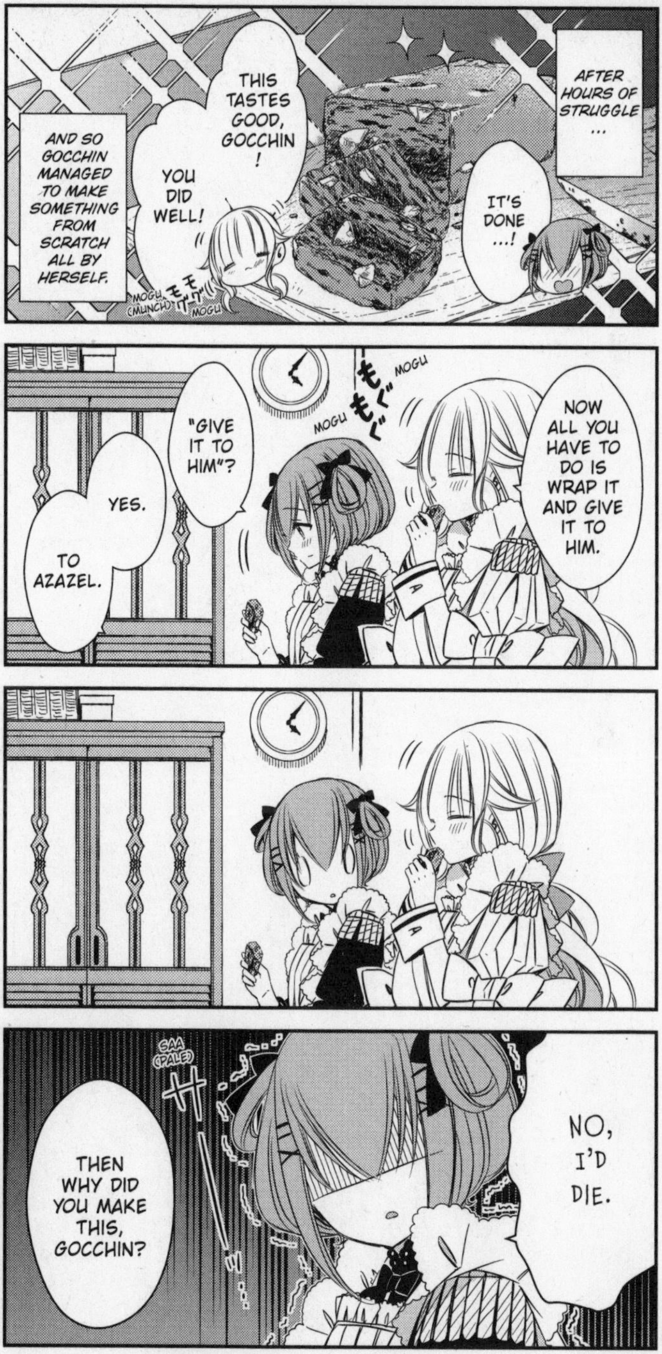
AFTER HOURS OF STRUGGLE...
IT'S DONE...!
THIS TASTES GOOD, GOCCHIN!
YOU DID WELL!
AND SO GOCCHIN MANAGED TO MAKE SOMETHING FROM SCRATCH ALL BY HERSELF.
MOGU (MUNCH) MOGU
NOW ALL YOU HAVE TO DO IS WRAP IT AND GIVE IT TO HIM.
もぐもぐ MOGU MOGU
"GIVE IT TO HIM"?
YES.
TO AZAZEL.
NO, I'D DIE.
SAA (PALED)
THEN WHY DID YOU MAKE THIS, GOCCHIN?

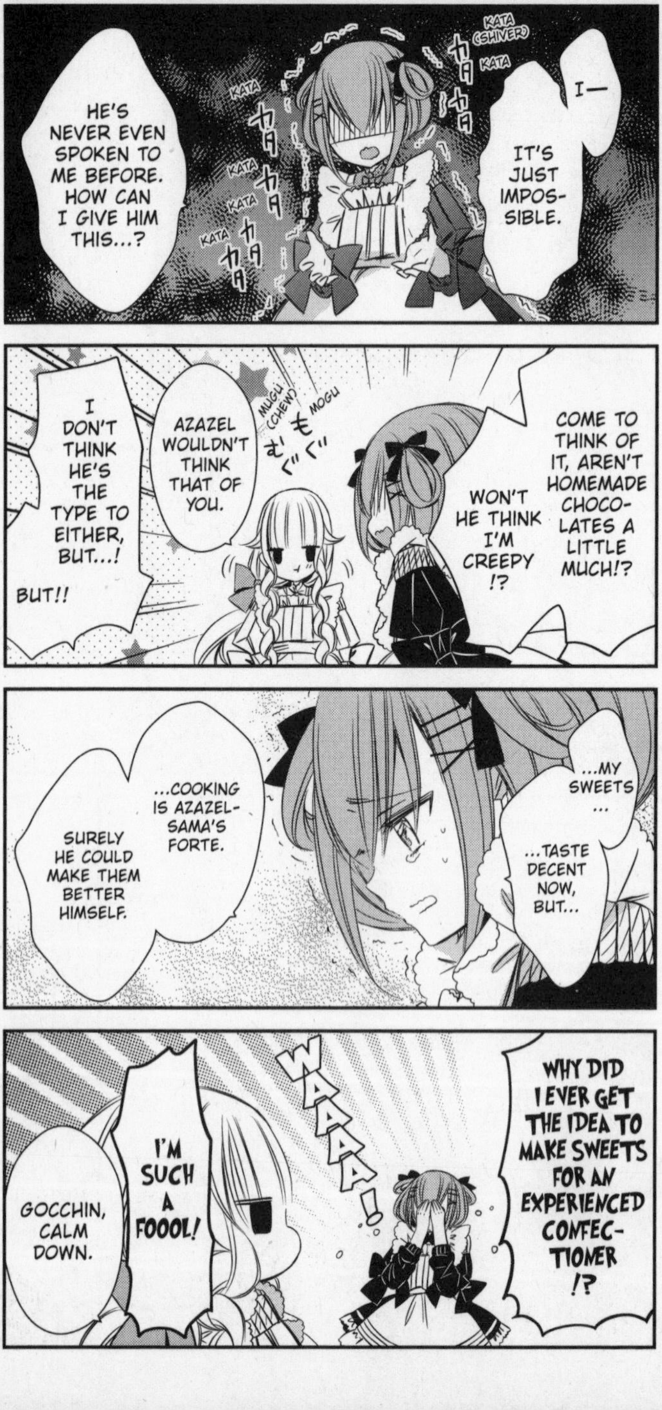
KATA (SHIVER)
KATA
I—
IT'S JUST IMPOS-SIBLE.
KATA
KATA
KATA
KATA
HE'S NEVER EVEN SPOKEN TO ME BEFORE. HOW CAN I GIVE HIM THIS...?
COME TO THINK OF IT, AREN'T HOMEMADE CHOCO-LATES A LITTLE MUCH!?
WON'T HE THINK I'M CREEPY!?
MOGU
MUGU (CHEW)
AZAZEL WOULDN'T THINK THAT OF YOU.
I DON'T THINK HE'S THE TYPE TO EITHER, BUT...!
BUT!!
...MY SWEETS...
...TASTE DECENT NOW, BUT...
...COOKING IS AZAZEL-SAMA'S FORTE.
SURELY HE COULD MAKE THEM BETTER HIMSELF.
WHY DID I EVER GET THE IDEA TO MAKE SWEETS FOR AN EXPERIENCED CONFEC-TIONER!?
WAAAA!
I'M SUCH A FOOOL!
GOCCHIN, CALM DOWN.

CALM DOWN

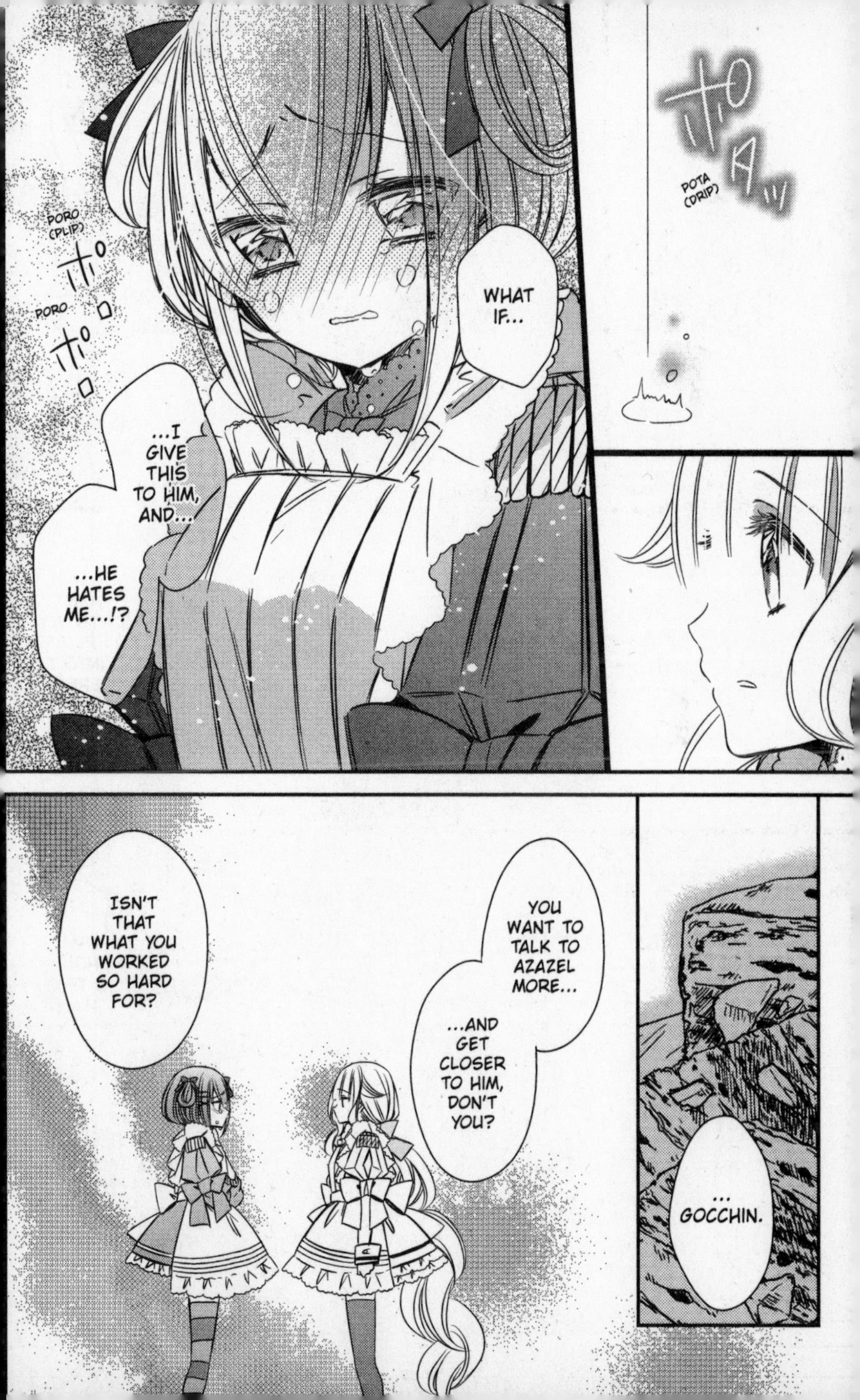
POTA (DRIP)
WHAT IF...
PORO (PLIP)
PORO
...I GIVE THIS TO HIM, AND...
...HE HATES ME...!?
... GOCCHIN.
YOU WANT TO TALK TO AZAZEL MORE...
...AND GET CLOSER TO HIM, DON'T YOU?
ISN'T THAT WHAT YOU WORKED SO HARD FOR?

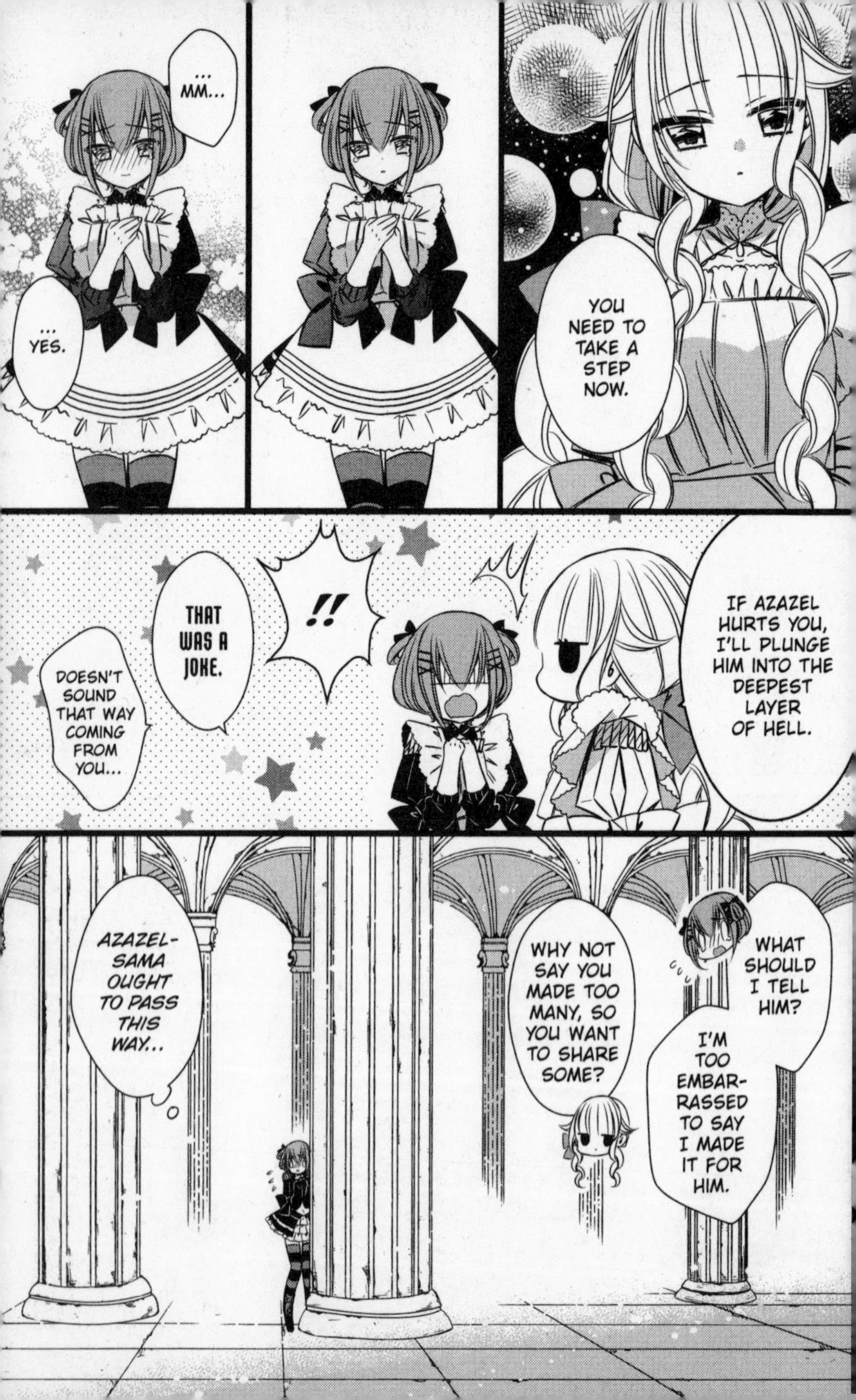
YOU NEED TO TAKE A STEP NOW.
... MM...
... YES.
IF AZAZEL HURTS YOU, I'LL PLUNGE HIM INTO THE DEEPEST LAYER OF HELL.
!!
THAT WAS A JOKE.
DOESN'T SOUND THAT WAY COMING FROM YOU...
WHAT SHOULD I TELL HIM?
I'M TOO EMBARRASSED TO SAY I MADE IT FOR HIM.
WHY NOT SAY YOU MADE TOO MANY, SO YOU WANT TO SHARE SOME?
AZAZEL-SAMA OUGHT TO PASS THIS WAY...

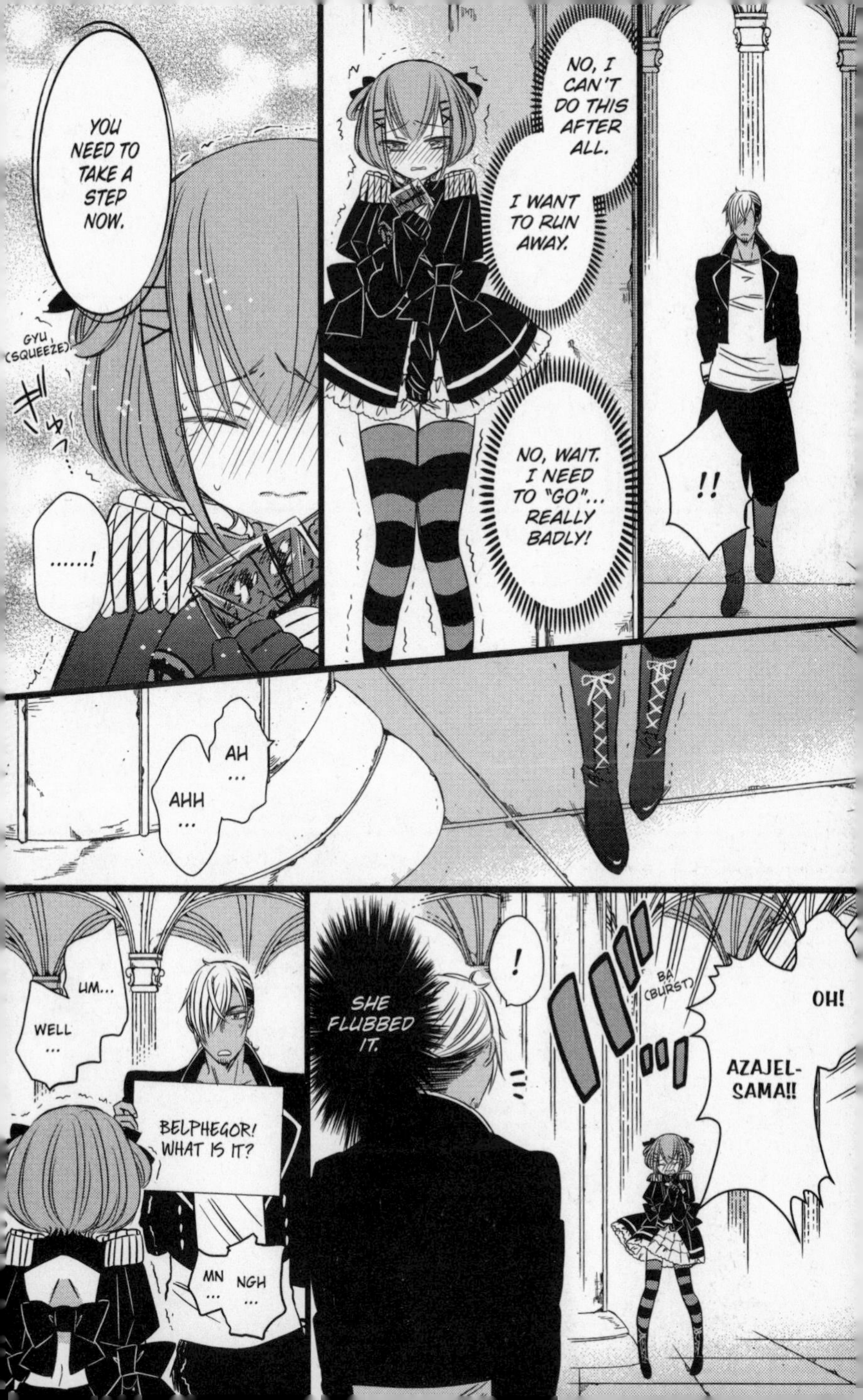
!!
NO, I CAN'T DO THIS AFTER ALL.
I WANT TO RUN AWAY.
NO, WAIT. I NEED TO "GO"... REALLY BADLY!
YOU NEED TO TAKE A STEP NOW.
GYU (SQUEEZE)
......!
AH... AHH...
OH!
AZAJEL-SAMA!!
BA (BURST)
!
SHE FLUBBED IT.
BELPHEGOR! WHAT IS IT?
UM... WELL...
MN... NGH...

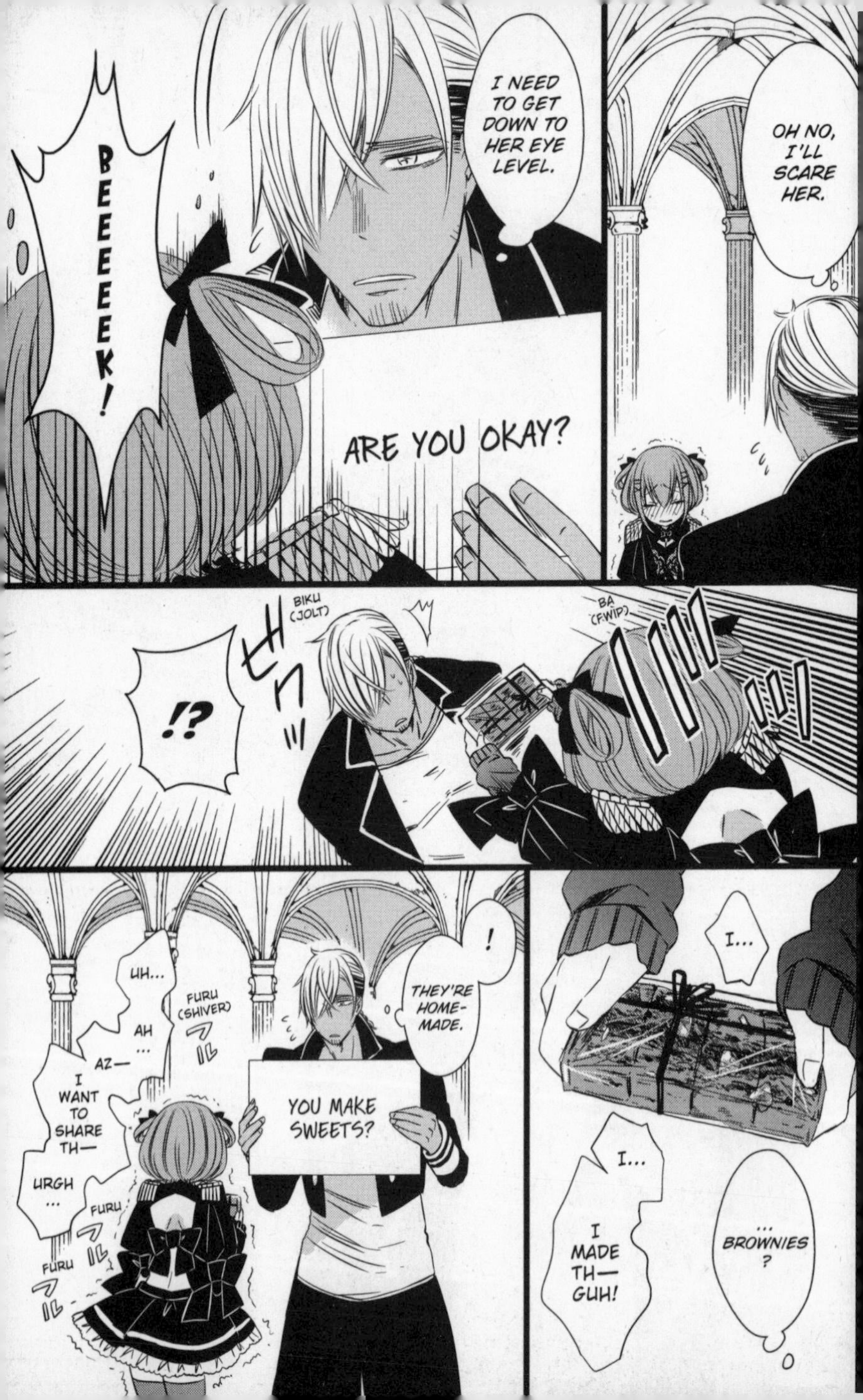
OH NO, I'LL SCARE HER.
I NEED TO GET DOWN TO HER EYE LEVEL.
ARE YOU OKAY?
BEEEEEK!
BA (F'WIP)
BIKU (JOLT)
!?
I...
I...
I MADE TH— GUH!
...BROWNIES?
!
THEY'RE HOME-MADE.
YOU MAKE SWEETS?
UH...
FURU (SHIVER)
AH ...
AZ—
I WANT TO SHARE TH—
URGH ...
FURU
FURU

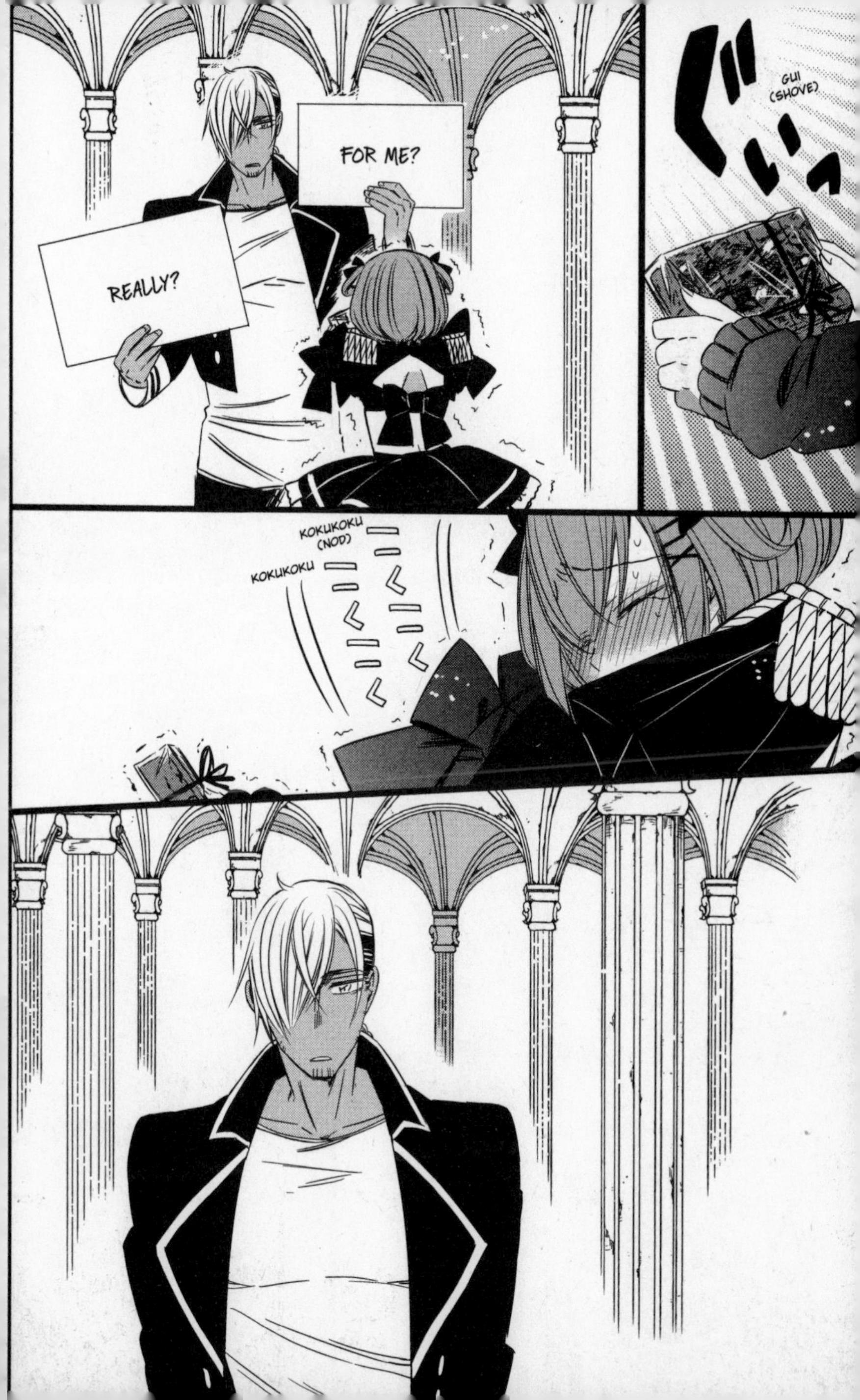
GUI
(SHOVE)
FOR ME?
REALLY?
KOKUKOKU
(NOD)
KOKUKOKU

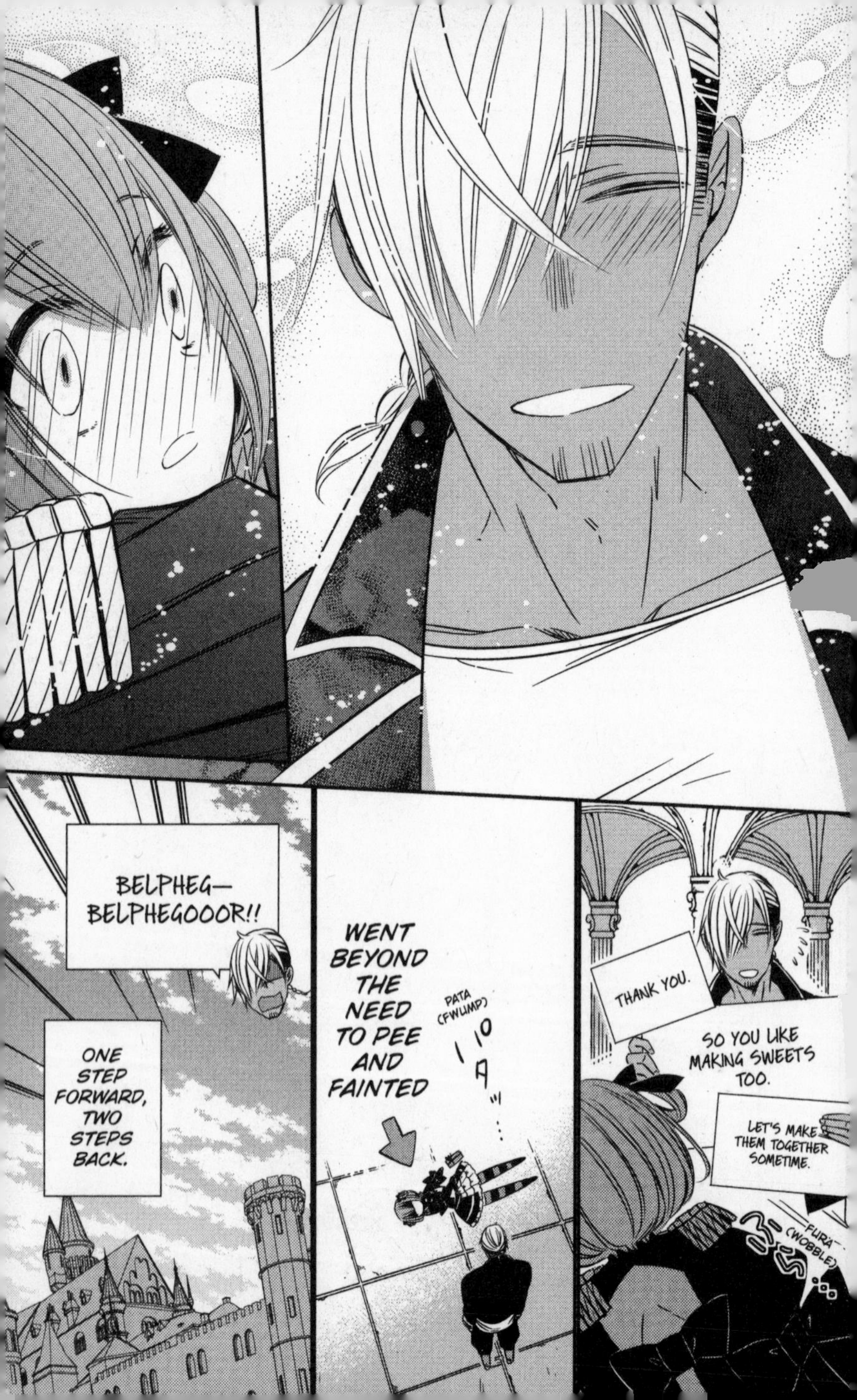
THANK YOU.
SO YOU LIKE MAKING SWEETS TOO.
LET'S MAKE THEM TOGETHER SOMETIME.
FURA (WOBBLE)
WENT BEYOND THE NEED TO PEE AND FAINTED
PATA (FWUMP)
BELPHEG— BELPHEGOOOR!!
ONE STEP FORWARD, TWO STEPS BACK.

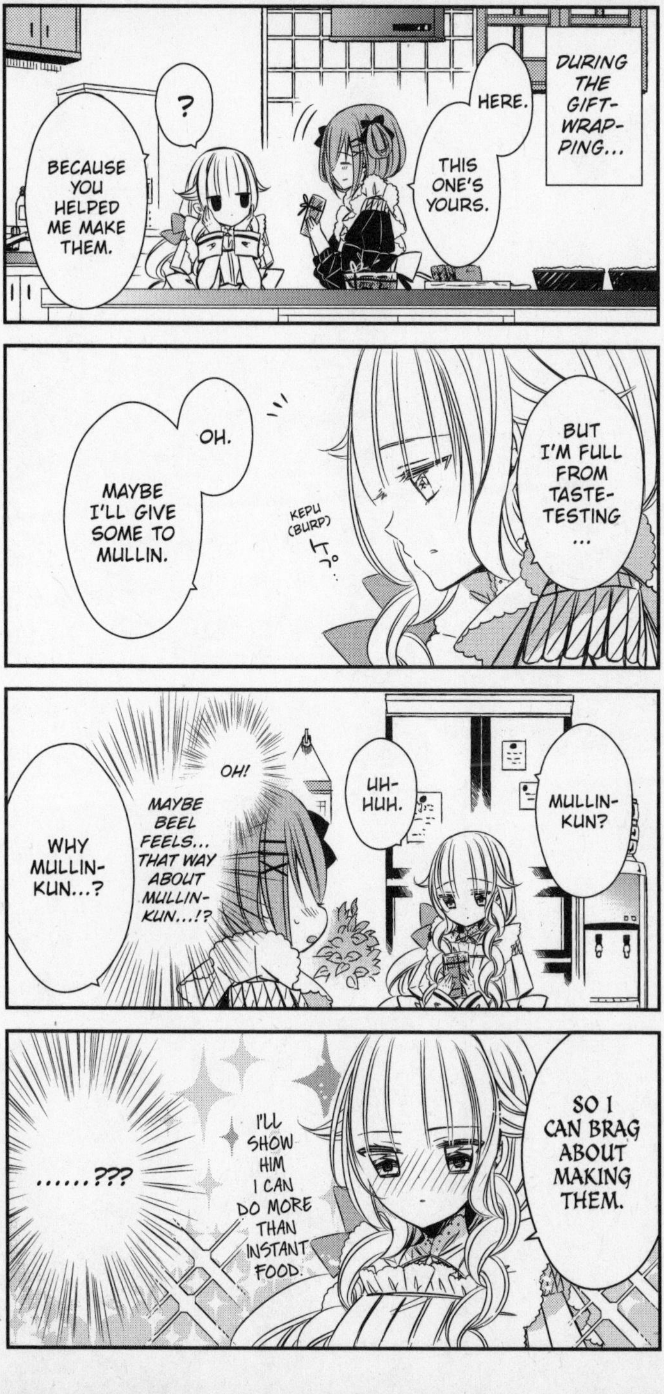
DURING THE GIFT-WRAPPING...
HERE.
THIS ONE'S YOURS.
?
BECAUSE YOU HELPED ME MAKE THEM.
BUT I'M FULL FROM TASTE-TESTING...
KEPU (BURP)
OH.
MAYBE I'LL GIVE SOME TO MULLIN.
MULLIN-KUN?
UH-HUH.
OH!
MAYBE BEEL FEELS... THAT WAY ABOUT MULLIN-KUN...!?
WHY MULLIN-KUN...?
SO I CAN BRAG ABOUT MAKING THEM.
I'LL SHOW HIM I CAN DO MORE THAN INSTANT FOOD.
......???

CHAPTER 10 BONUS MANGA

AT THE SUPER-MARKET TO BUY MORE CHOCOLATE ...
YOU WANT TO BUY ICE CREAM?
LET'S SPLIT IT BETWEEN US.
WRAPPER: ICE MILK "TWIN MILK" / TWICE AS MUCH MILK!!

As Miss Beelzebub Likes

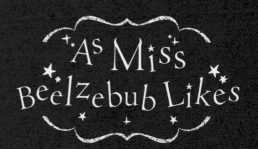

CHAPTER 11

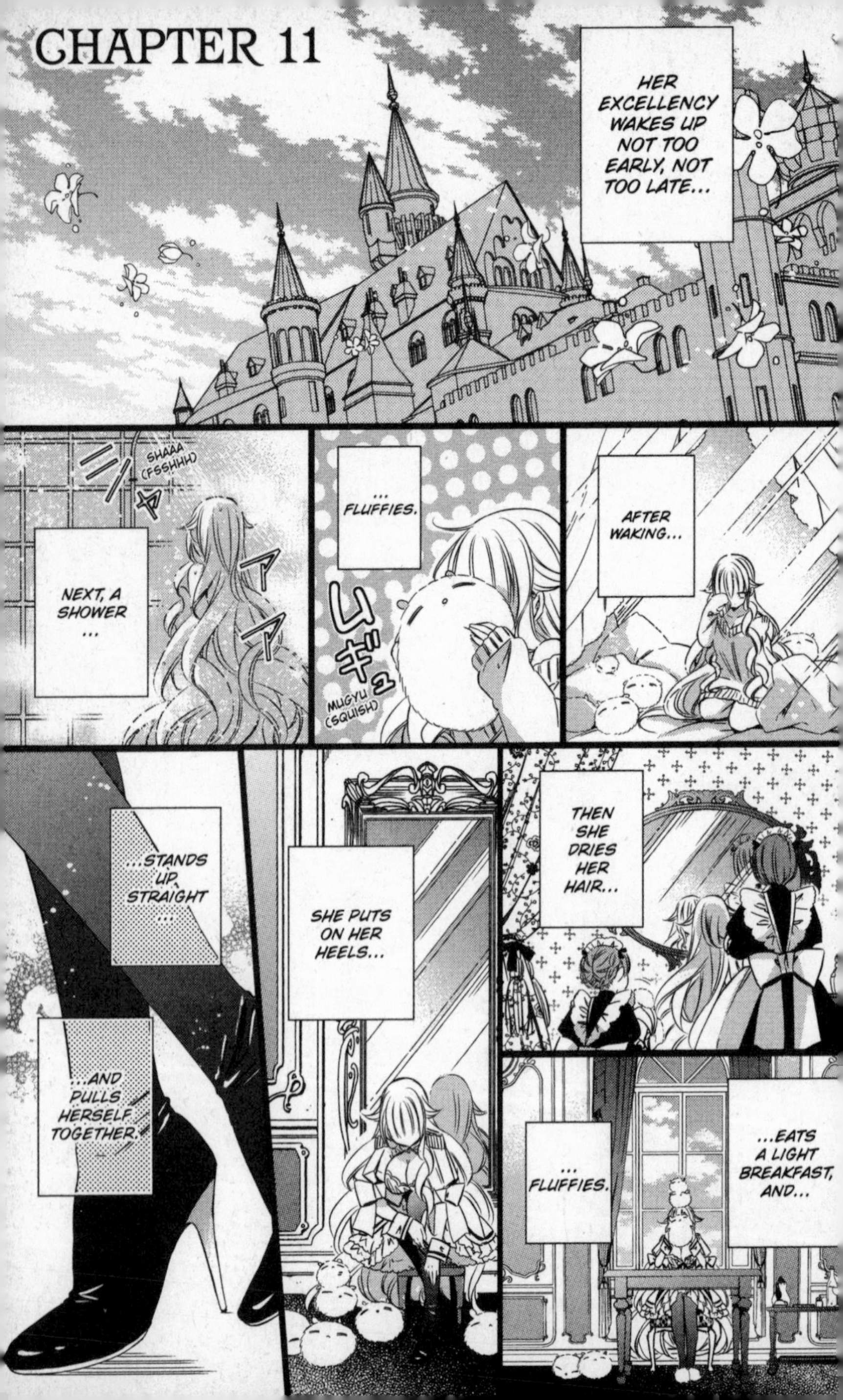

HER EXCELLENCY WAKES UP NOT TOO EARLY, NOT TOO LATE...
AFTER WAKING...
... FLUFFIES.
ムギュ
MUGYU (SQUISH)
NEXT, A SHOWER ...
SHAAA (FSSHHH)
THEN SHE DRIES HER HAIR...
...EATS A LIGHT BREAKFAST, AND...
... FLUFFIES.
SHE PUTS ON HER HEELS...
...STANDS UP STRAIGHT ...
...AND PULLS HERSELF TOGETHER.

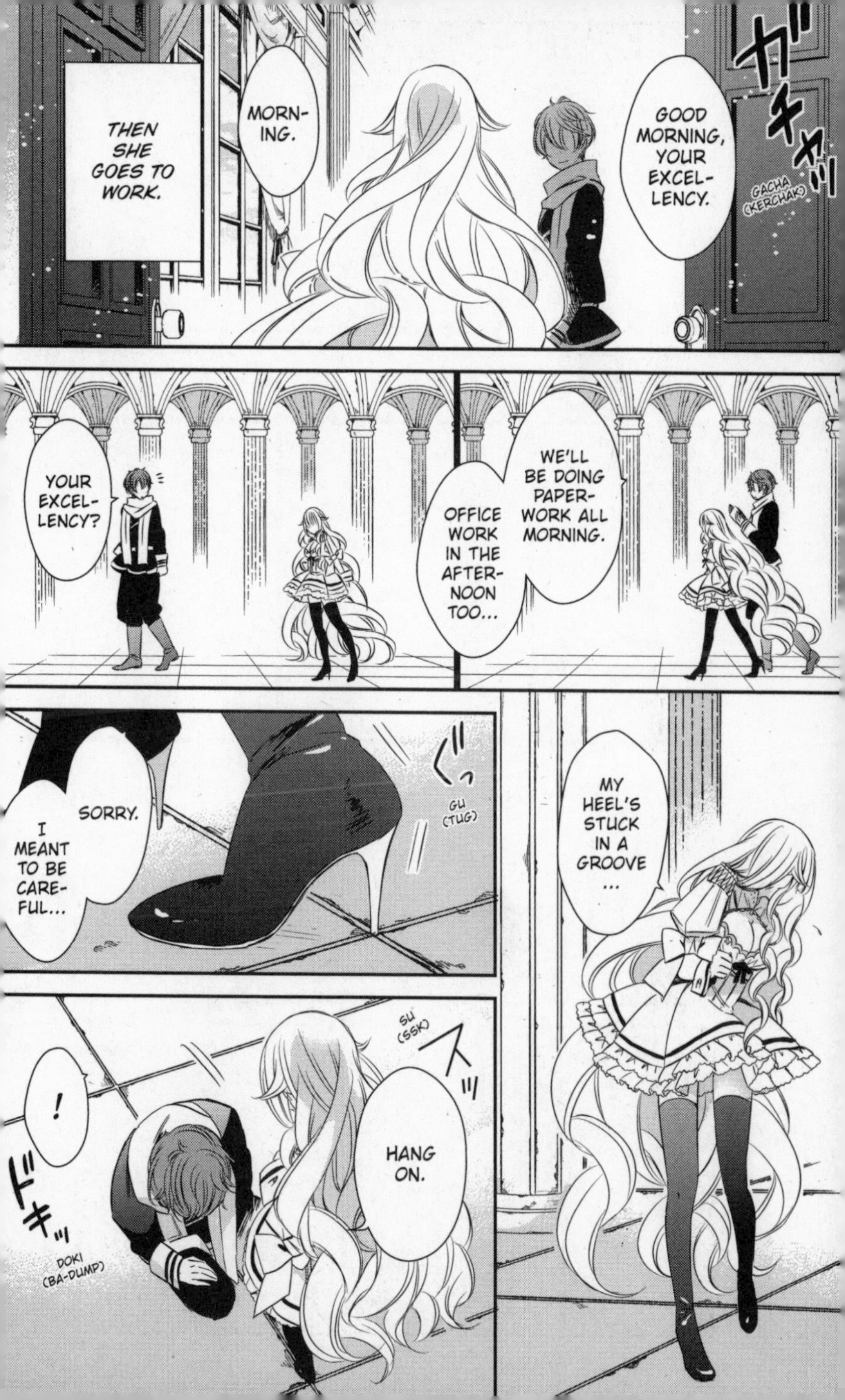
ガチャッ
GACHA (KERCHAK)
GOOD MORNING, YOUR EXCEL-LENCY.
MORN-ING.
THEN SHE GOES TO WORK.
WE'LL BE DOING PAPER-WORK ALL MORNING.
OFFICE WORK IN THE AFTER-NOON TOO...
YOUR EXCEL-LENCY?
MY HEEL'S STUCK IN A GROOVE ...
ぐっ
GU (TUG)
SORRY.
I MEANT TO BE CARE-FUL...
スッ
SU (SSK)
HANG ON.
!
ドキッ
DOKI (BA-DUMP)

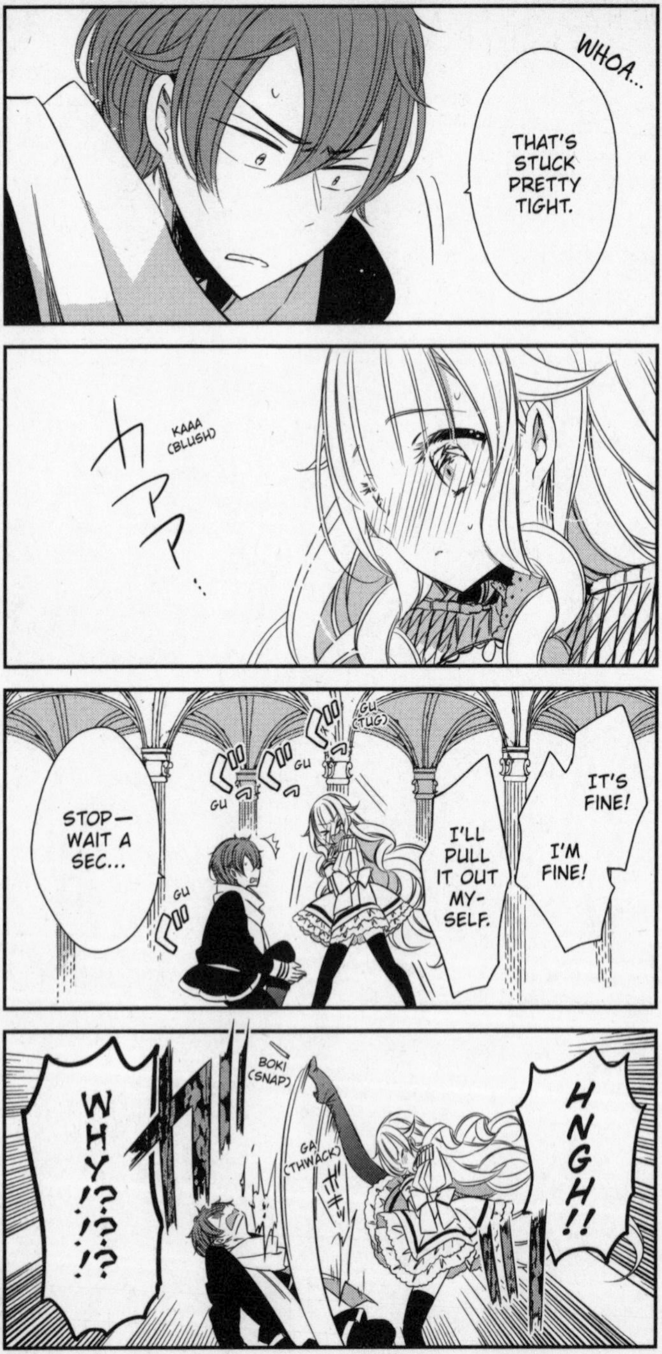
WHOA...
THAT'S STUCK PRETTY TIGHT.
カァァ…
KAAA (BLUSH)
IT'S FINE!
I'M FINE!
I'LL PULL IT OUT MY-SELF.
GU (TUG)
GU
GU
GU
STOP— WAIT A SEC...
HNGH!!
BOKI (SNAP)
GA (THWACK)
ガキッ
WHY!?!?!?

EVER HELPFUL

HE TRIED HIS BEST

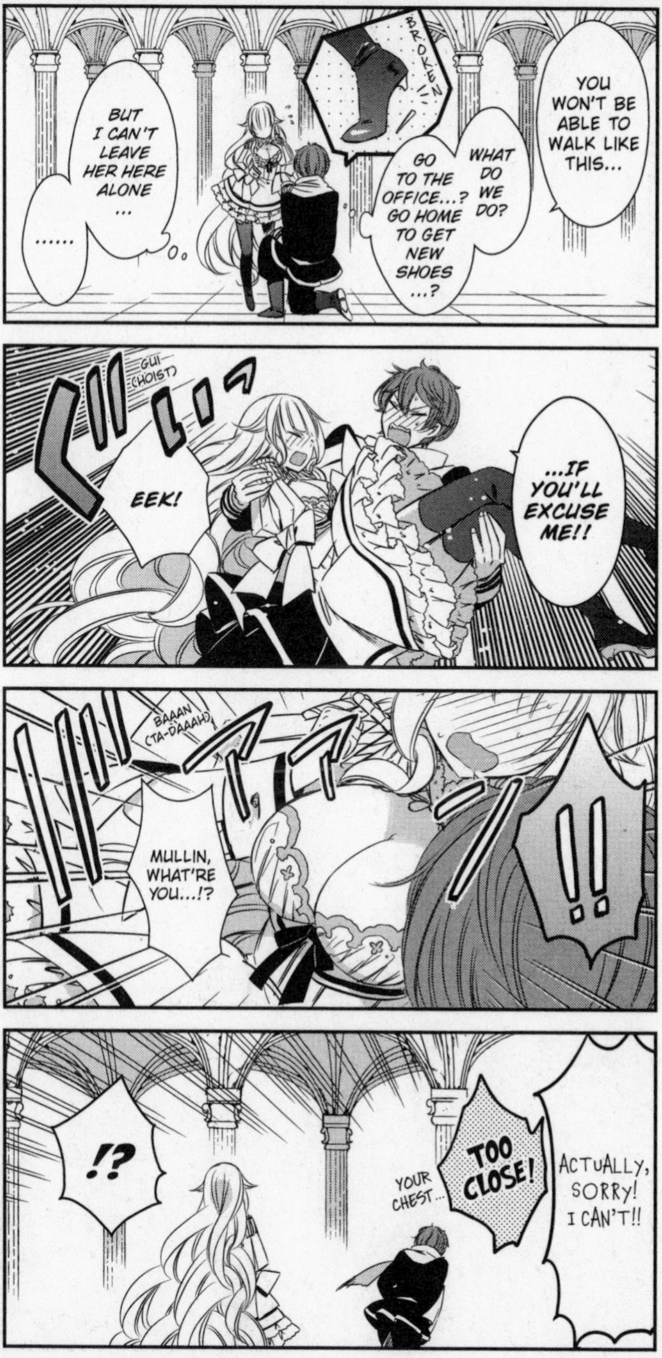
YOU WON'T BE ABLE TO WALK LIKE THIS...
BROKEN
WHAT DO WE DO?
GO TO THE OFFICE...? GO HOME TO GET NEW SHOES...?
BUT I CAN'T LEAVE HER HERE ALONE...
......
...IF YOU'LL EXCUSE ME!!
GUI (HOIST)
EEK!
!!
BAAAN (TA-DAAAH)
MULLIN, WHAT'RE YOU...!?
ACTUALLY, SORRY! I CAN'T!!
TOO CLOSE!
YOUR CHEST...
!?

WHAT'LL YOU DO?

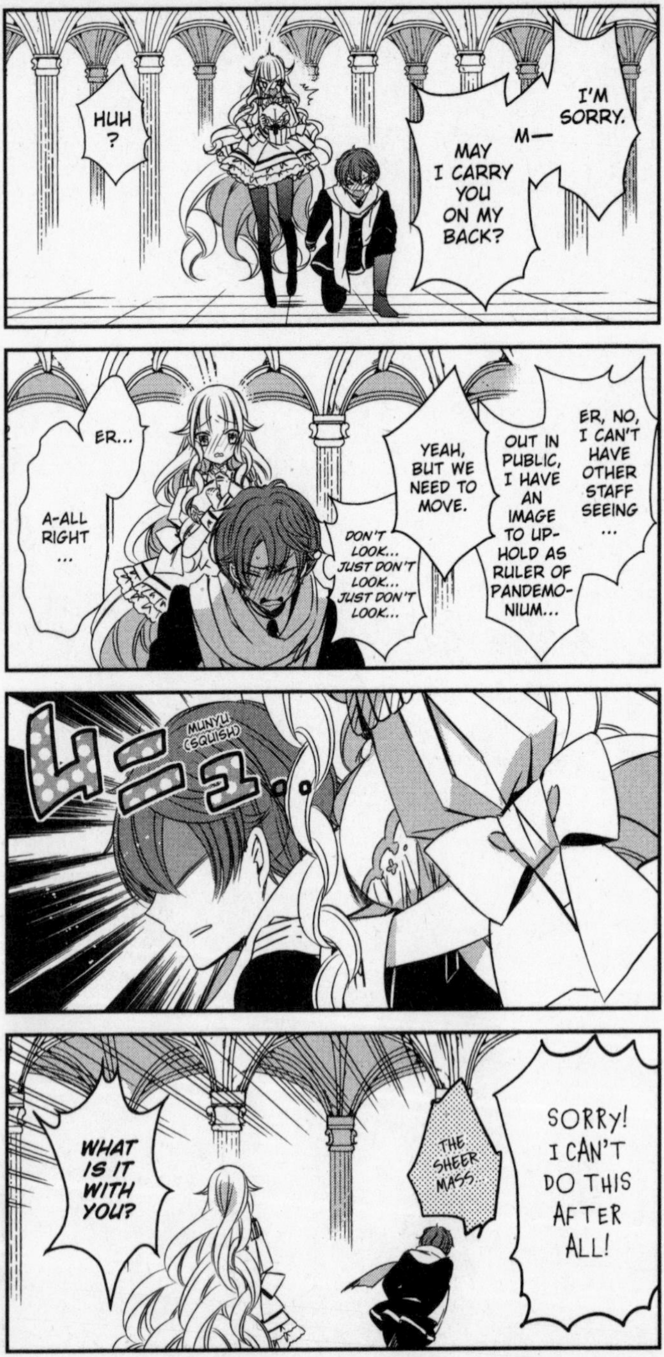
I'M SORRY.
M— MAY I CARRY YOU ON MY BACK?
HUH?
ER, NO, I CAN'T HAVE OTHER STAFF SEEING...
OUT IN PUBLIC, I HAVE AN IMAGE TO UPHOLD AS RULER OF PANDEMONIUM...
YEAH, BUT WE NEED TO MOVE.
DON'T LOOK... JUST DON'T LOOK... JUST DON'T LOOK...
ER...
A-ALL RIGHT...
ムニュ。。
MUNYU (SQUISH)
SORRY! I CAN'T DO THIS AFTER ALL!
THE SHEER MASS
WHAT IS IT WITH YOU?

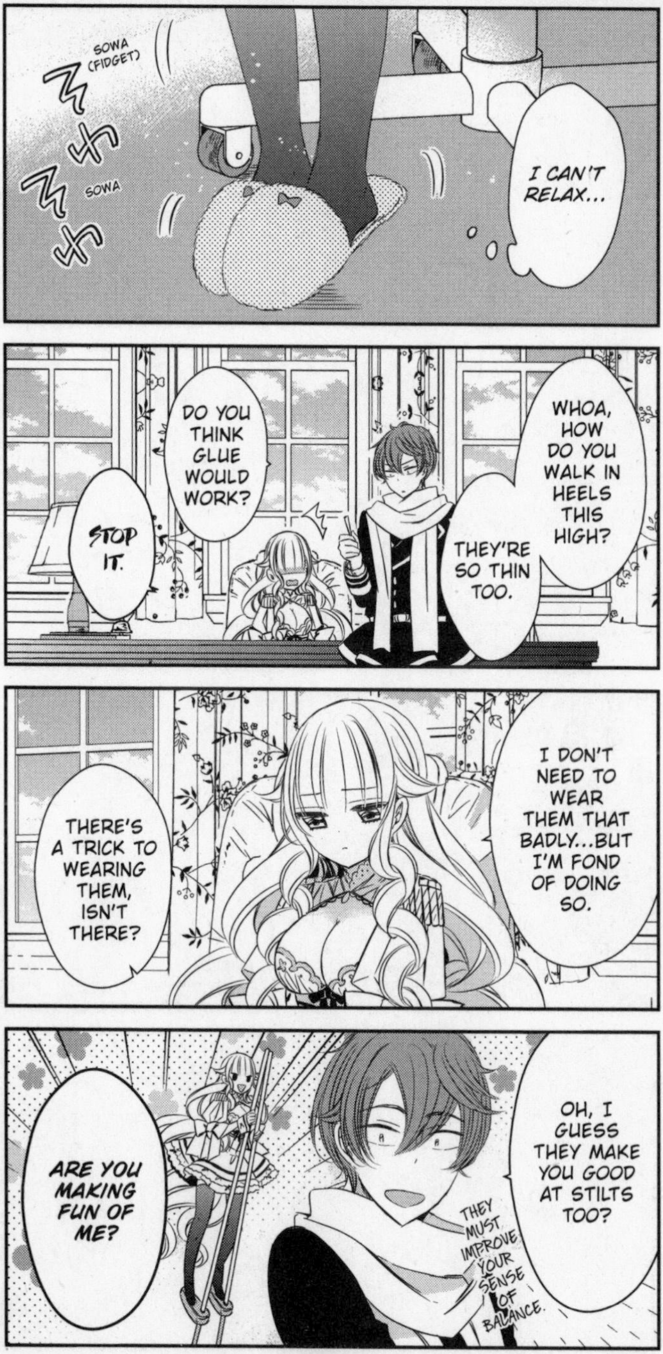
SOWA (FIDGET)
SOWA
I CAN'T RELAX...
WHOA, HOW DO YOU WALK IN HEELS THIS HIGH?
THEY'RE SO THIN TOO.
DO YOU THINK GLUE WOULD WORK?
STOP IT.
I DON'T NEED TO WEAR THEM THAT BADLY...BUT I'M FOND OF DOING SO.
THERE'S A TRICK TO WEARING THEM, ISN'T THERE?
OH, I GUESS THEY MAKE YOU GOOD AT STILTS TOO?
THEY MUST IMPROVE YOUR SENSE OF BALANCE.
ARE YOU MAKING FUN OF ME?

ONEE-SAMA

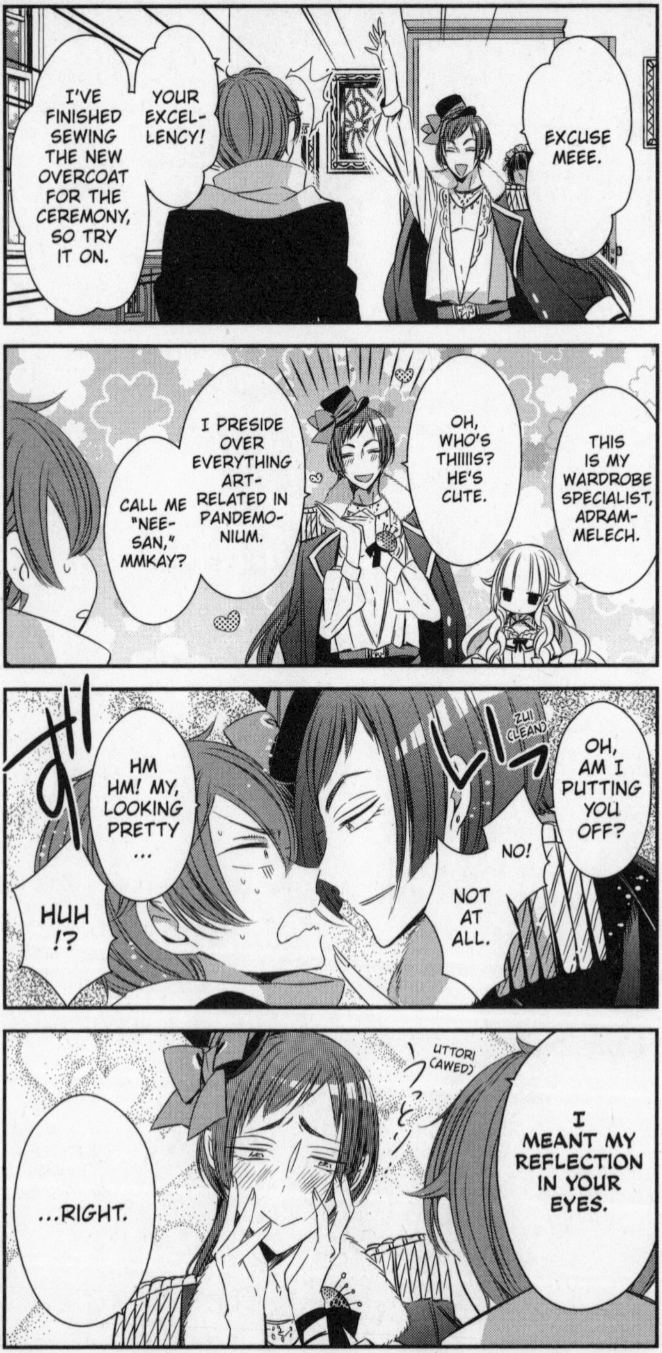
EXCUSE MEEE.
YOUR EXCELLENCY!
I'VE FINISHED SEWING THE NEW OVERCOAT FOR THE CEREMONY, SO TRY IT ON.
THIS IS MY WARDROBE SPECIALIST, ADRAMMELECH.
OH, WHO'S THIIIIS? HE'S CUTE.
I PRESIDE OVER EVERYTHING ART-RELATED IN PANDEMONIUM.
CALL ME "NEE-SAN," MMKAY?
ZUI (LEAN)
OH, AM I PUTTING YOU OFF?
NO!
NOT AT ALL.
HM HM! MY, LOOKING PRETTY ...
HUH !?
UTTORI (AWED)
I MEANT MY REFLECTION IN YOUR EYES.
...RIGHT.

THE FINEST TASTE, HUH?

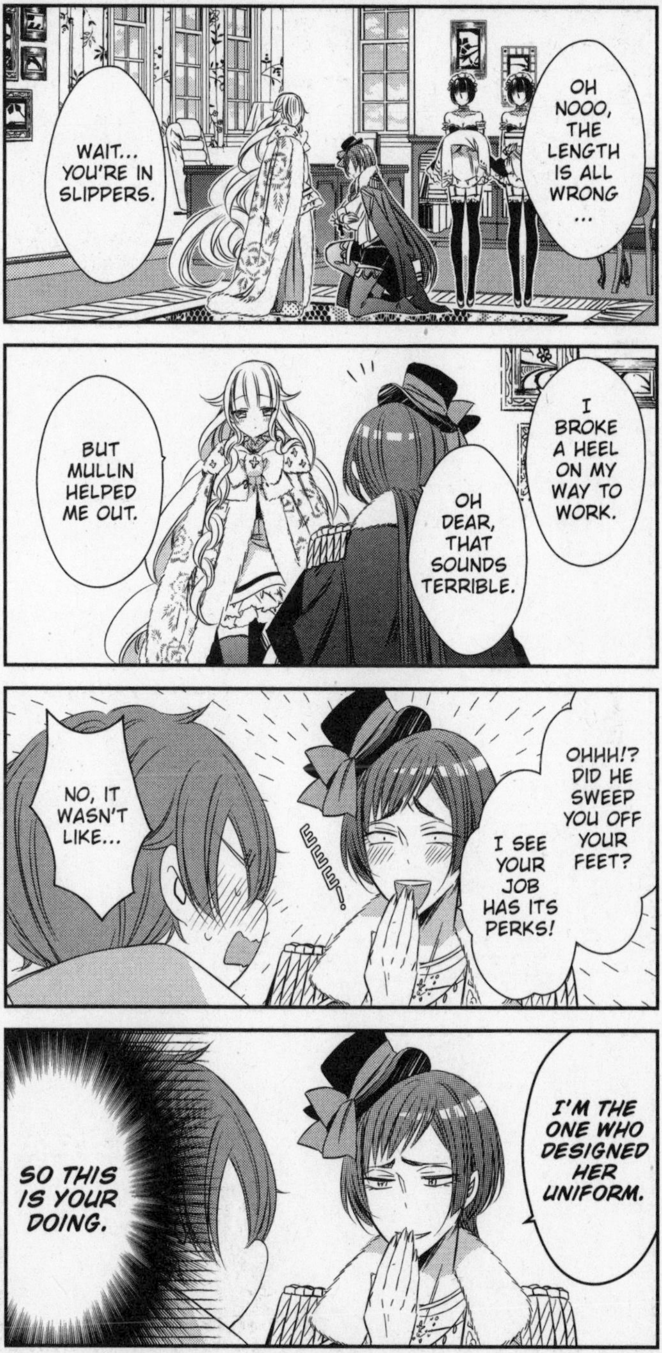
OH NOOO, THE LENGTH IS ALL WRONG ...
WAIT... YOU'RE IN SLIPPERS.
I BROKE A HEEL ON MY WAY TO WORK.
OH DEAR, THAT SOUNDS TERRIBLE.
BUT MULLIN HELPED ME OUT.
OHHH!? DID HE SWEEP YOU OFF YOUR FEET?
I SEE YOUR JOB HAS ITS PERKS!
NO, IT WASN'T LIKE...
I'M THE ONE WHO DESIGNED HER UNIFORM.
SO THIS IS YOUR DOING.

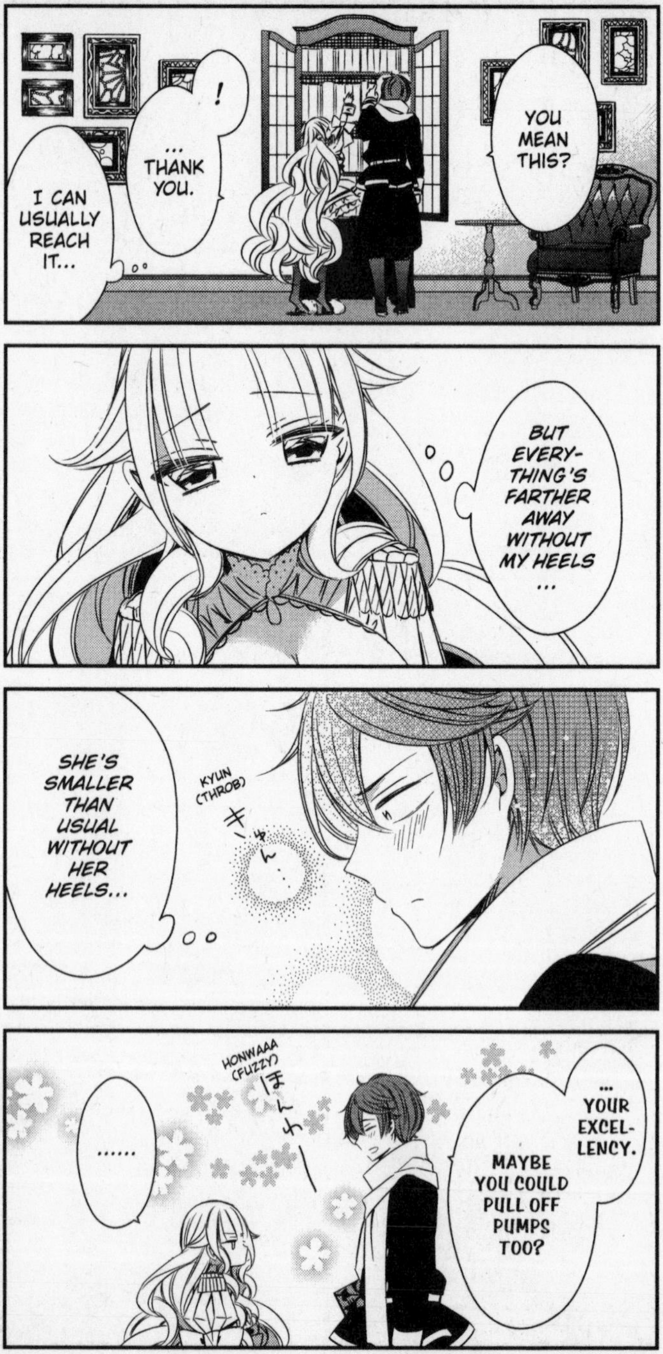
YOU MEAN THIS?
!
... THANK YOU.
I CAN USUALLY REACH IT...
BUT EVERYTHING'S FARTHER AWAY WITHOUT MY HEELS ...
KYUN (THROB)
きゅん…
SHE'S SMALLER THAN USUAL WITHOUT HER HEELS...
... YOUR EXCELLENCY.
MAYBE YOU COULD PULL OFF PUMPS TOO?
HONWAAA (FUZZY)
ほんわー
......

NINE CENTIMETERS' WORTH

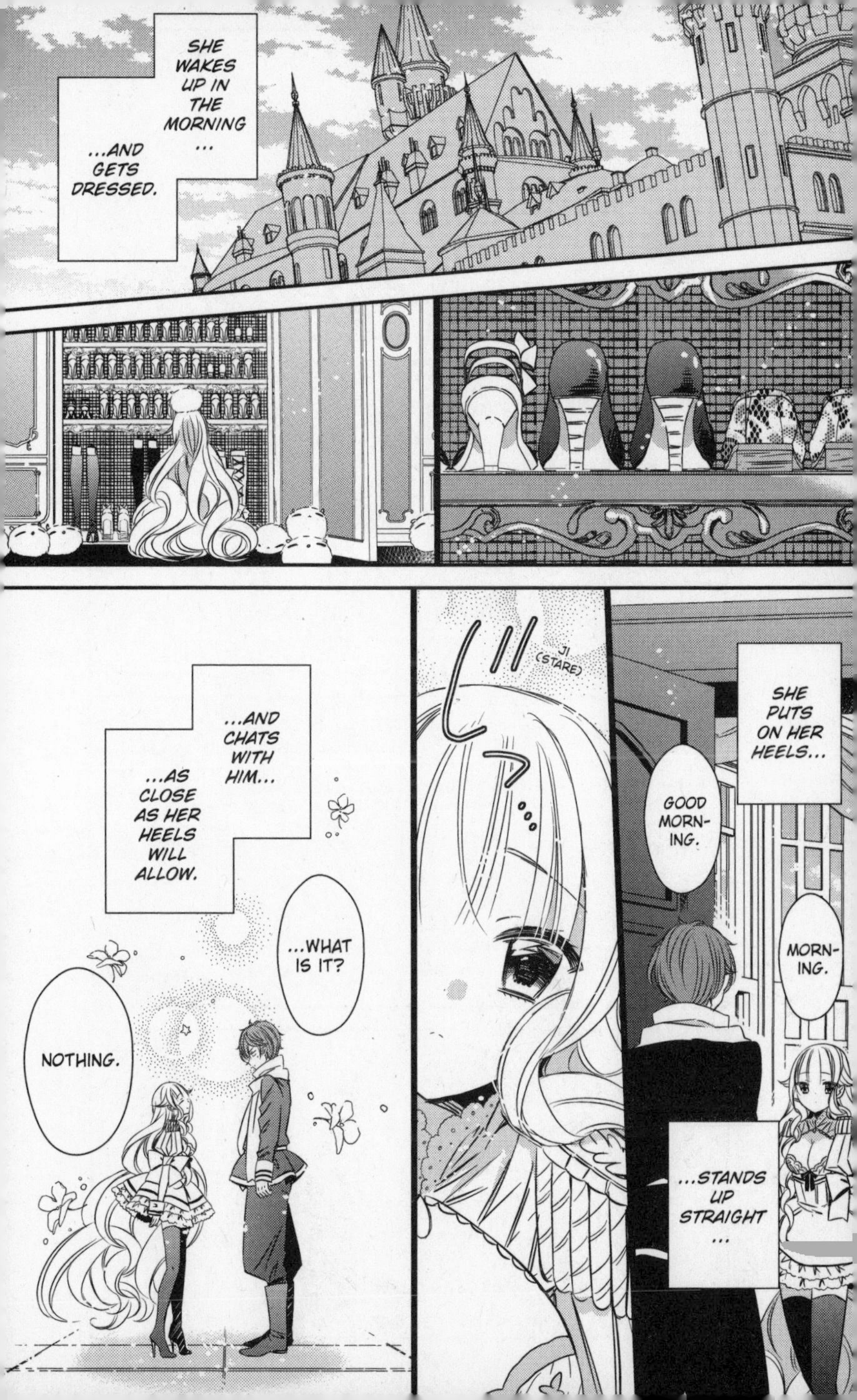
SHE WAKES UP IN THE MORNING...
...AND GETS DRESSED.
SHE PUTS ON HER HEELS...
GOOD MORN-ING.
MORN-ING.
...STANDS UP STRAIGHT...
JI (STARE)
...AND CHATS WITH HIM...
...AS CLOSE AS HER HEELS WILL ALLOW.
...WHAT IS IT?
NOTHING.

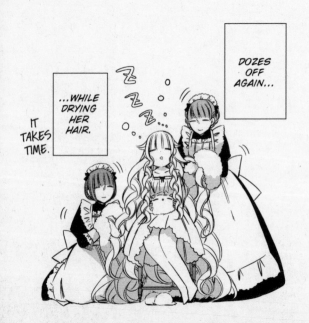

DOZES OFF AGAIN...
...WHILE DRYING HER HAIR.
IT TAKES TIME.

As Miss Beelzebub Likes

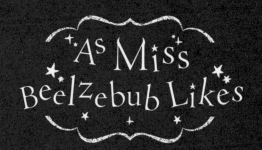

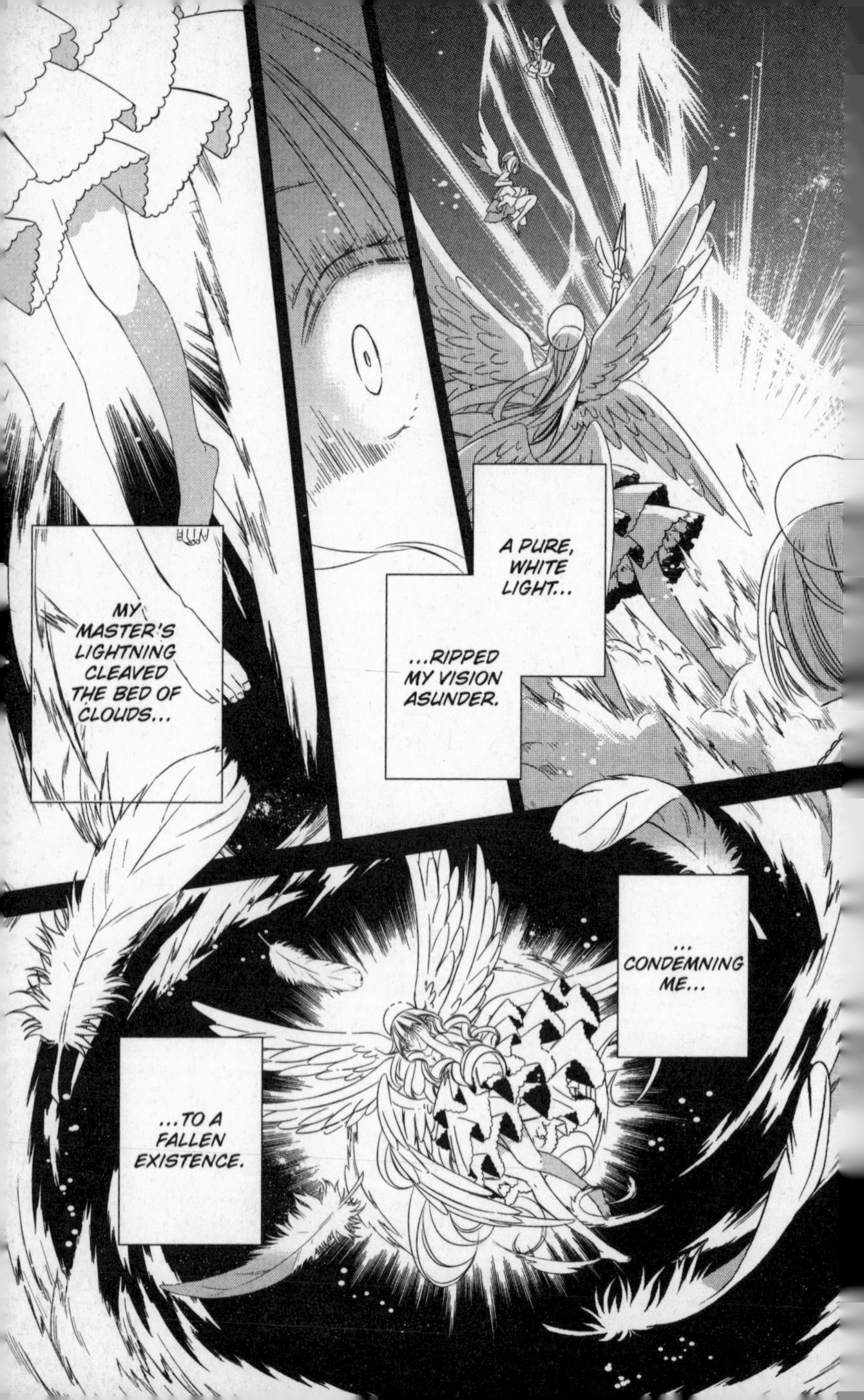
A PURE, WHITE LIGHT...
...RIPPED MY VISION ASUNDER.
MY MASTER'S LIGHTNING CLEAVED THE BED OF CLOUDS...
...CONDEMNING ME...
...TO A FALLEN EXISTENCE.

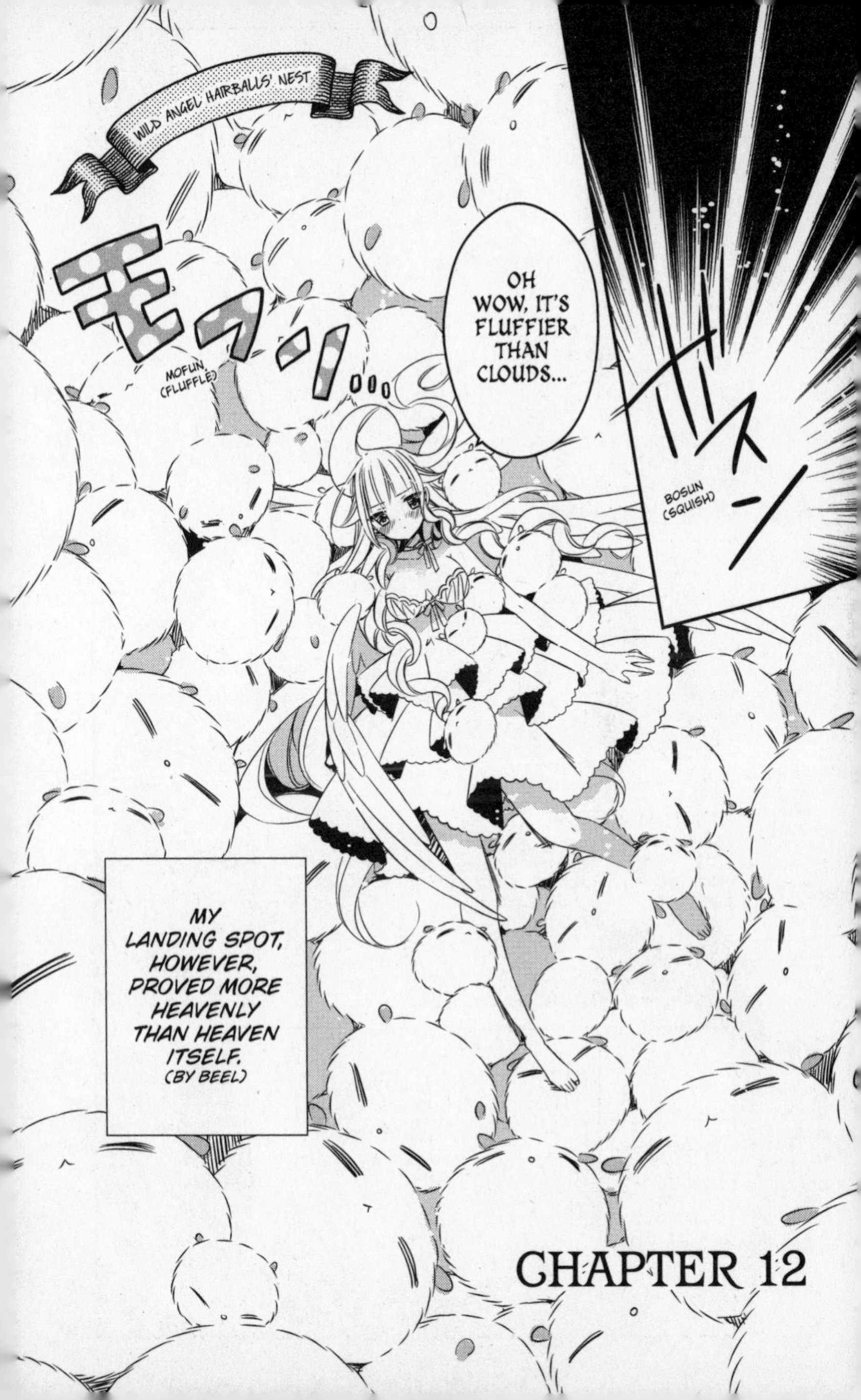
BOSUN (SQUISH)
OH WOW, IT'S FLUFFIER THAN CLOUDS...
WILD ANGEL HAIRBALLS' NEST
MOFUN (FLUFFLE)
MY LANDING SPOT, HOWEVER, PROVED MORE HEAVENLY THAN HEAVEN ITSELF. (BY BEEL)
CHAPTER 12

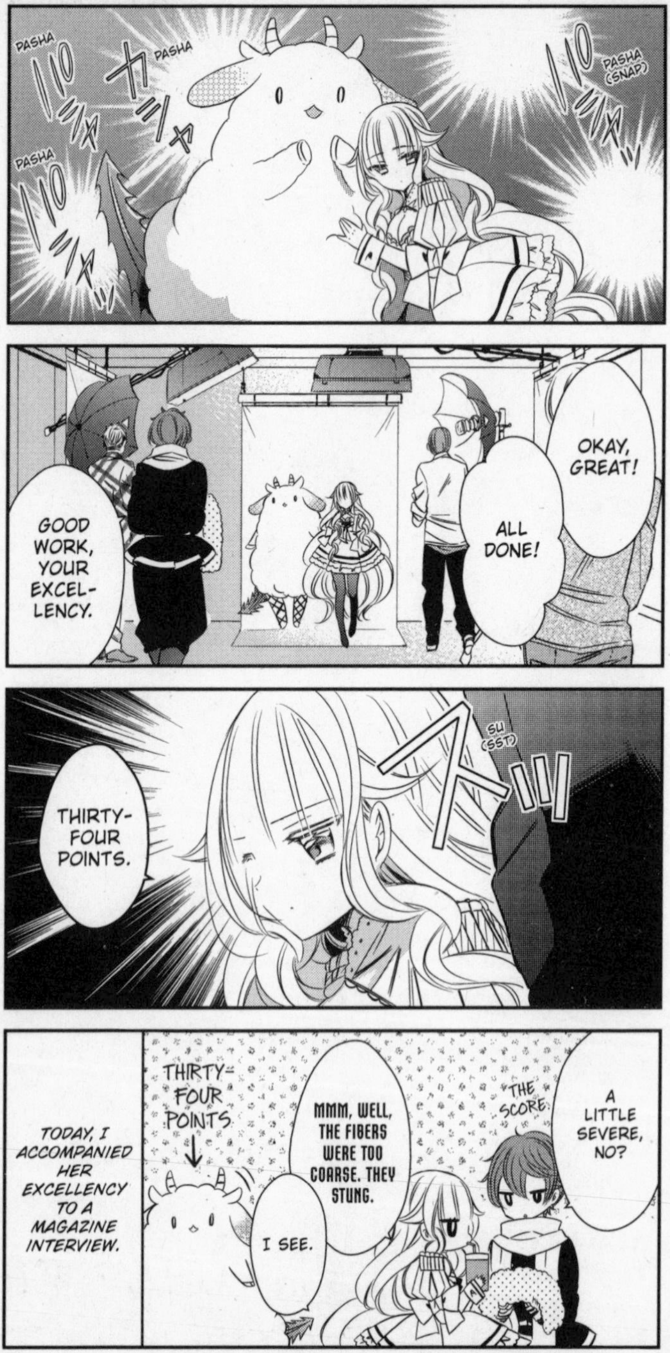
PASHA (SNAP)
PASHA
PASHA
PASHA
OKAY, GREAT!
ALL DONE!
GOOD WORK, YOUR EXCELLENCY.
SU (SST)
THIRTY-FOUR POINTS.
A LITTLE SEVERE, NO?
THE SCORE
MMM, WELL, THE FIBERS WERE TOO COARSE. THEY STUNG.
THIRTY-FOUR POINTS
I SEE.
TODAY, I ACCOMPANIED HER EXCELLENCY TO A MAGAZINE INTERVIEW.

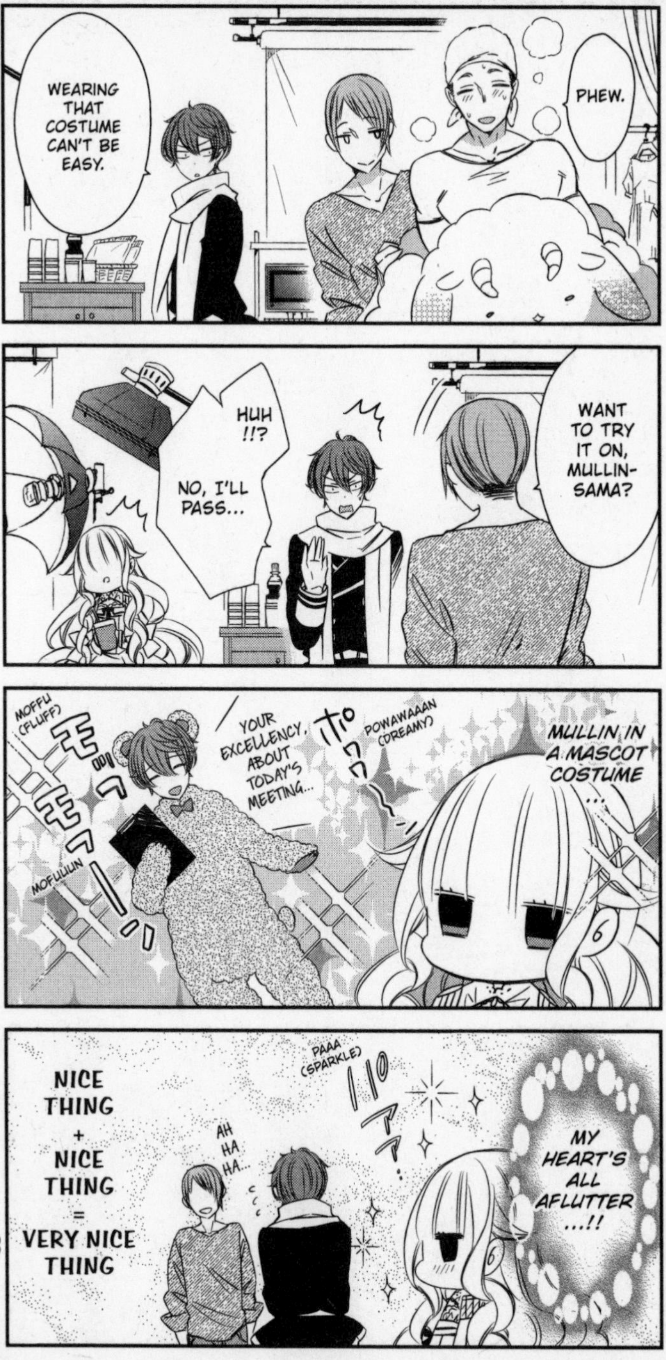
PHEW.
WEARING THAT COSTUME CAN'T BE EASY.
WANT TO TRY IT ON, MULLIN-SAMA?
HUH!!?
NO, I'LL PASS...
MULLIN IN A MASCOT COSTUME...
POWAWAAAN (DREAMY)
YOUR EXCELLENCY, ABOUT TODAY'S MEETING...
MOFFU (FLUFF)
MOFUUUN
MY HEART'S ALL AFLUTTER...!!
PAAA (SPARKLE)
AH HA HA...
NICE THING + NICE THING = VERY NICE THING

THE POWER OF ATTACHED DOCUMENTS

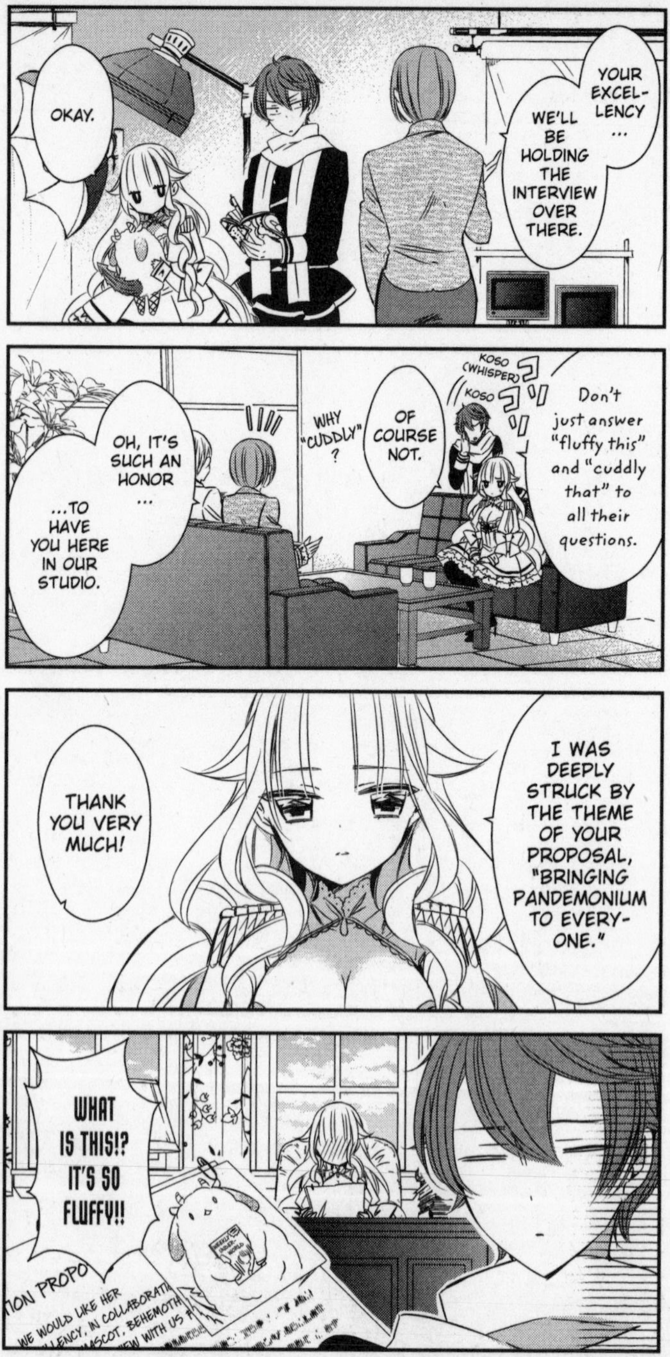
YOUR EXCELLENCY ... WE'LL BE HOLDING THE INTERVIEW OVER THERE.
OKAY.
Don't just answer "fluffy this" and "cuddly that" to all their questions.
KOSO (WHISPER)
KOSO
OF COURSE NOT.
WHY "CUDDLY"?
OH, IT'S SUCH AN HONOR ...
...TO HAVE YOU HERE IN OUR STUDIO.
I WAS DEEPLY STRUCK BY THE THEME OF YOUR PROPOSAL, "BRINGING PANDEMONIUM TO EVERYONE."
THANK YOU VERY MUCH!
WHAT IS THIS!? IT'S SO FLUFFY!!
WE WOULD LIKE HER

HE WITHSTOOD IT

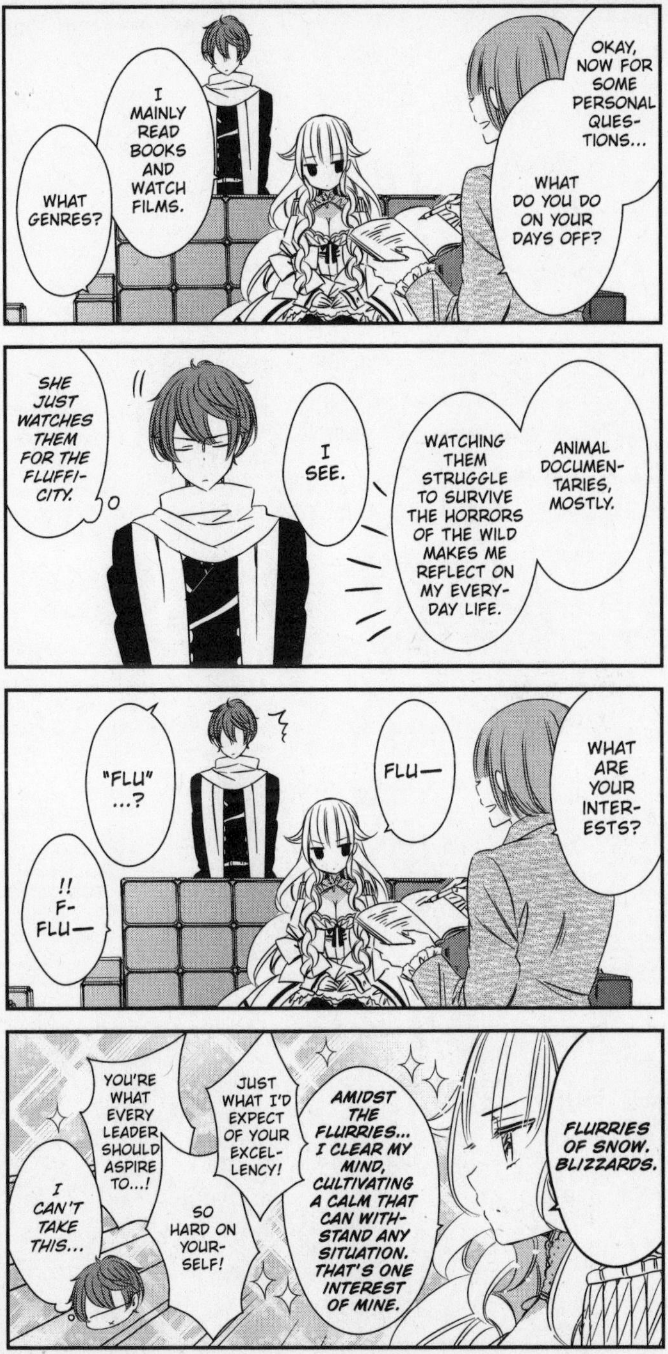

OKAY, NOW FOR SOME PERSONAL QUESTIONS...
WHAT DO YOU DO ON YOUR DAYS OFF?
I MAINLY READ BOOKS AND WATCH FILMS.
WHAT GENRES?
ANIMAL DOCUMENTARIES, MOSTLY.
WATCHING THEM STRUGGLE TO SURVIVE THE HORRORS OF THE WILD MAKES ME REFLECT ON MY EVERYDAY LIFE.
I SEE.
SHE JUST WATCHES THEM FOR THE FLUFFICITY.
WHAT ARE YOUR INTERESTS?
FLU—
"FLU" ...?
!! F-FLU—
FLURRIES OF SNOW. BLIZZARDS.
AMIDST THE FLURRIES... I CLEAR MY MIND, CULTIVATING A CALM THAT CAN WITHSTAND ANY SITUATION. THAT'S ONE INTEREST OF MINE.
JUST WHAT I'D EXPECT OF YOUR EXCELLENCY!
YOU'RE WHAT EVERY LEADER SHOULD ASPIRE TO...!
SO HARD ON YOURSELF!
I CAN'T TAKE THIS...

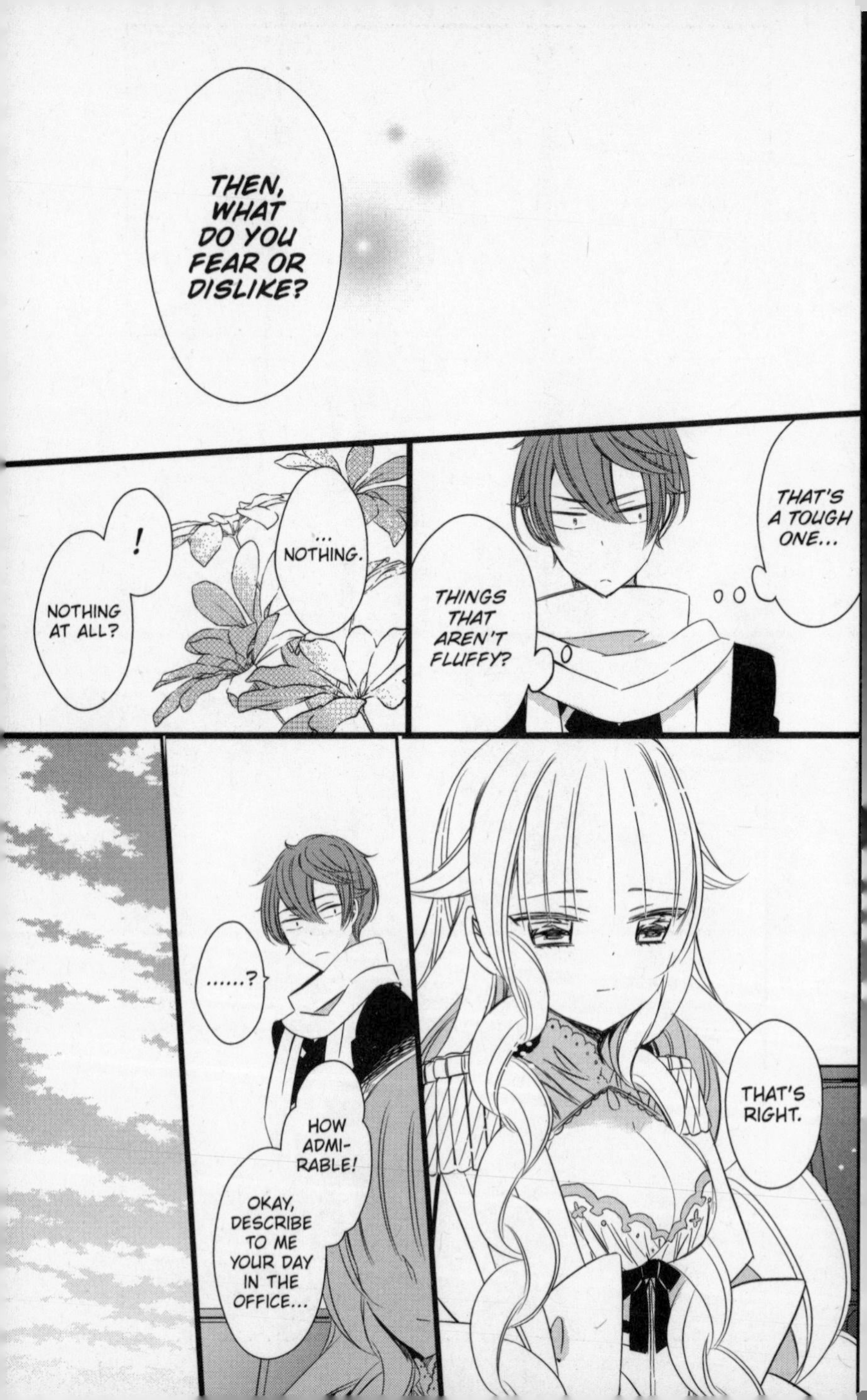
THEN, WHAT DO YOU FEAR OR DISLIKE?
THAT'S A TOUGH ONE...
THINGS THAT AREN'T FLUFFY?
... NOTHING.
!
NOTHING AT ALL?
THAT'S RIGHT.
......?
HOW ADMI-RABLE!
OKAY, DESCRIBE TO ME YOUR DAY IN THE OFFICE...

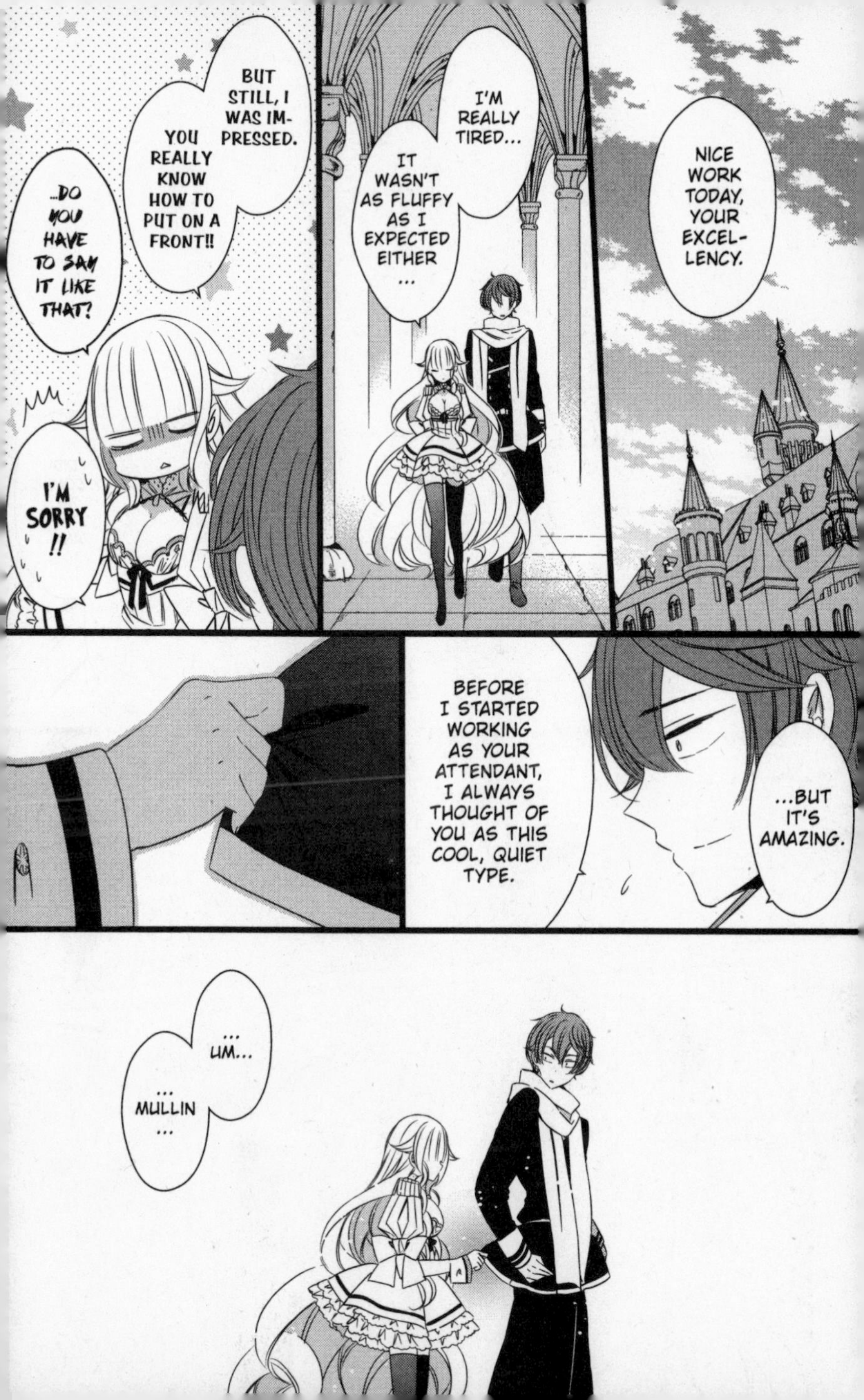
NICE WORK TODAY, YOUR EXCELLENCY.
I'M REALLY TIRED...
IT WASN'T AS FLUFFY AS I EXPECTED EITHER...
BUT STILL, I WAS IMPRESSED.
YOU REALLY KNOW HOW TO PUT ON A FRONT!!
...DO YOU HAVE TO SAY IT LIKE THAT?
I'M SORRY!!
BEFORE I STARTED WORKING AS YOUR ATTENDANT, I ALWAYS THOUGHT OF YOU AS THIS COOL, QUIET TYPE.
...BUT IT'S AMAZING.
... UM...
... MULLIN ...

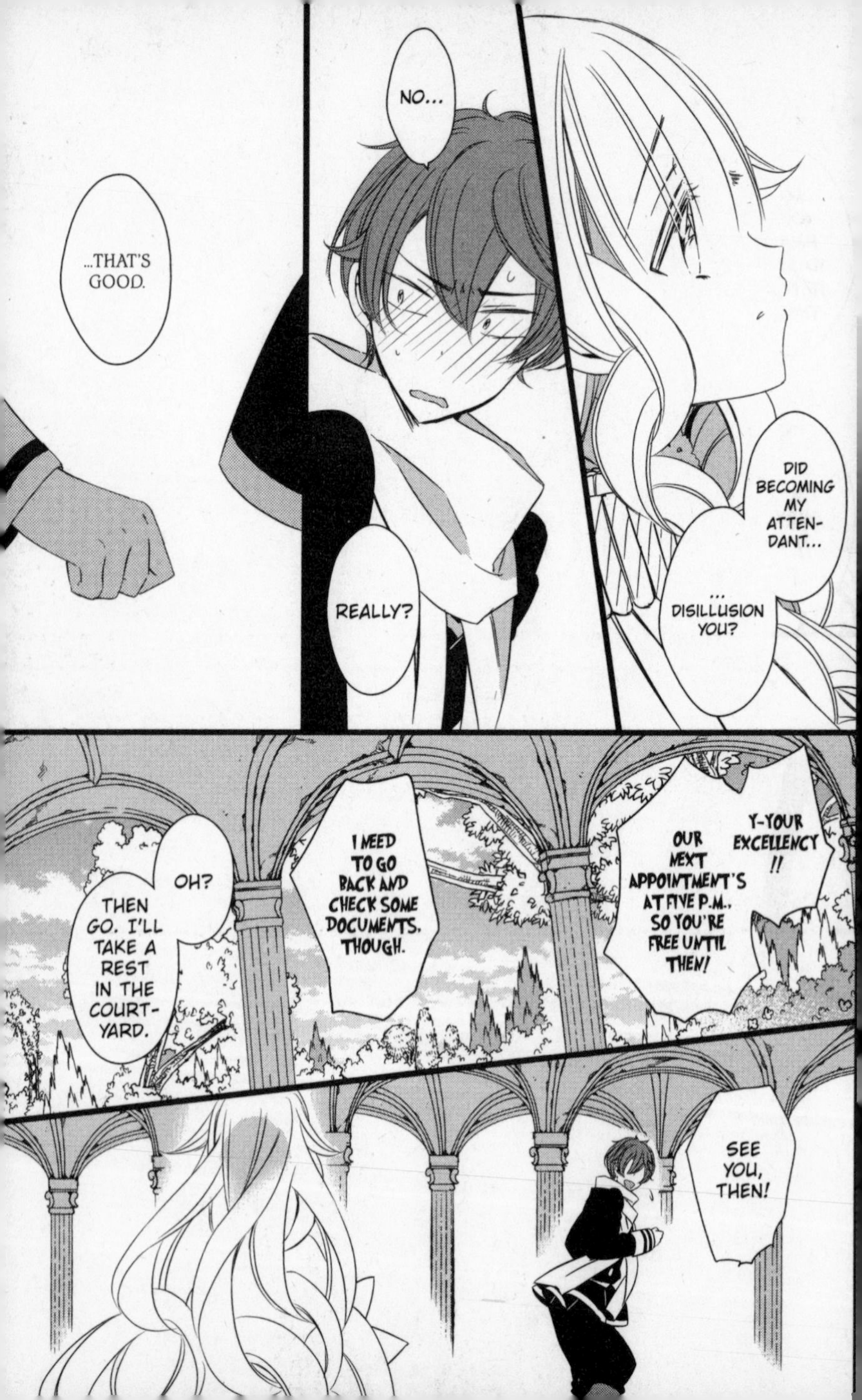
DID BECOMING MY ATTENDANT...
...DISILLUSION YOU?
NO...
REALLY?
...THAT'S GOOD.
Y-YOUR EXCELLENCY!!
OUR NEXT APPOINTMENT'S AT FIVE P.M., SO YOU'RE FREE UNTIL THEN!
I NEED TO GO BACK AND CHECK SOME DOCUMENTS, THOUGH.
OH?
THEN GO. I'LL TAKE A REST IN THE COURTYARD.
SEE YOU, THEN!

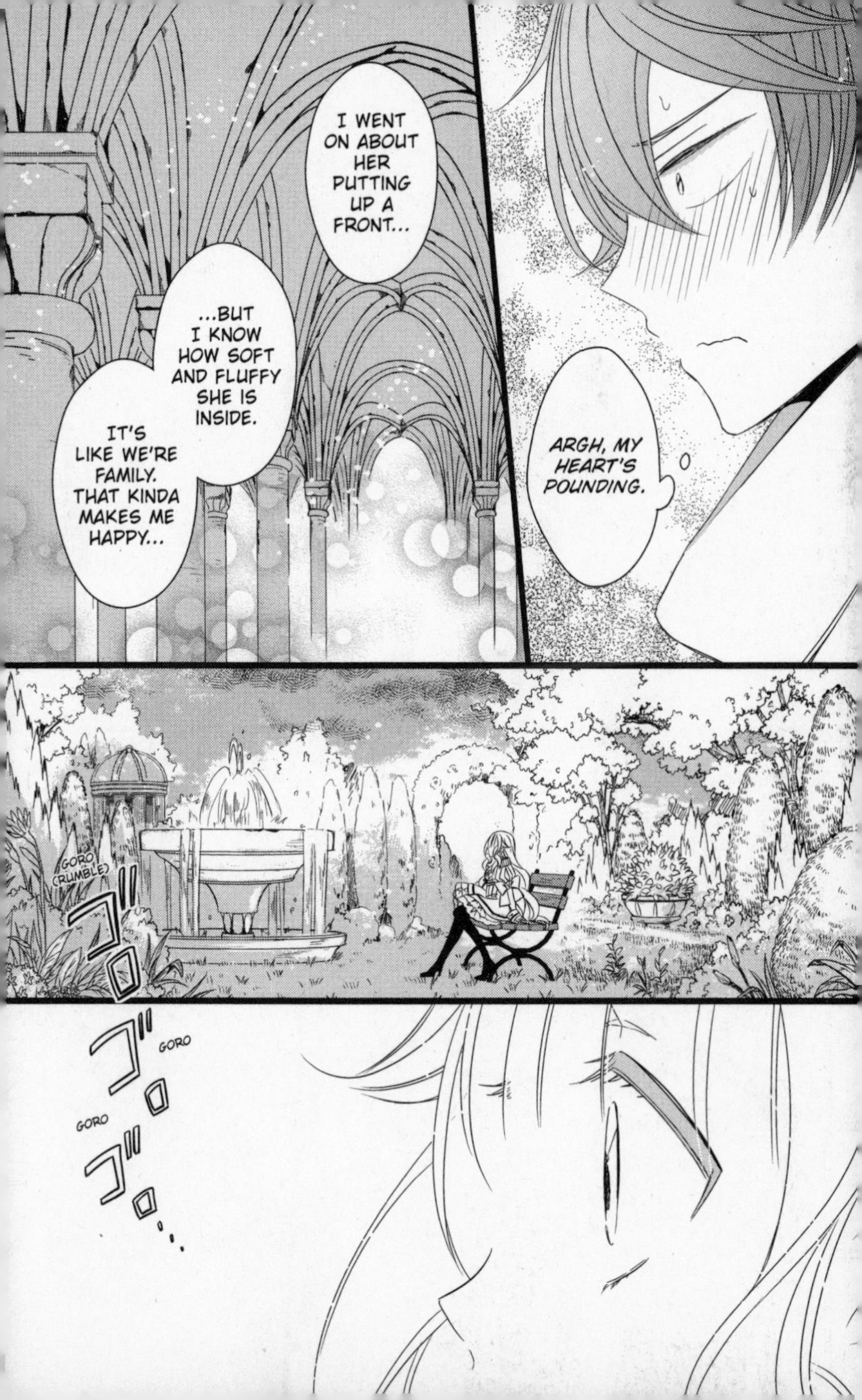

ARGH, MY HEART'S POUNDING.
I WENT ON ABOUT HER PUTTING UP A FRONT...
...BUT I KNOW HOW SOFT AND FLUFFY SHE IS INSIDE.
IT'S LIKE WE'RE FAMILY. THAT KINDA MAKES ME HAPPY...
GORO (RUMBLE)
GORO
GORO

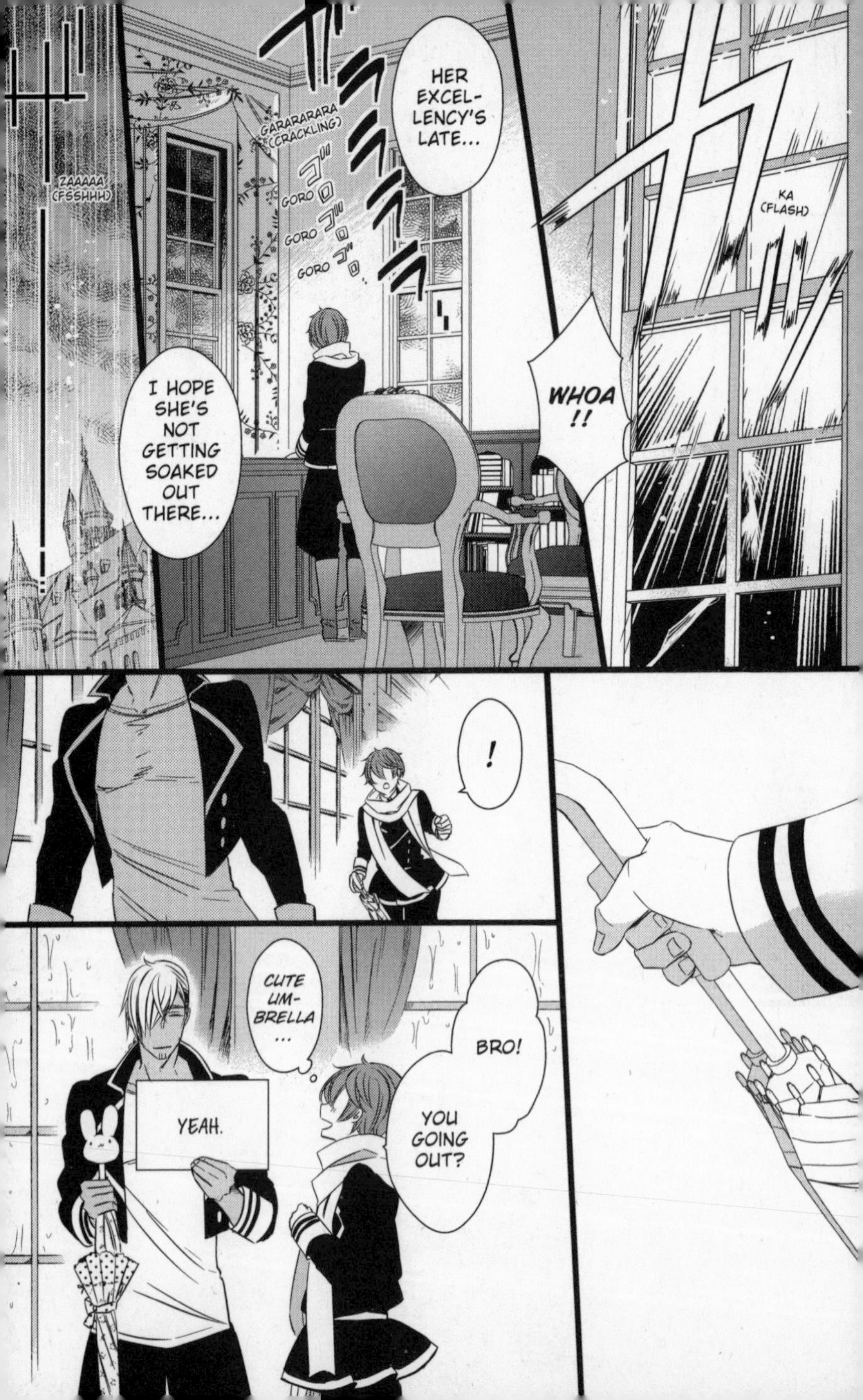

KA (FLASH)
WHOA!!
HER EXCEL-LENCY'S LATE...
GARARARARA (CRACKLING)
GORO GORO GORO
ZAAAAA (FSSHHH)
I HOPE SHE'S NOT GETTING SOAKED OUT THERE...
!
BRO!
YOU GOING OUT?
CUTE UM-BRELLA...
YEAH.

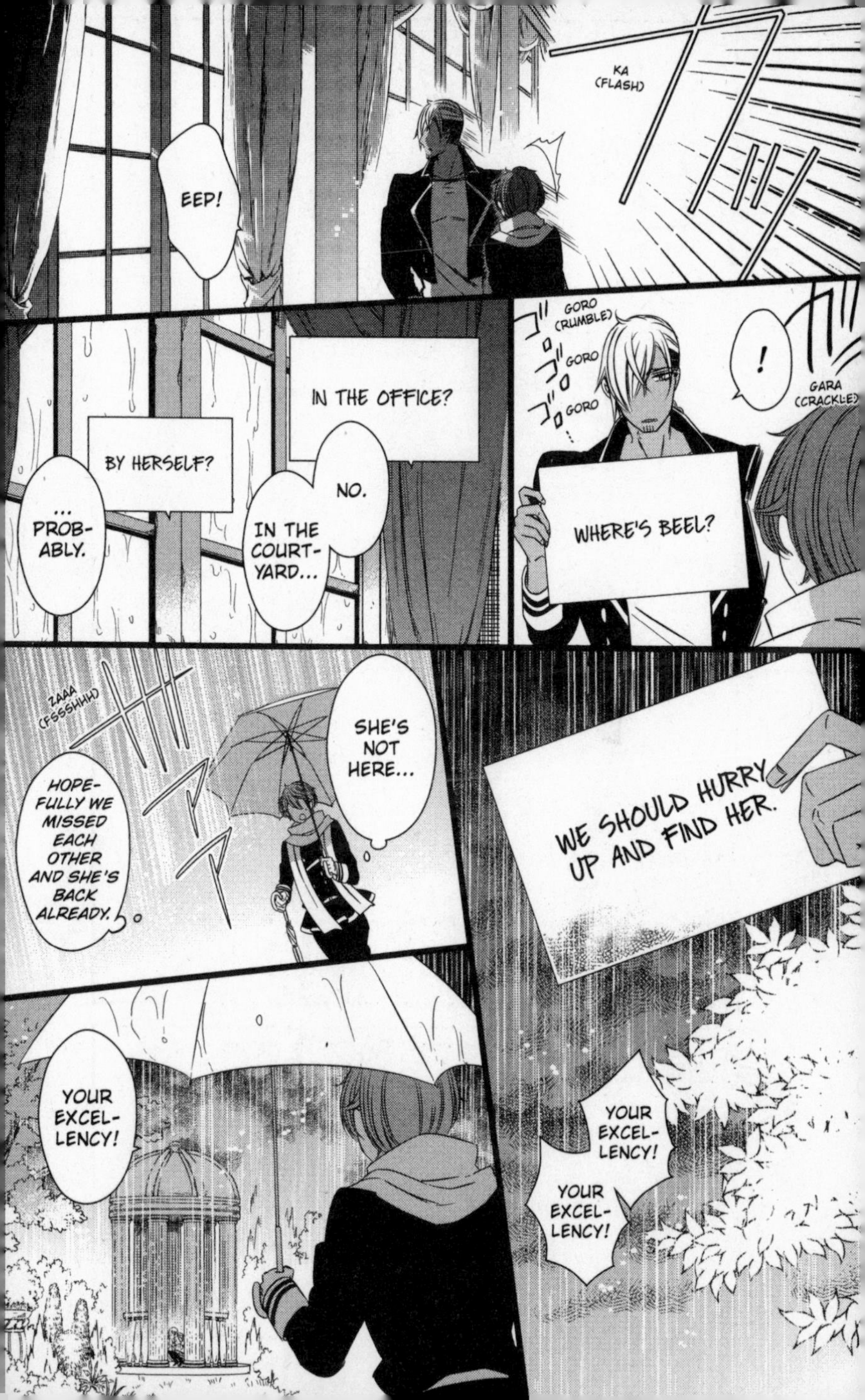
KA (FLASH)
EEP!
GORO (RUMBLE)
GORO
GORO
!
GARA (CRACKLE)
WHERE'S BEEL?
IN THE OFFICE?
NO.
IN THE COURTYARD...
BY HERSELF?
... PROBABLY.
WE SHOULD HURRY UP AND FIND HER.
YOUR EXCELLENCY!
YOUR EXCELLENCY!
ZAAA (FSSSHHH)
SHE'S NOT HERE...
HOPEFULLY WE MISSED EACH OTHER AND SHE'S BACK ALREADY.
YOUR EXCELLENCY!

DRIPPING WET

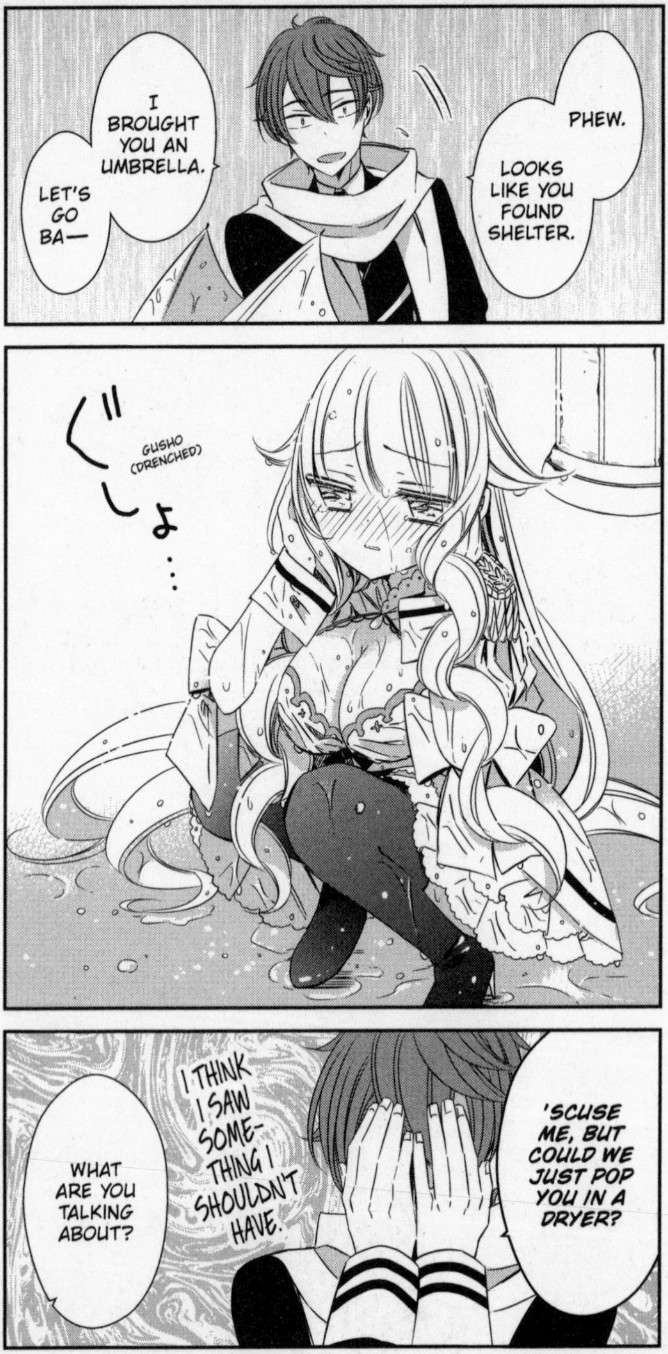
PHEW.
LOOKS LIKE YOU FOUND SHELTER.
I BROUGHT YOU AN UMBRELLA.
LET'S GO BA—
ぐしょ…
GUSHO (DRENCHED)
'SCUSE ME, BUT COULD WE JUST POP YOU IN A DRYER?
I THINK I SAW SOME-THING I SHOULDN'T HAVE.
WHAT ARE YOU TALKING ABOUT?

HE-SAID, SHE-SAID (IN THE RAIN)

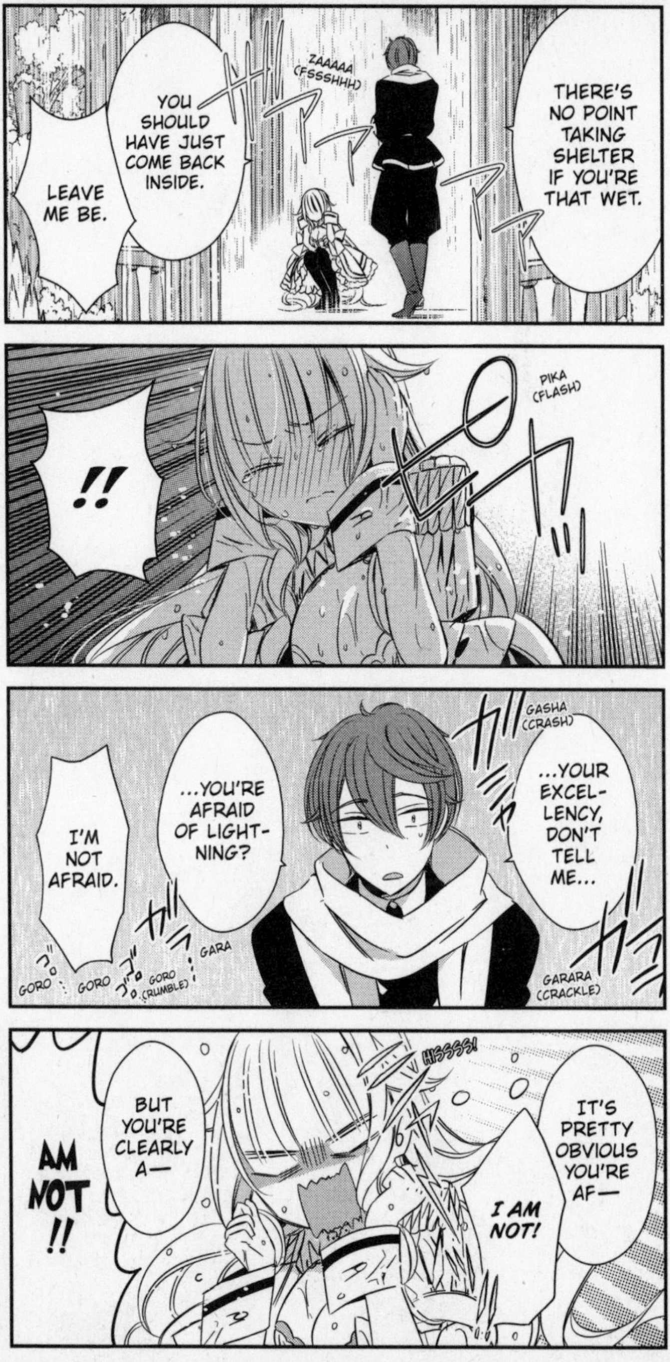
THERE'S NO POINT TAKING SHELTER IF YOU'RE THAT WET.
ZAAAAA (FSSSHHH)
YOU SHOULD HAVE JUST COME BACK INSIDE.
LEAVE ME BE.
PIKA (FLASH)
!!
GASHA (CRASH)
...YOUR EXCEL-LENCY, DON'T TELL ME...
GARARA (CRACKLE)
...YOU'RE AFRAID OF LIGHT-NING?
GARA
I'M NOT AFRAID.
GORO GORO GORO (RUMBLE)
HISSSS!
IT'S PRETTY OBVIOUS YOU'RE AF—
I AM NOT!
BUT YOU'RE CLEARLY A—
AM NOT!!

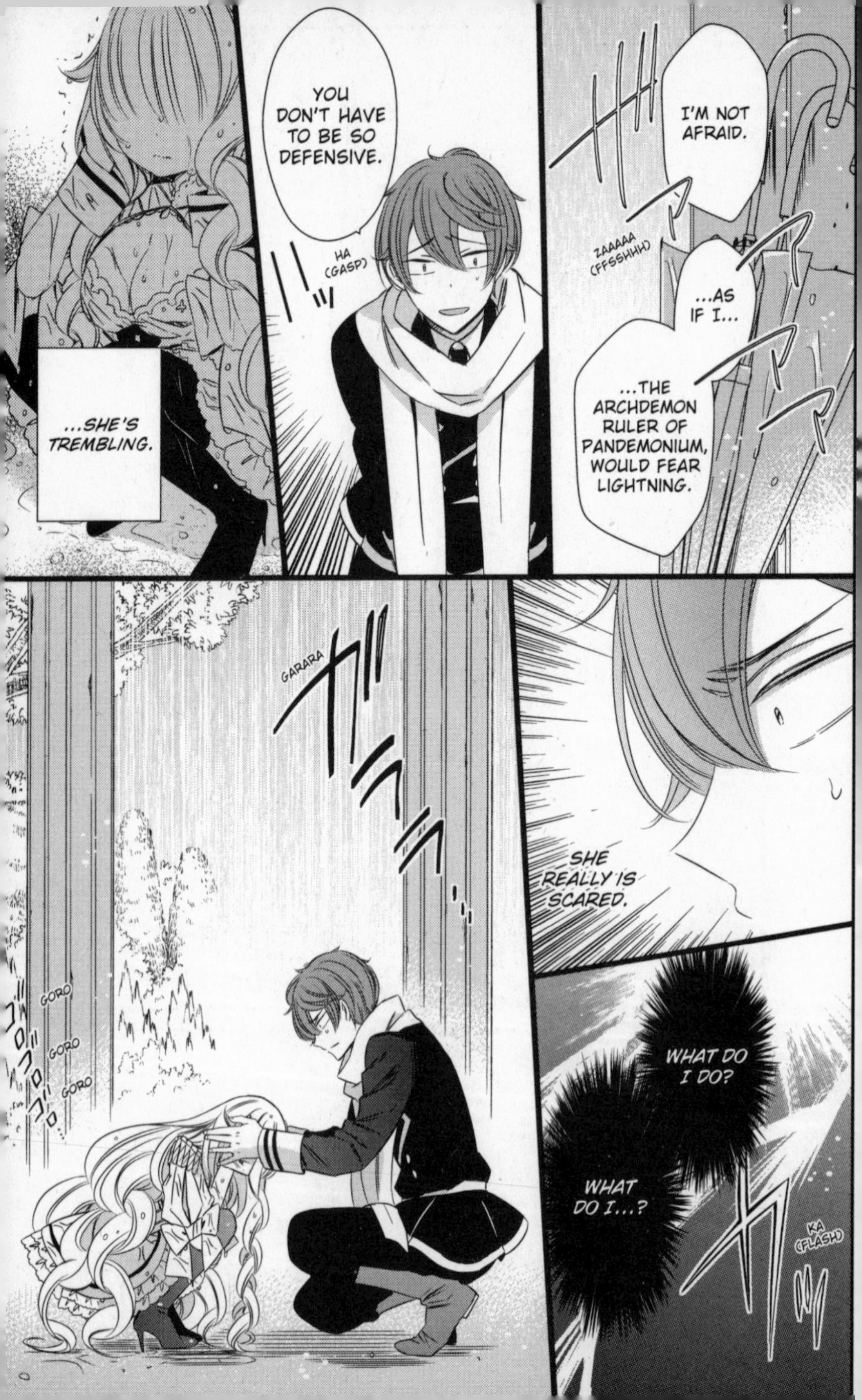
I'M NOT AFRAID.
ZAAAAAA (FFSSHHH)
...AS IF I...
...THE ARCHDEMON RULER OF PANDEMONIUM, WOULD FEAR LIGHTNING.
YOU DON'T HAVE TO BE SO DEFENSIVE.
HA (GASP)
...SHE'S TREMBLING.
SHE REALLY IS SCARED.
WHAT DO I DO?
WHAT DO I...?
KA (FLASH)
GARARA
GORO
GORO
GORO

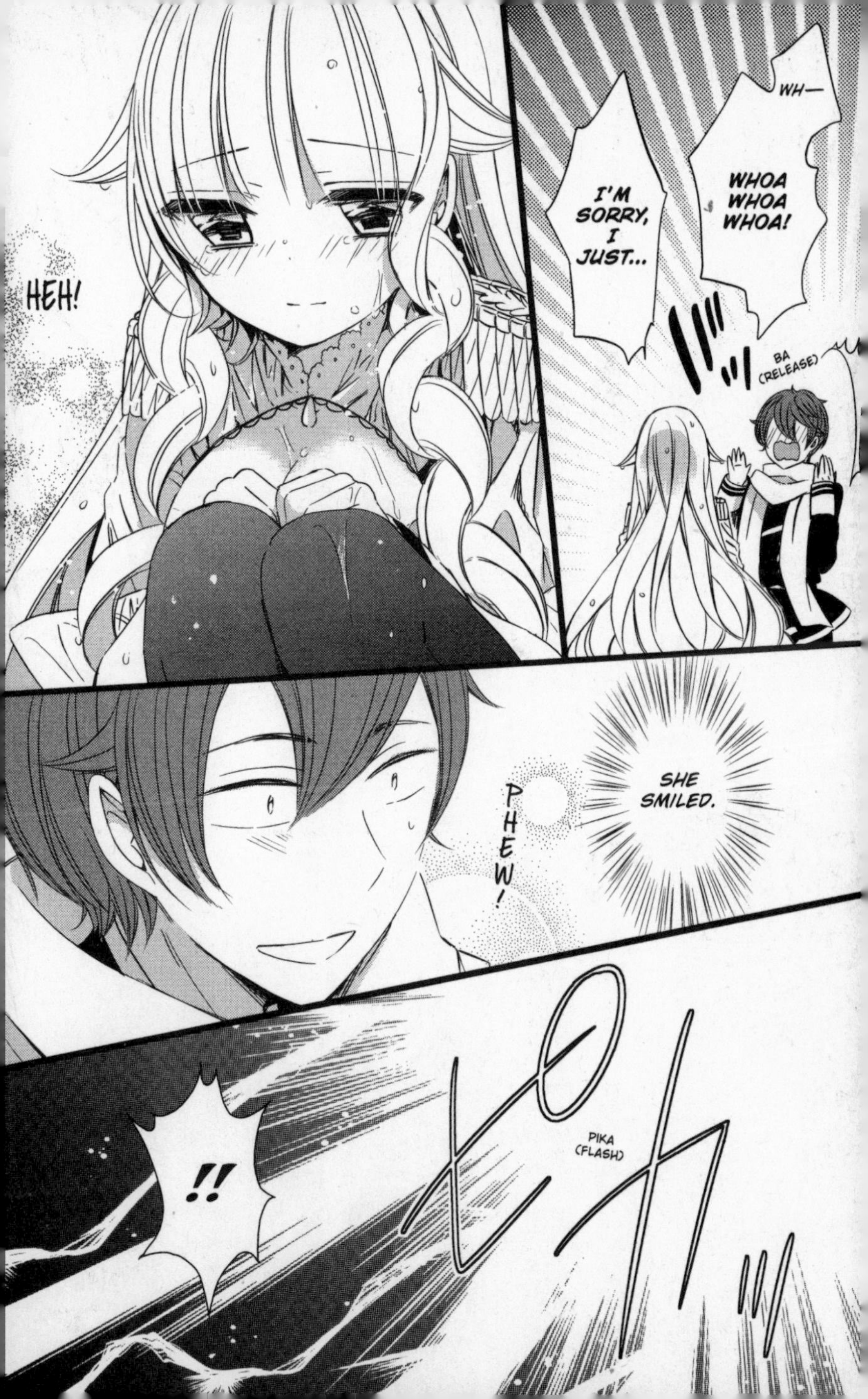
WH—
WHOA WHOA WHOA!
I'M SORRY, I JUST...
BA (RELEASE)
HEH!
SHE SMILED.
PHEW!
PIKA (FLASH)
!!

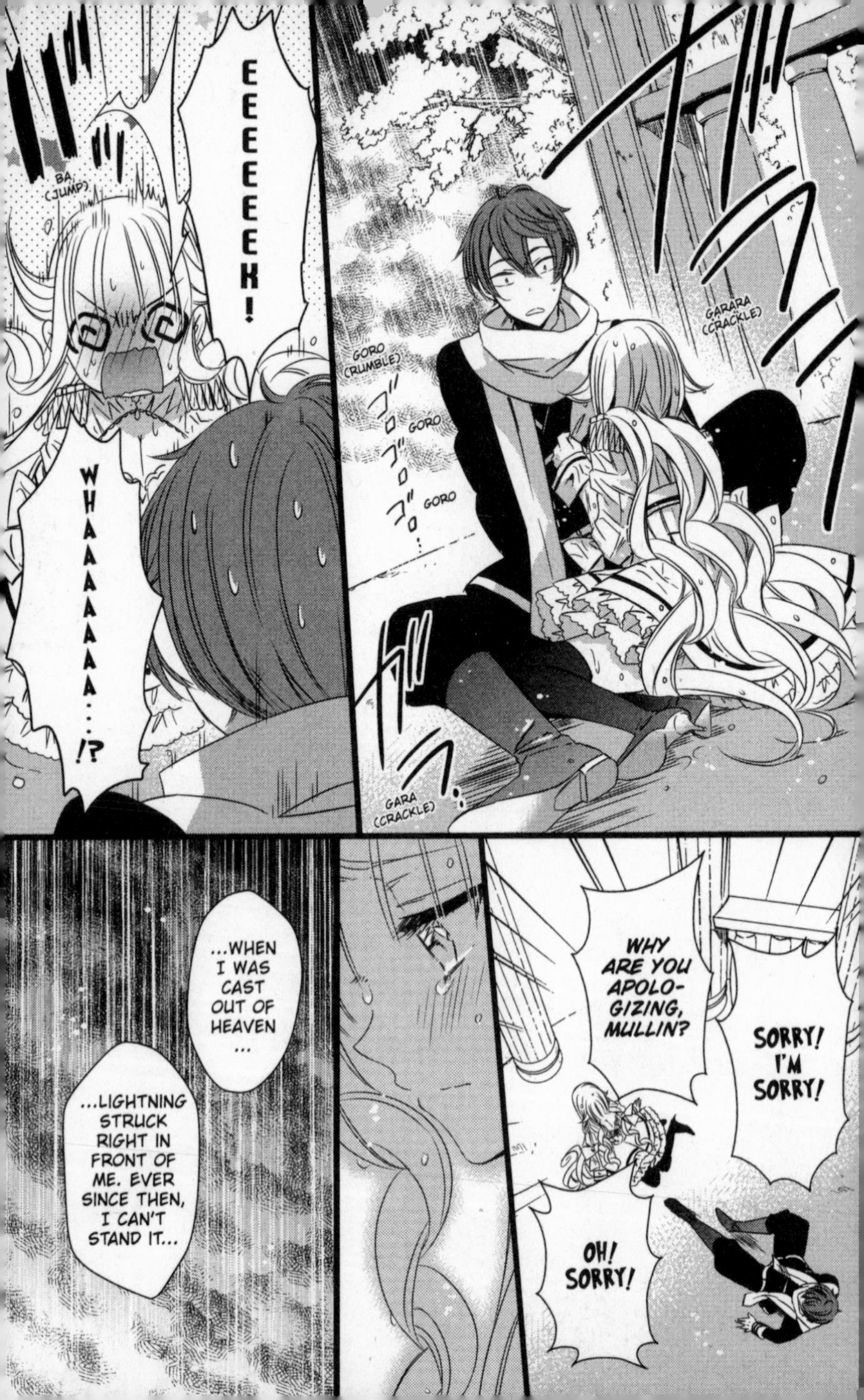
GARARA (CRACKLE)
GORO (RUMBLE)
GORO
GORO
GARA (CRACKLE)
EEEEEEEEK!
BA (JUMP)
WHAAAAAAAAA...!?
SORRY! I'M SORRY!
WHY ARE YOU APOLOGIZING, MULLIN?
OH! SORRY!
...WHEN I WAS CAST OUT OF HEAVEN...
...LIGHTNING STRUCK RIGHT IN FRONT OF ME. EVER SINCE THEN, I CAN'T STAND IT...

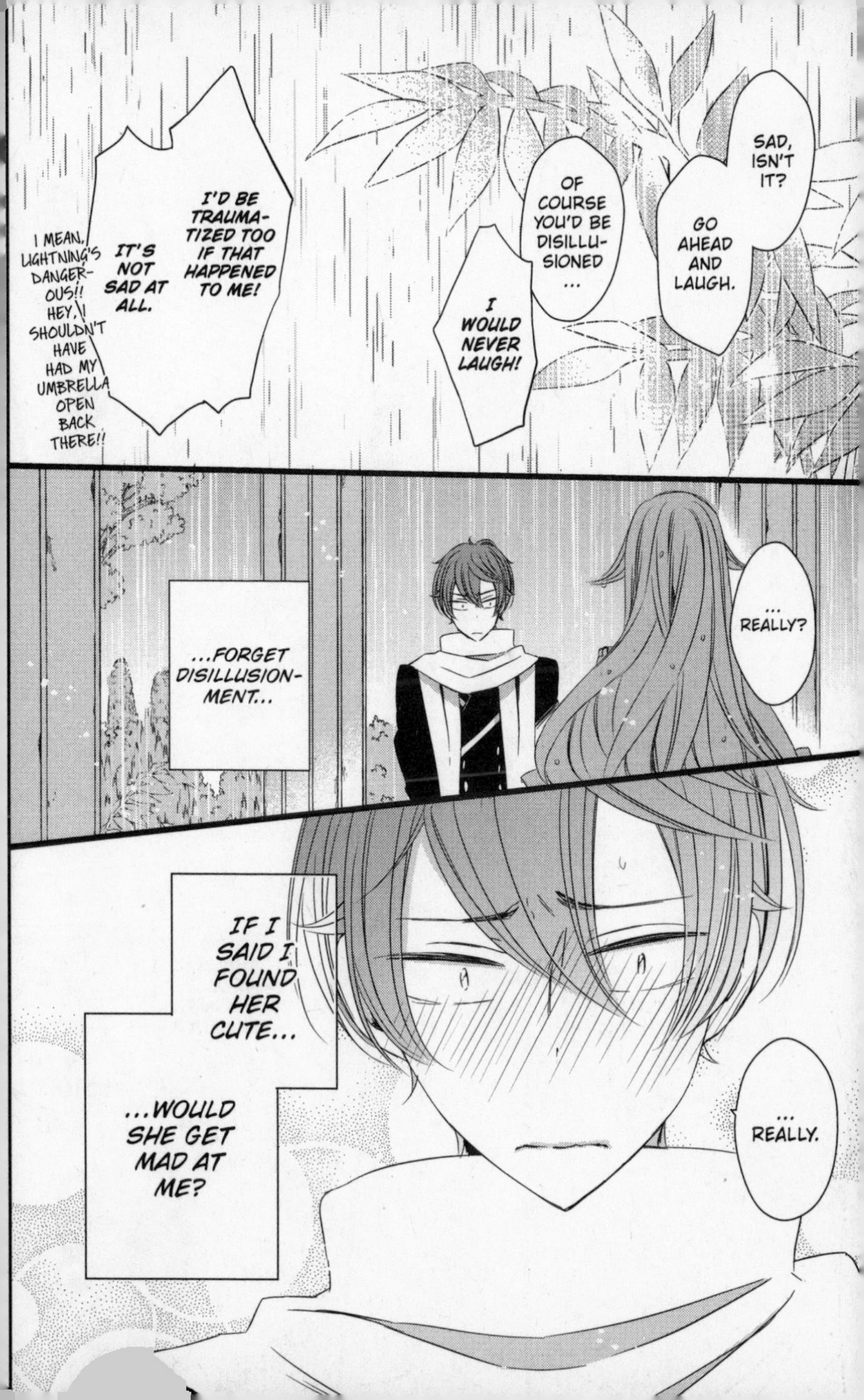
SAD, ISN'T IT?
GO AHEAD AND LAUGH.
OF COURSE YOU'D BE DISILLUSIONED ...
I WOULD NEVER LAUGH!
I'D BE TRAUMATIZED TOO IF THAT HAPPENED TO ME!
IT'S NOT SAD AT ALL.
I MEAN, LIGHTNING'S DANGEROUS!! HEY, I SHOULDN'T HAVE HAD MY UMBRELLA OPEN BACK THERE!!
...REALLY?
...FORGET DISILLUSIONMENT...
...REALLY.
IF I SAID I FOUND HER CUTE...
...WOULD SHE GET MAD AT ME?

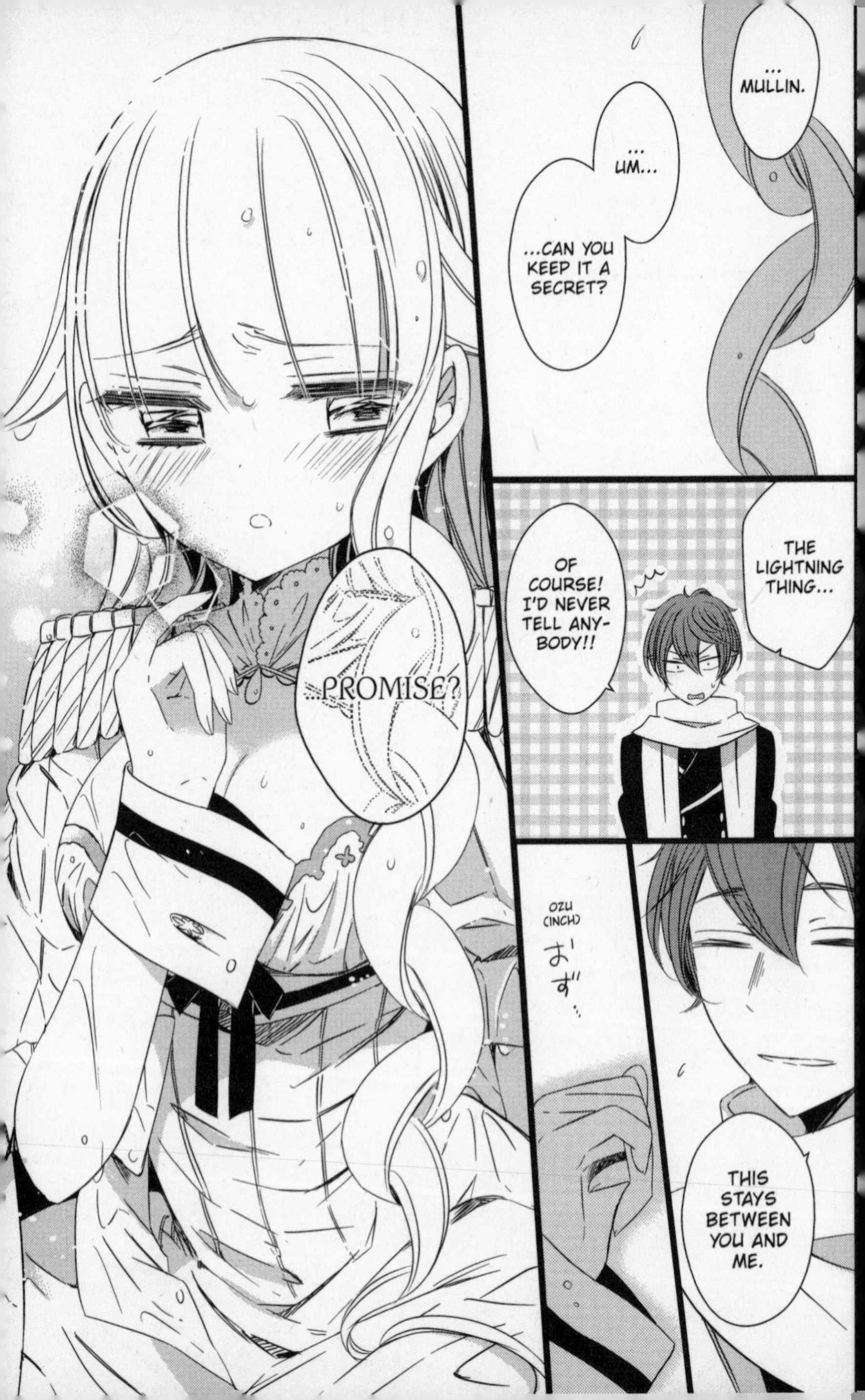
...MULLIN.
...UM...
...CAN YOU KEEP IT A SECRET?
THE LIGHTNING THING...
OF COURSE! I'D NEVER TELL ANYBODY!!
OZU (INCH)
おず…
THIS STAYS BETWEEN YOU AND ME.
...PROMISE?

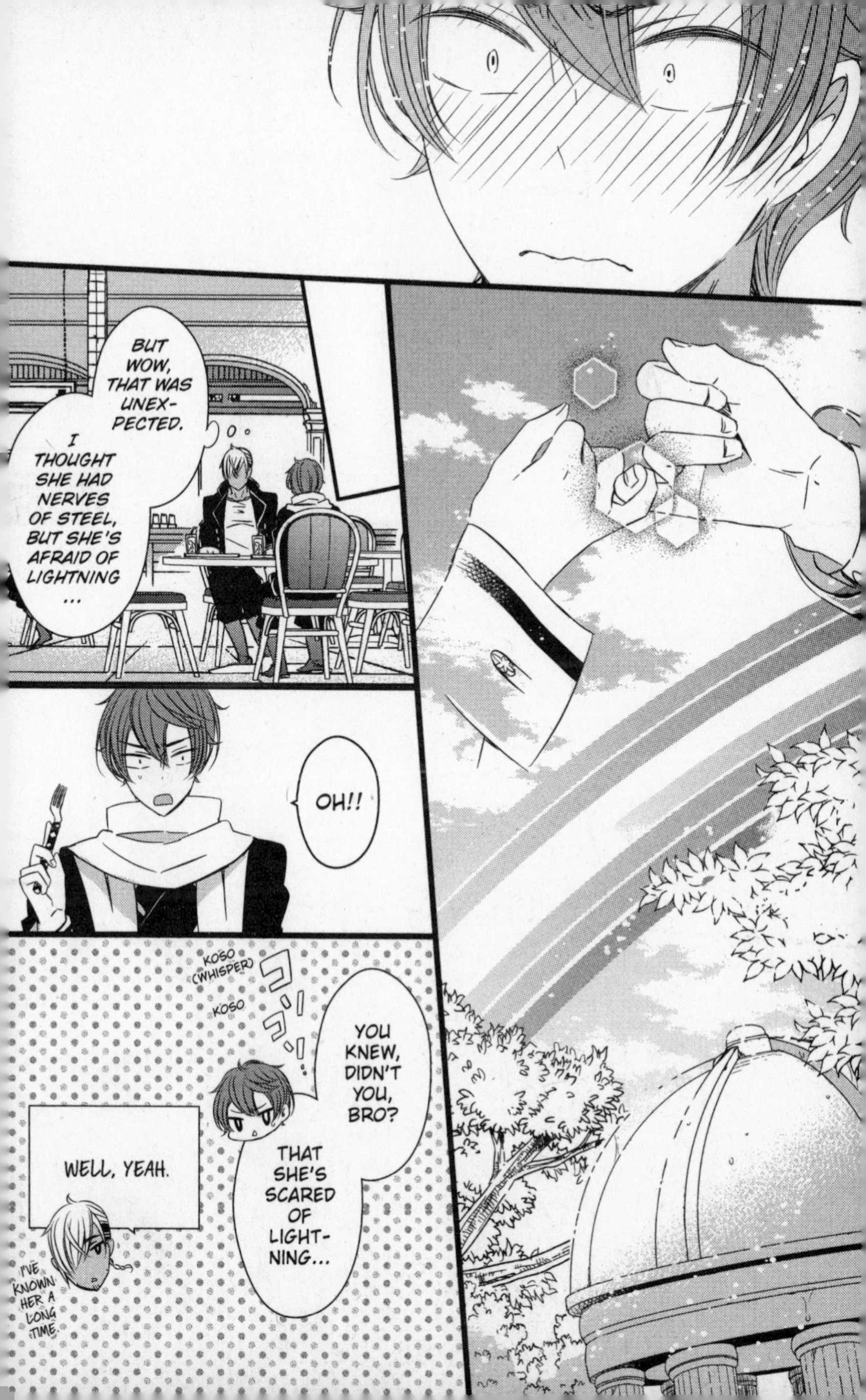
BUT WOW, THAT WAS UNEXPECTED.
I THOUGHT SHE HAD NERVES OF STEEL, BUT SHE'S AFRAID OF LIGHTNING...
OH!!
KOSO (WHISPER)
KOSO
YOU KNEW, DIDN'T YOU, BRO?
THAT SHE'S SCARED OF LIGHTNING...
WELL, YEAH.
I'VE KNOWN HER A LONG TIME.

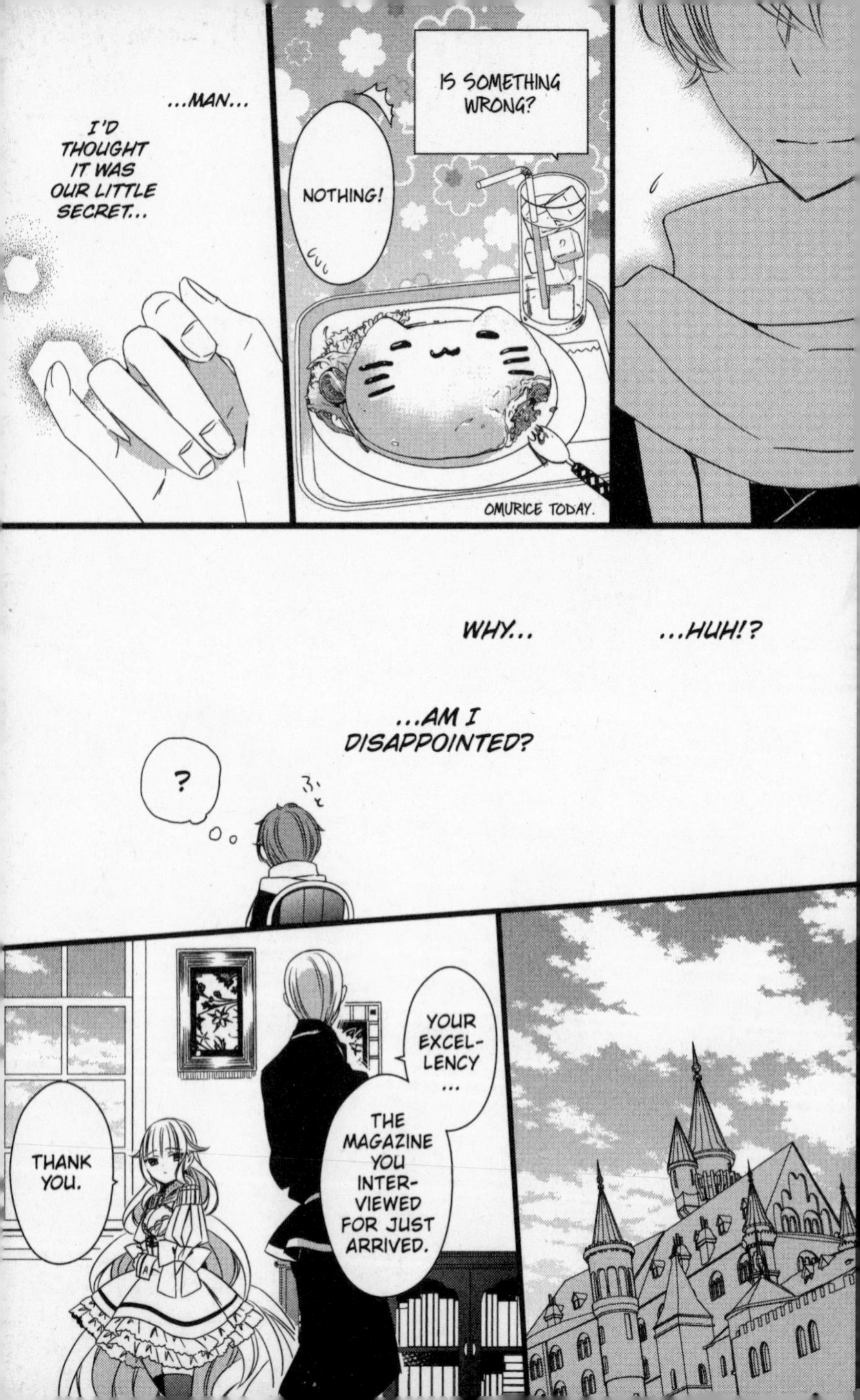
IS SOMETHING WRONG?
NOTHING!
OMURICE TODAY.
...MAN...
I'D THOUGHT IT WAS OUR LITTLE SECRET...
...HUH!?
WHY...
...AM I DISAPPOINTED?
?
YOUR EXCEL-LENCY ...
THE MAGAZINE YOU INTER-VIEWED FOR JUST ARRIVED.
THANK YOU.

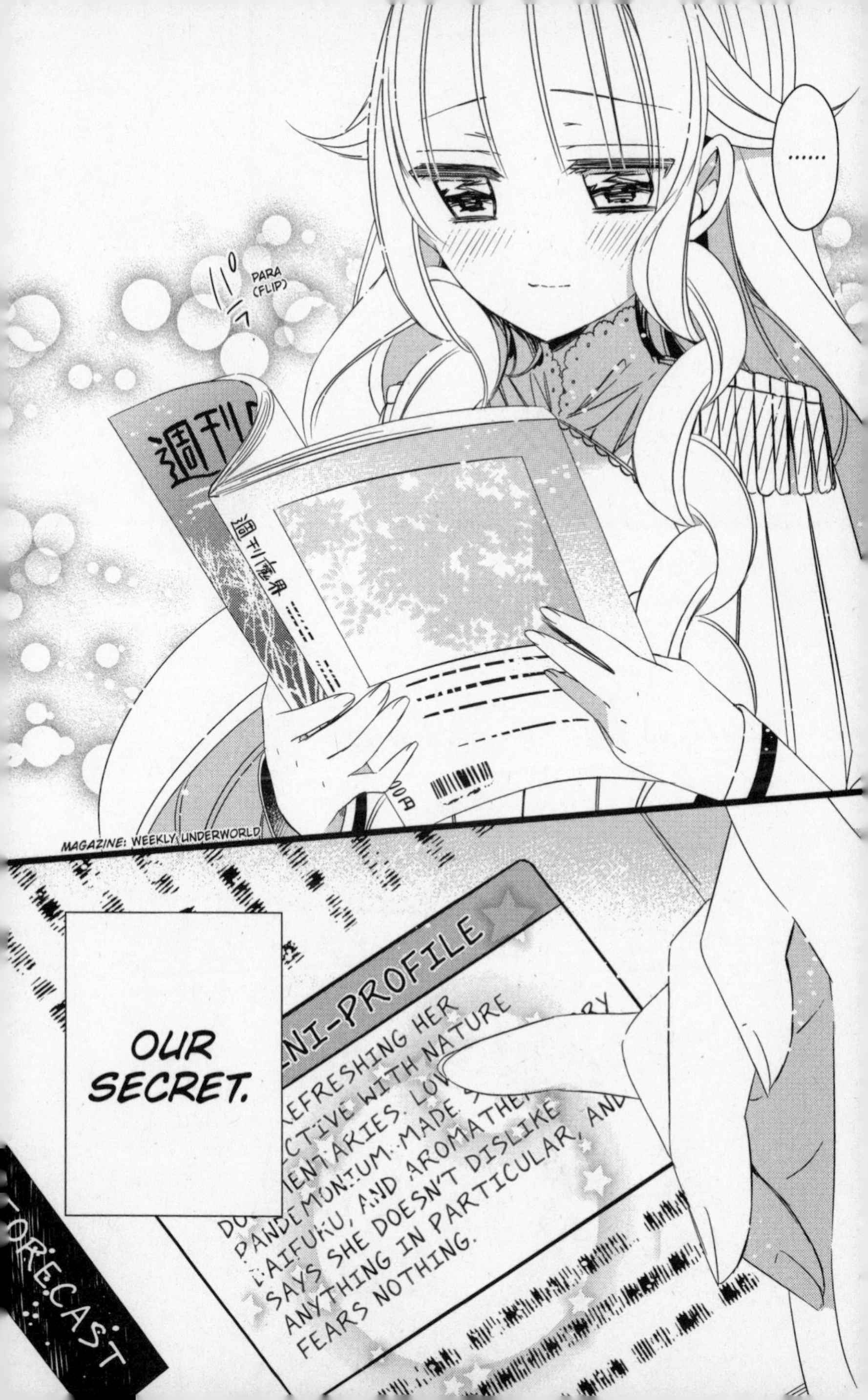
......
PARA (FLIP)
MAGAZINE: WEEKLY UNDERWORLD
OUR SECRET.
NI-PROFILE
REFRESHING HER
CTIVE WITH NATURE
MENTARIES. LOV
PANDEMONIUM MADE
DAIFUKU, AND AROMATHER
SAYS SHE DOESN'T DISLIKE
ANYTHING IN PARTICULAR, AND
FEARS NOTHING.
FORECAST

VERY
LEGGY.

SEXY
BIKINI
MODEL
BEHEMOTH-
TAN.

As Miss Beelzebub Likes

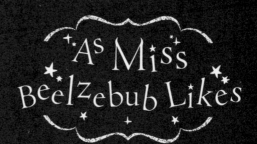

WAKE UP, QUICK!

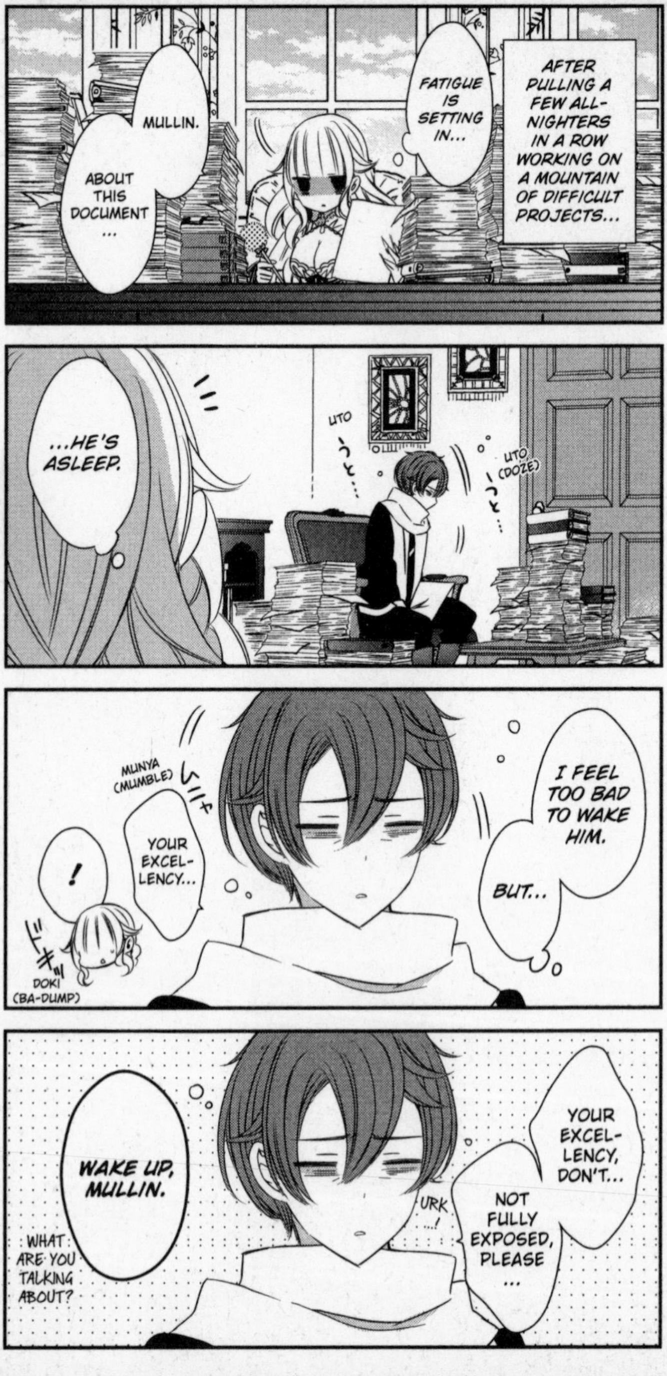
AFTER PULLING A FEW ALL-NIGHTERS IN A ROW WORKING ON A MOUNTAIN OF DIFFICULT PROJECTS...
FATIGUE IS SETTING IN...
MULLIN.
ABOUT THIS DOCUMENT...
UTO (DOZE)
UTO
...HE'S ASLEEP.
I FEEL TOO BAD TO WAKE HIM.
BUT...
MUNYA (MUMBLE)
YOUR EXCELLENCY...
!
DOKI (BA-DUMP)
YOUR EXCELLENCY, DON'T...
NOT FULLY EXPOSED, PLEASE...
URK...!
WAKE UP, MULLIN.
WHAT ARE YOU TALKING ABOUT?

CHAPTER 13

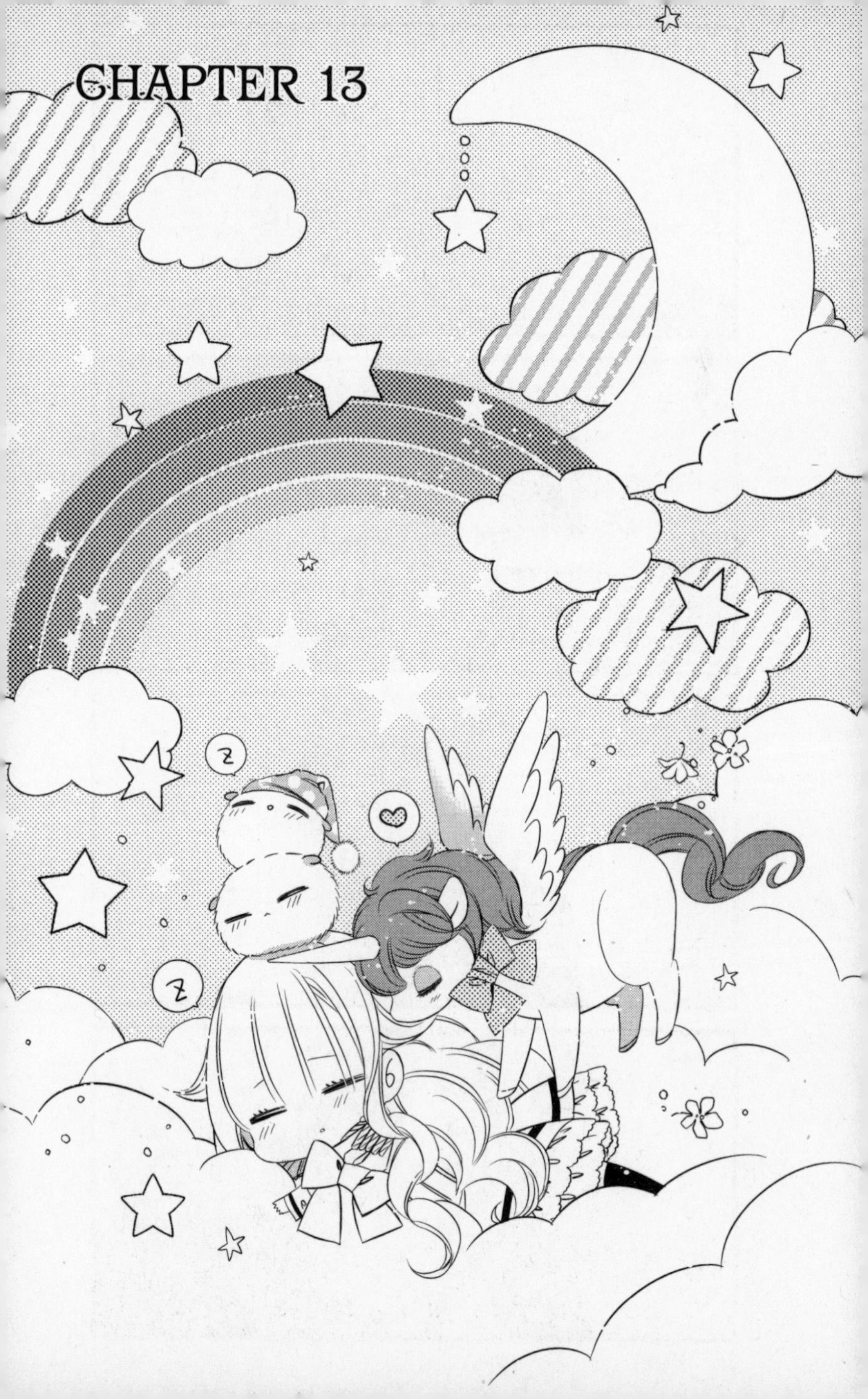
z
z

SIS MEETS BRO

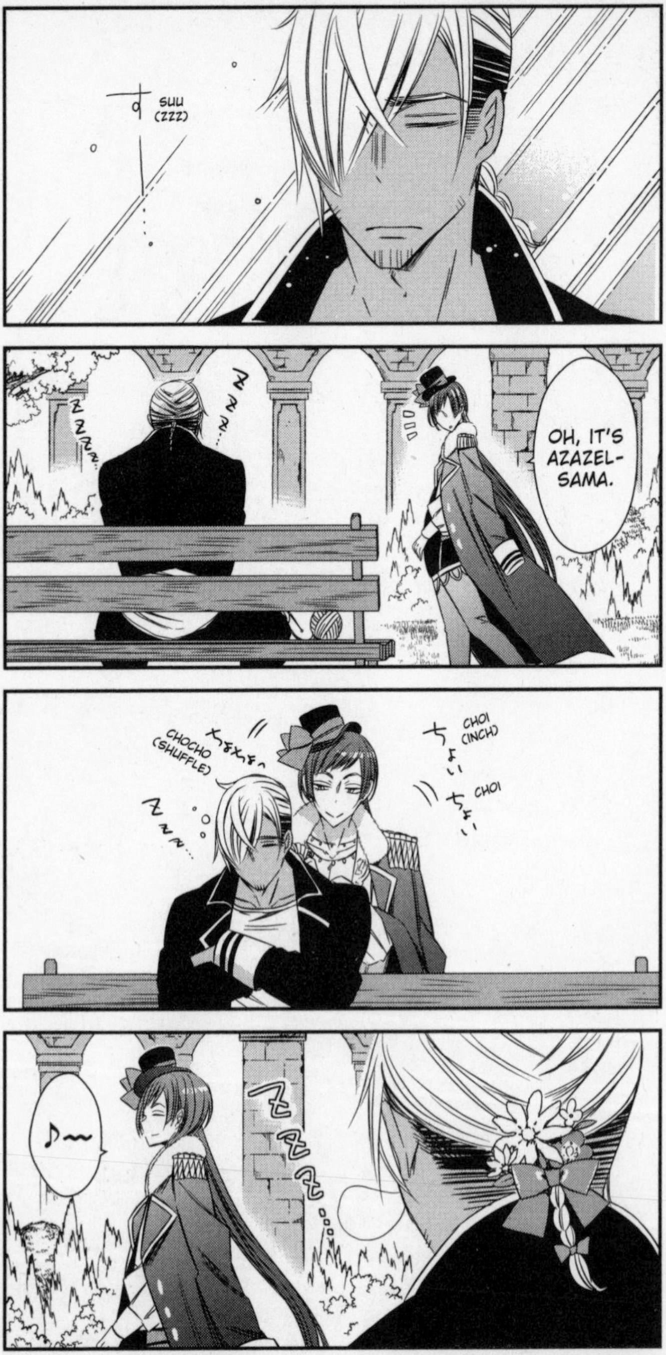
す
SUU (ZZZ)
ZZZ...
ZZZZ...
OH, IT'S AZAZEL-SAMA.
ちょい
CHOI (INCH)
ちょい
CHOI
ちょこちょこ
CHOCHO (SHUFFLE)
Z z z...
♪~~
Z z z z...

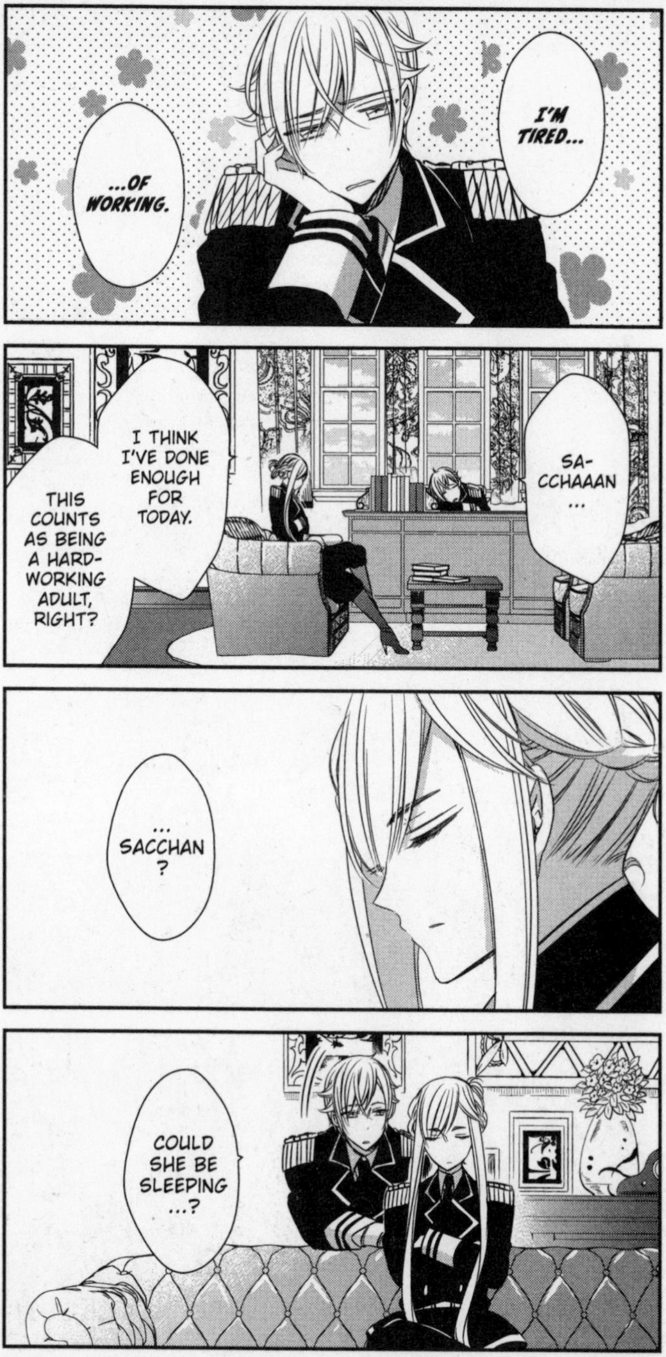
I'M TIRED...
...OF WORKING.
SA-CCHAAAN...
I THINK I'VE DONE ENOUGH FOR TODAY.
THIS COUNTS AS BEING A HARD-WORKING ADULT, RIGHT?
...SACCHAN?
COULD SHE BE SLEEPING...?

THE USUAL PATTERN

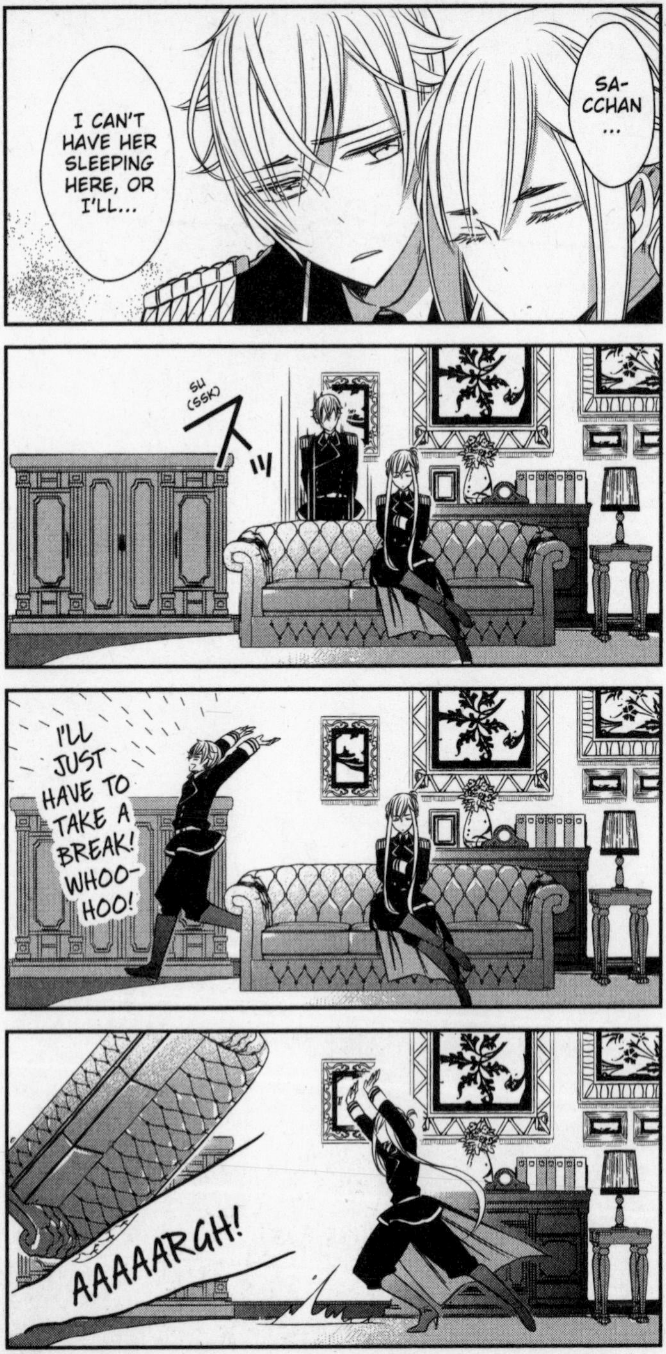

SA-CCHAN...
I CAN'T HAVE HER SLEEPING HERE, OR I'LL...
スッ
SU (SSK)
I'LL JUST HAVE TO TAKE A BREAK! WHOO-HOO!
AAAAARGH!

BRO AND GOR

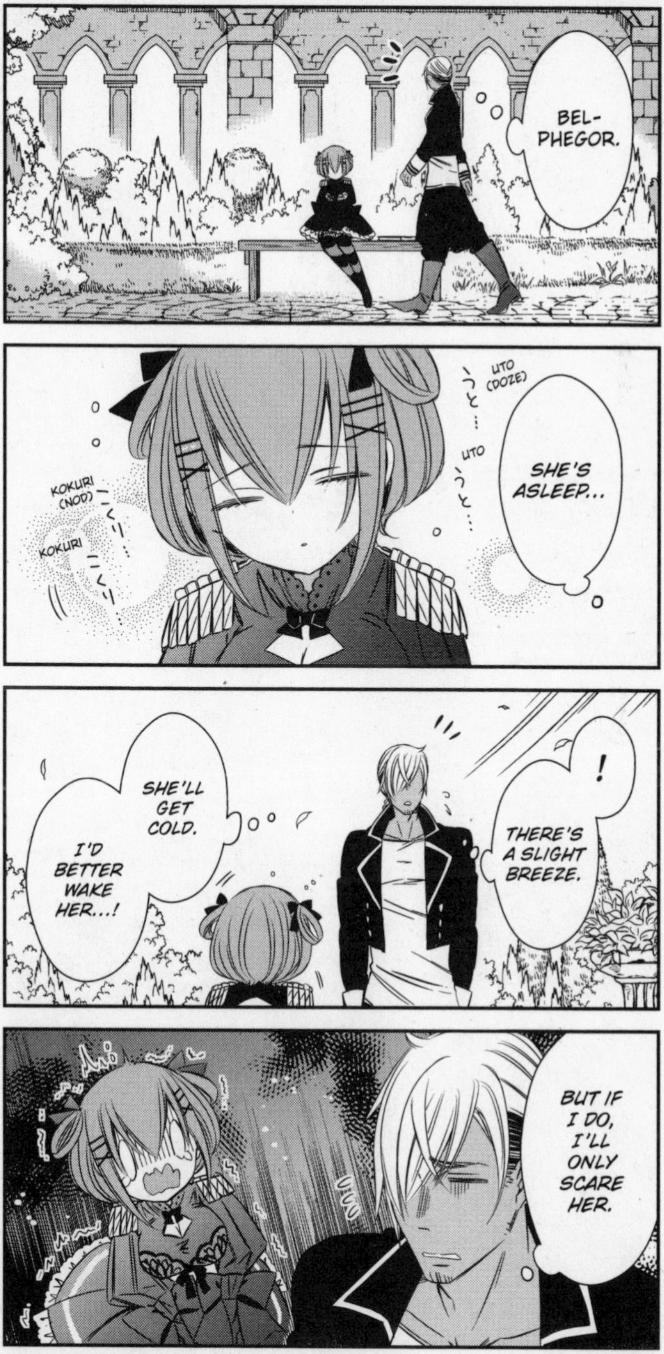
BEL-PHEGOR.
SHE'S ASLEEP...
うと… UTO (DOZE)
うと… UTO
こくり… KOKURI (NOD)
こくり… KOKURI
!
THERE'S A SLIGHT BREEZE.
SHE'LL GET COLD.
I'D BETTER WAKE HER...!
BUT IF I DO, I'LL ONLY SCARE HER.

WARMTH

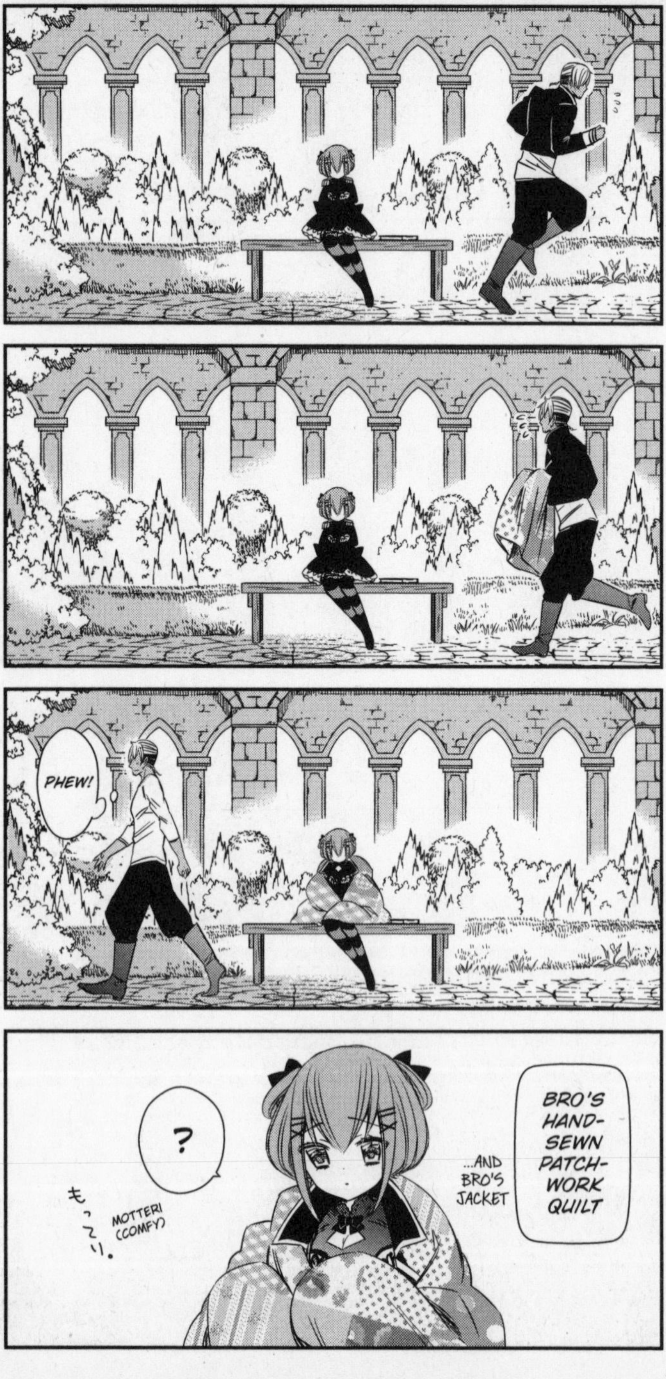
PHEW!
BRO'S HAND-SEWN PATCH-WORK QUILT
...AND BRO'S JACKET
?
もってり。
MOTTERI (COMFY)

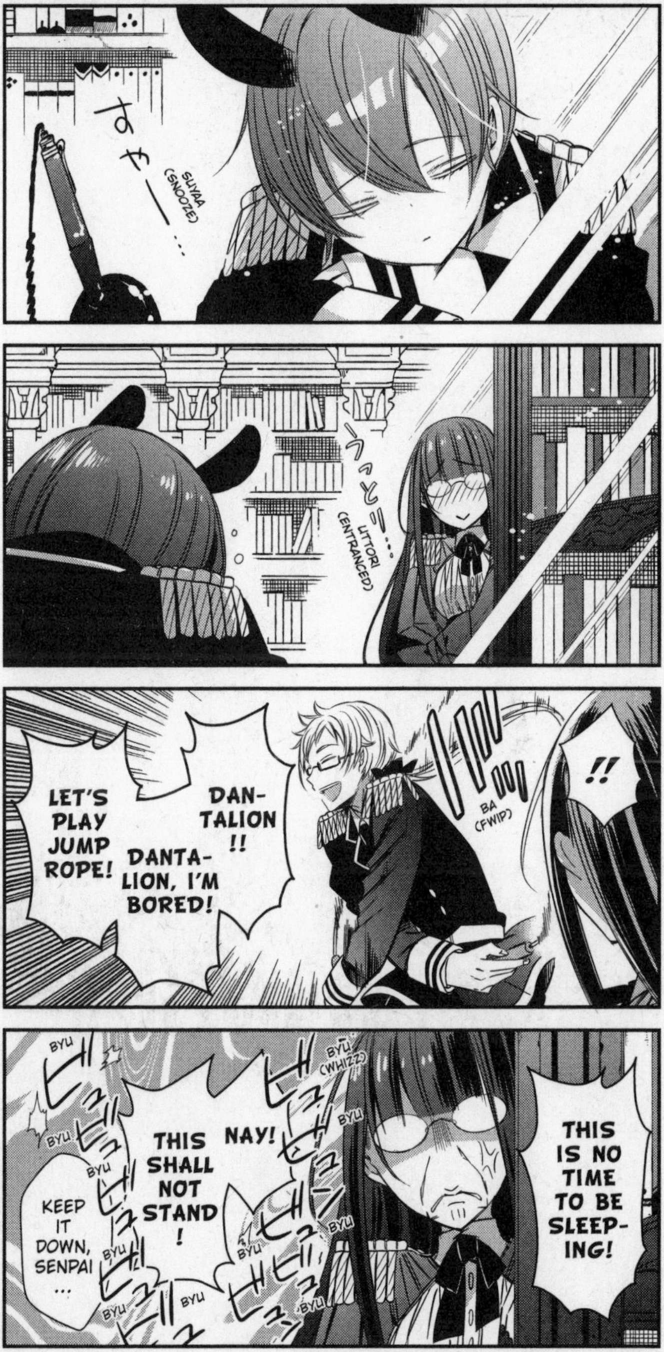
すやー…
SUYAA (SNOOZE)
うっとり…
UTTORI (ENTRANCED)
!!
BA (FWIP)
DANTALION!!
DANTALION, I'M BORED!
LET'S PLAY JUMP ROPE!
THIS IS NO TIME TO BE SLEEPING!
BYU (WHIZZ)
BYU
NAY!
THIS SHALL NOT STAND!
BYU
BYU
BYU
BYU
BYU
BYU
BYU
BYU
KEEP IT DOWN, SENPAI...

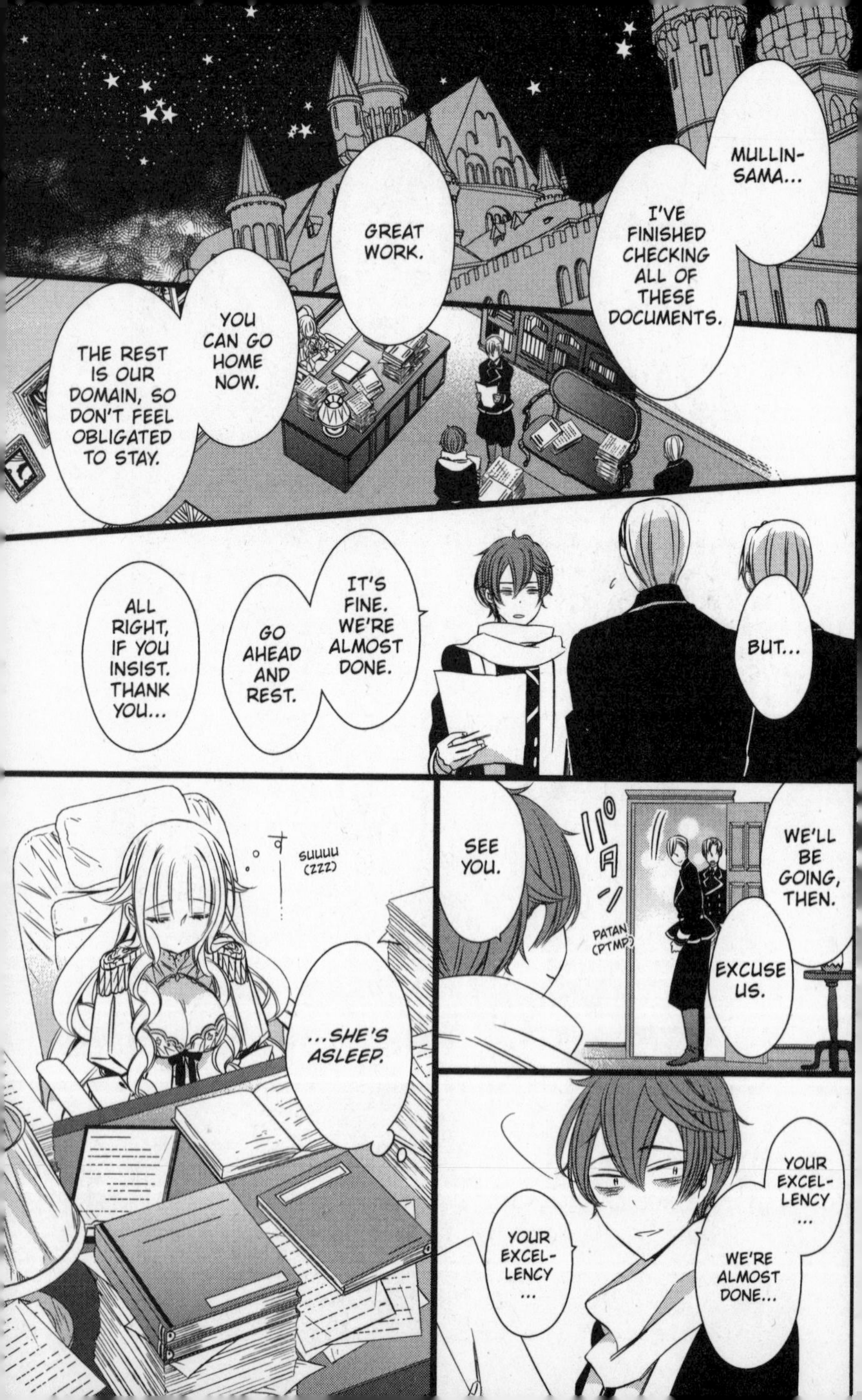
MULLIN-SAMA...
I'VE FINISHED CHECKING ALL OF THESE DOCUMENTS.
GREAT WORK.
YOU CAN GO HOME NOW.
THE REST IS OUR DOMAIN, SO DON'T FEEL OBLIGATED TO STAY.
BUT...
IT'S FINE. WE'RE ALMOST DONE.
GO AHEAD AND REST.
ALL RIGHT, IF YOU INSIST. THANK YOU...
WE'LL BE GOING, THEN.
EXCUSE US.
SEE YOU.
PATAN (PTMP)
YOUR EXCEL-LENCY...
WE'RE ALMOST DONE...
YOUR EXCEL-LENCY...
SUUUU (ZZZ)
...SHE'S ASLEEP.

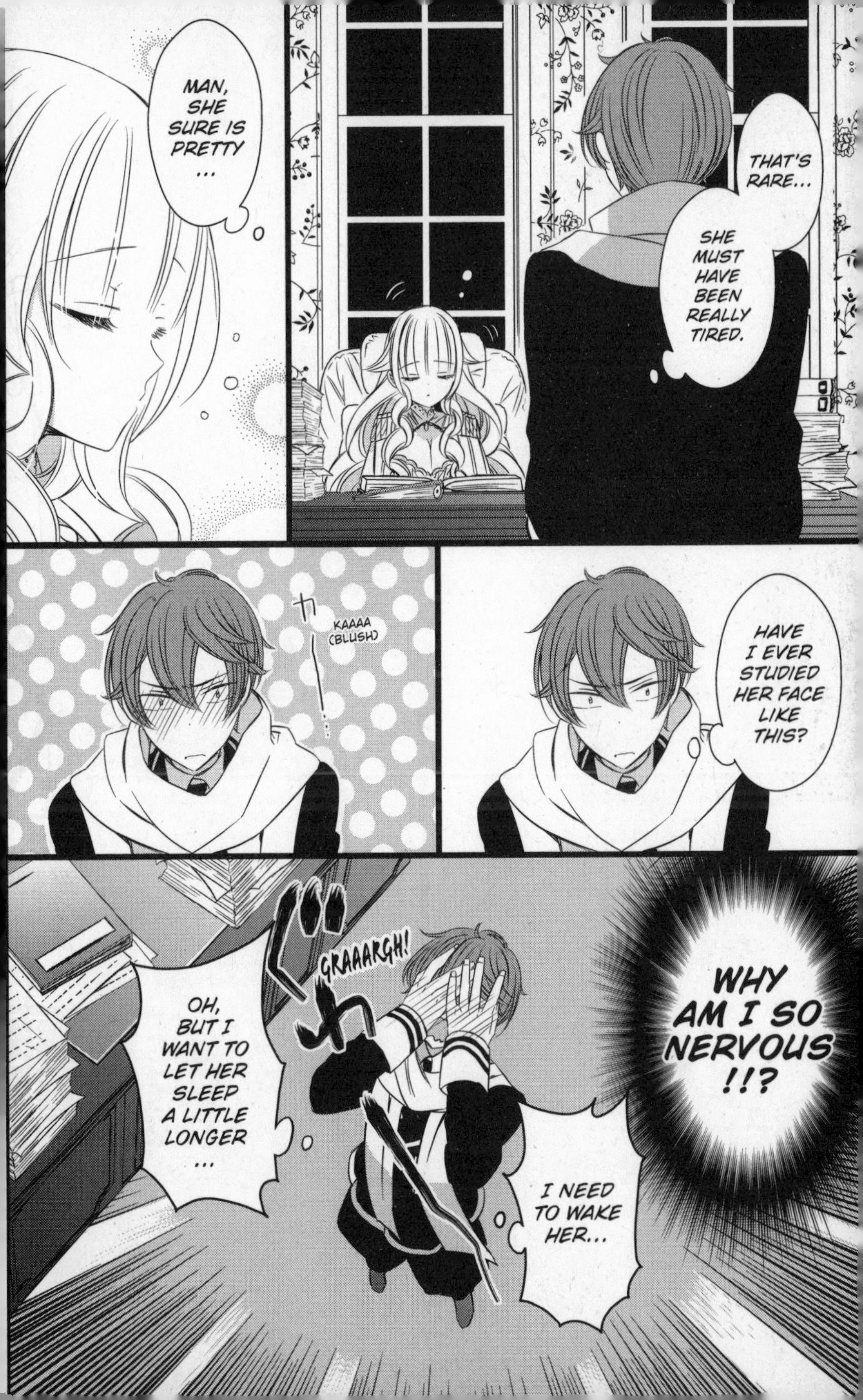

THAT'S RARE...
SHE MUST HAVE BEEN REALLY TIRED.
MAN, SHE SURE IS PRETTY ...
HAVE I EVER STUDIED HER FACE LIKE THIS?
KAAAA (BLUSH)
WHY AM I SO NERVOUS !!?
GRAAARGH!
I NEED TO WAKE HER...
OH, BUT I WANT TO LET HER SLEEP A LITTLE LONGER ...

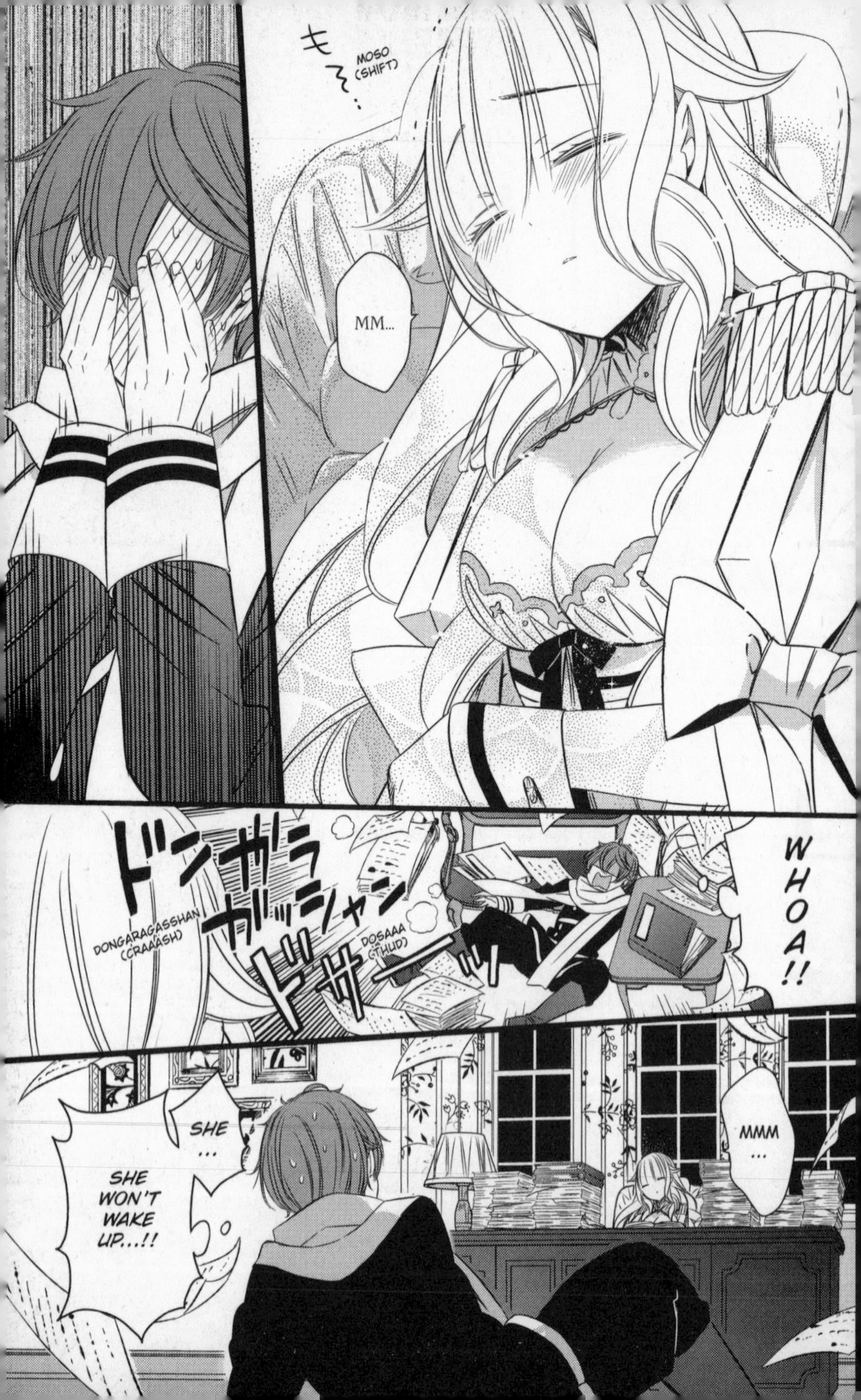

MOSO (SHIFT)
MM...
WHOA!!
ドサー
DOSAAA (THUD)
ドンガラガッシャン
DONGARAGASSHAN (CRAASH)
MMM...
SHE...
SHE WON'T WAKE UP...!!

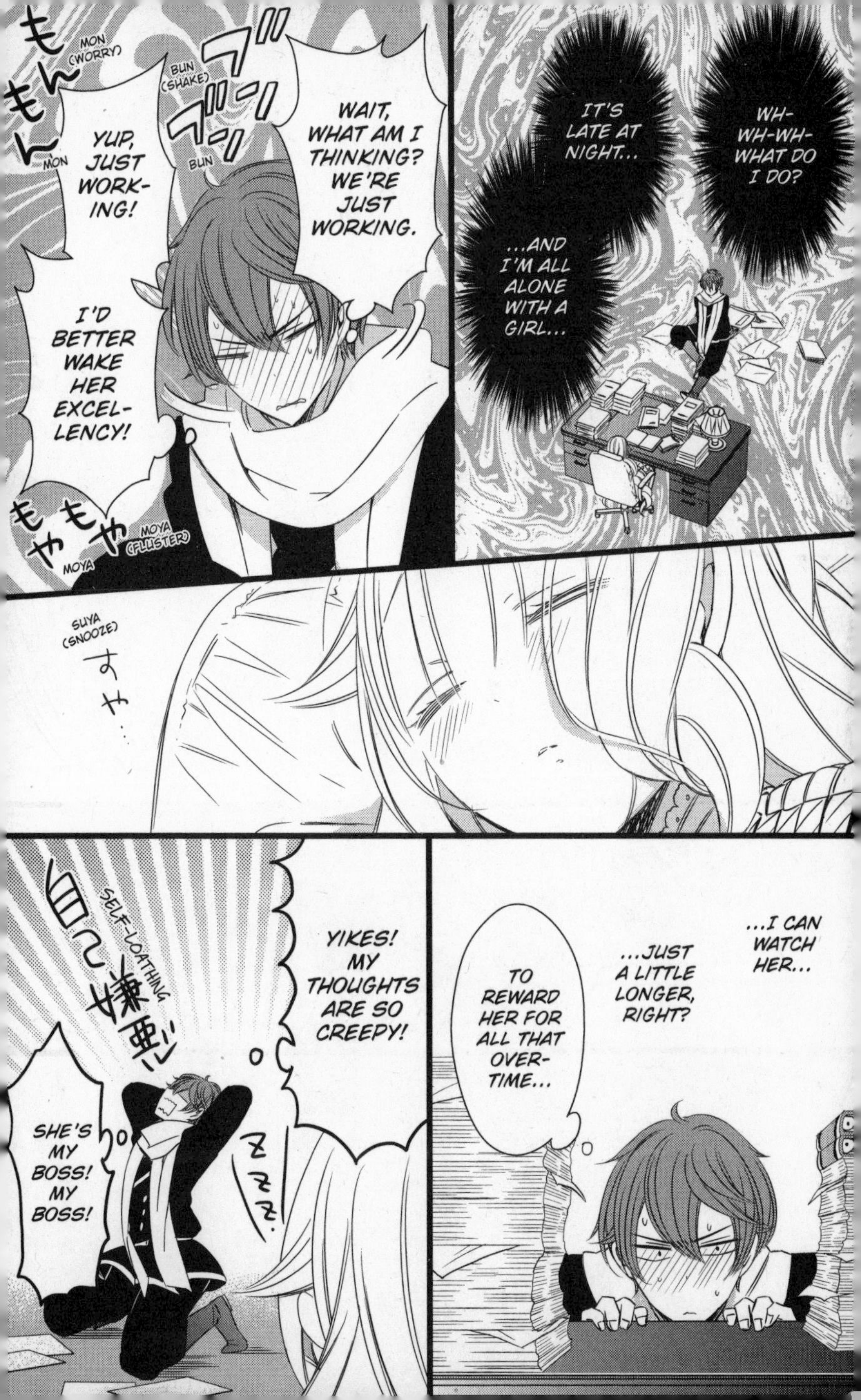
IT'S LATE AT NIGHT...
...AND I'M ALL ALONE WITH A GIRL...
WH-WH-WH-WHAT DO I DO?
WAIT, WHAT AM I THINKING? WE'RE JUST WORKING.
ブンブン
BUN (SHAKE) BUN
YUP, JUST WORKING!
もんもん
MON (WORRY) MON
I'D BETTER WAKE HER EXCELLENCY!
もやもや
MOYA (FLUSTER) MOYA
すや…
SUYA (SNOOZE)
...I CAN WATCH HER...
...JUST A LITTLE LONGER, RIGHT?
TO REWARD HER FOR ALL THAT OVER-TIME...
YIKES! MY THOUGHTS ARE SO CREEPY!
自己嫌悪
SELF-LOATHING
SHE'S MY BOSS! MY BOSS!
zzz

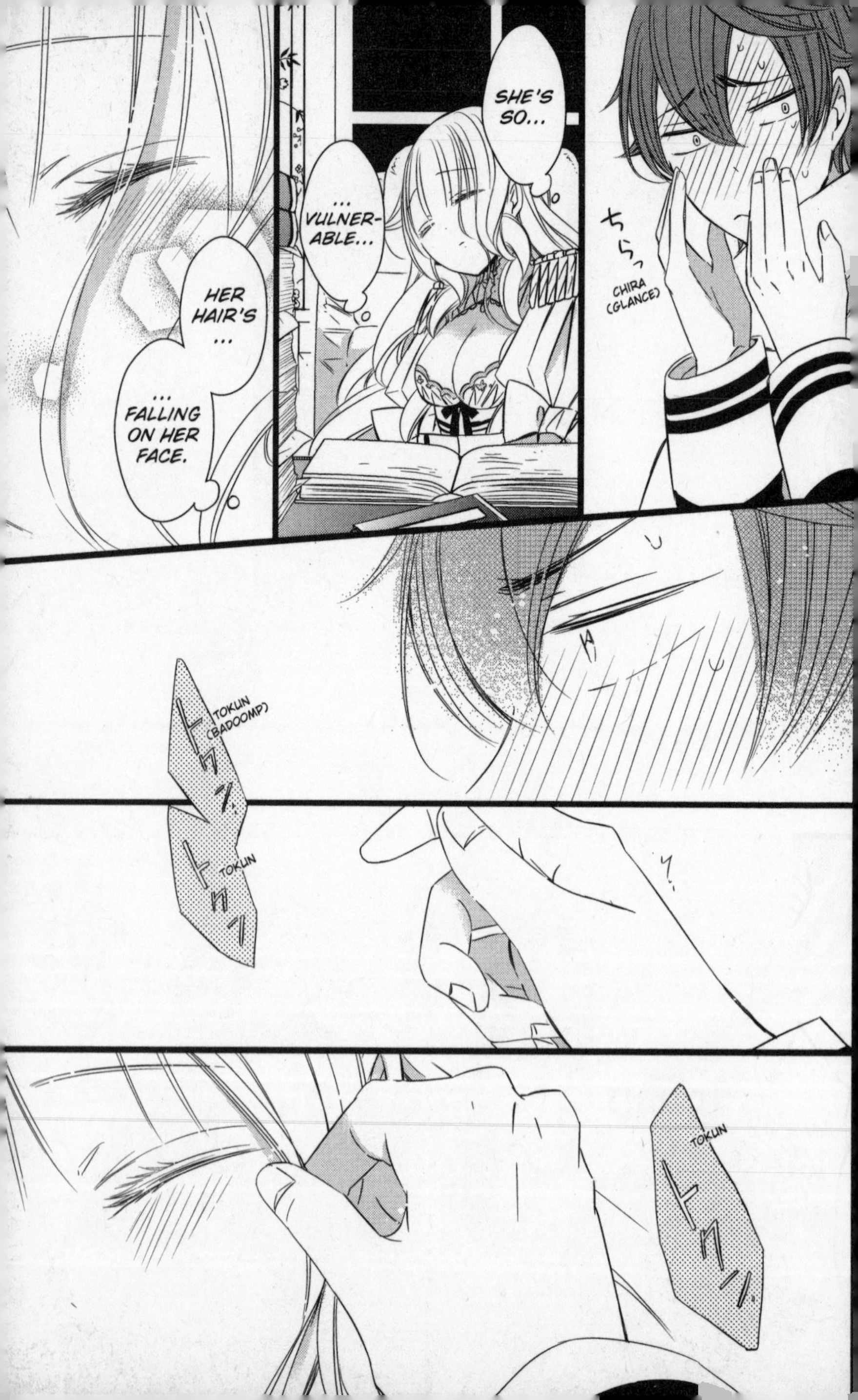
ちらっ
CHIRA (GLANCE)
SHE'S SO...
... VULNERABLE...
HER HAIR'S ...
... FALLING ON HER FACE.
TOKUN (BADOOMP)
TOKUN
TOKUN

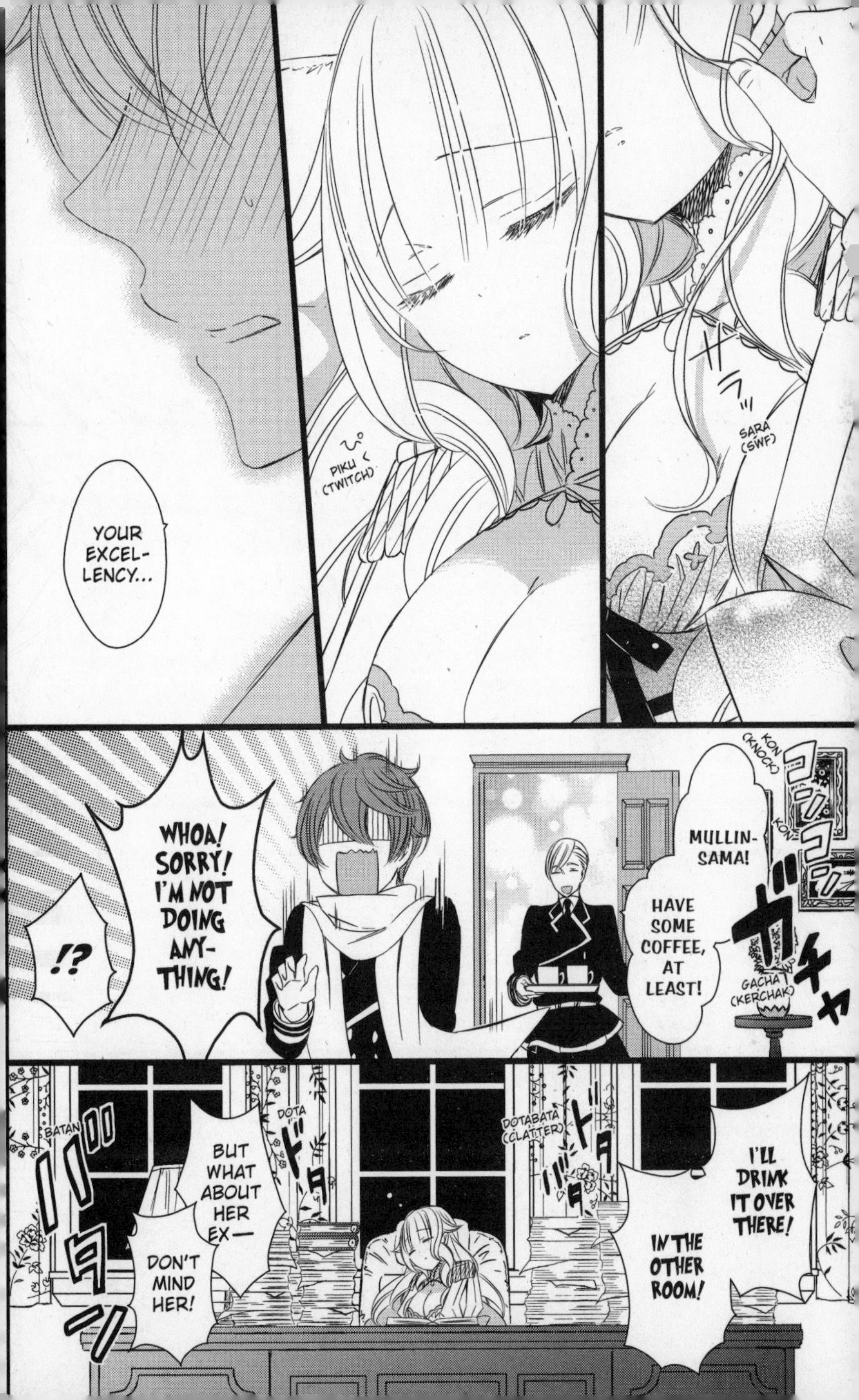
SARA (SWF)
ぴく
PIKU (TWITCH)
YOUR EXCEL-LENCY...
KON (KNOCK)
KON
MULLIN-SAMA!
HAVE SOME COFFEE, AT LEAST!
GACHA (KERCHAK)
WHOA! SORRY! I'M NOT DOING ANY-THING!
!?
I'LL DRINK IT OVER THERE!
IN THE OTHER ROOM!
DOTABATA (CLATTER)
DOTA
BUT WHAT ABOUT HER EX—
DON'T MIND HER!
BATAN

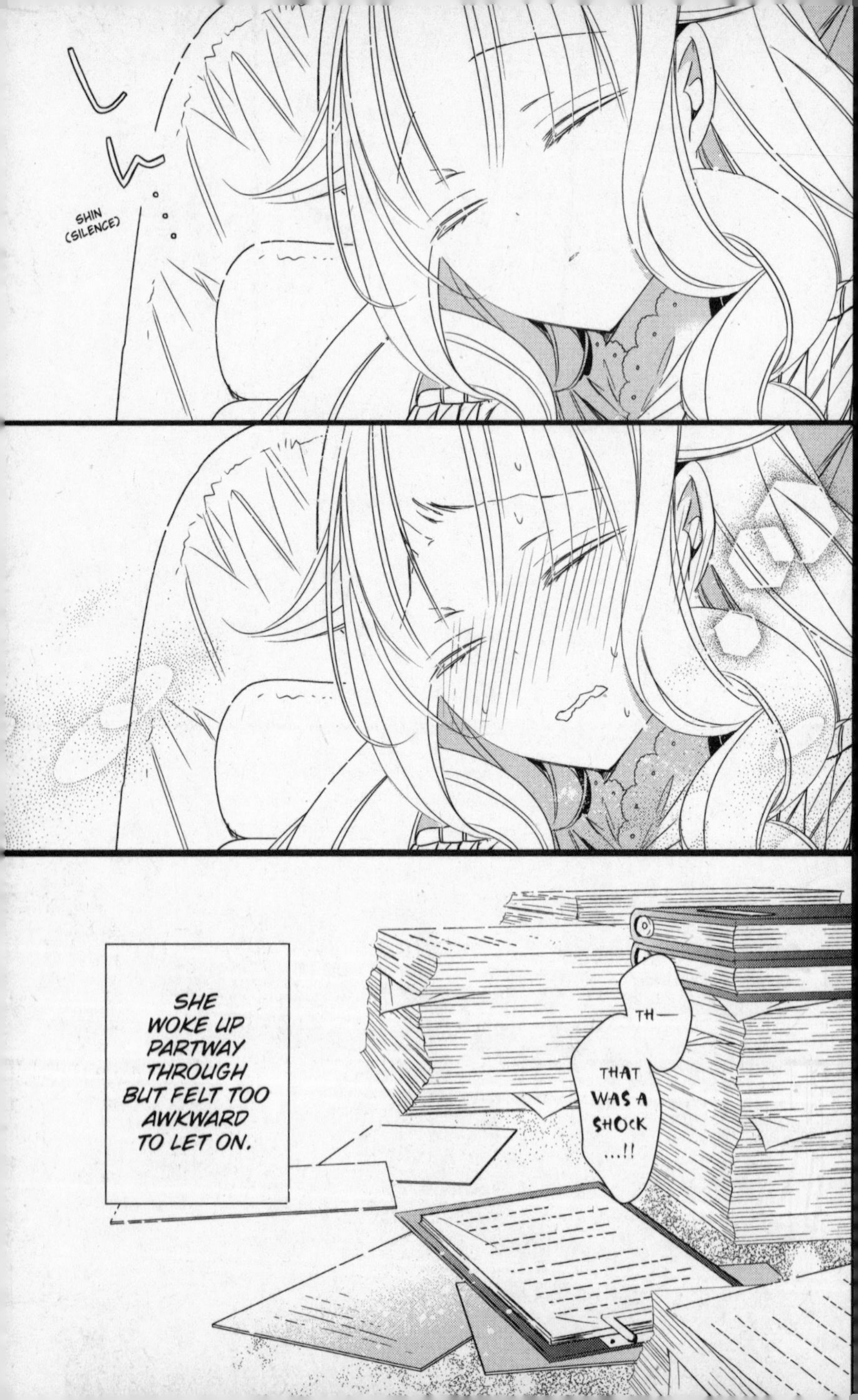
SHIN (SILENCE)
TH— THAT WAS A SHOCK ...!!
SHE WOKE UP PARTWAY THROUGH BUT FELT TOO AWKWARD TO LET ON.

As Miss Beelzebub Likes

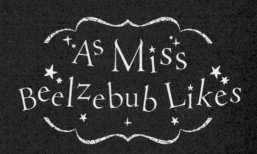

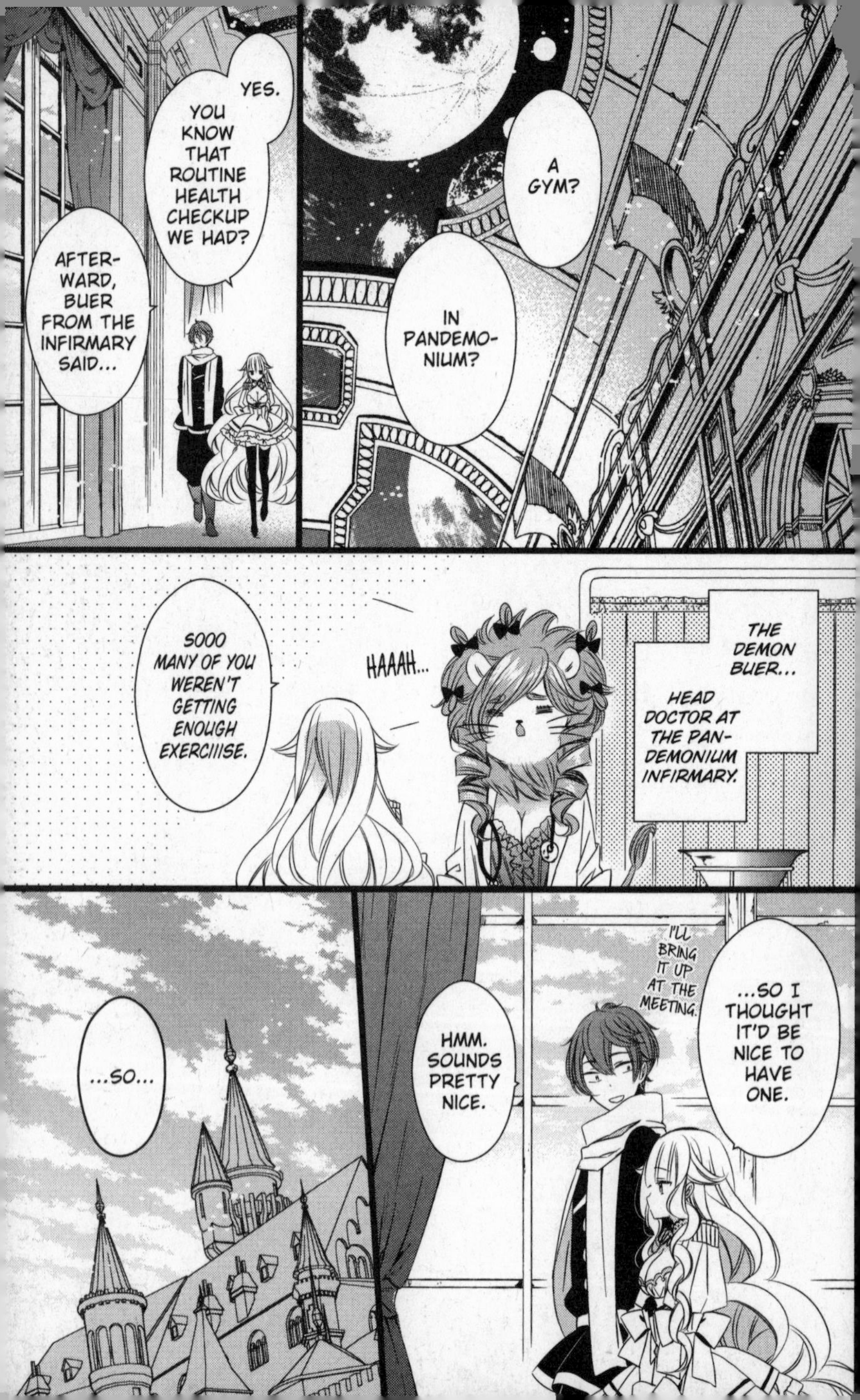
A GYM?
IN PANDEMONIUM?
YES.
YOU KNOW THAT ROUTINE HEALTH CHECKUP WE HAD?
AFTERWARD, BUER FROM THE INFIRMARY SAID...
THE DEMON BUER...
HEAD DOCTOR AT THE PANDEMONIUM INFIRMARY.
HAAAH...
SOOO MANY OF YOU WEREN'T GETTING ENOUGH EXERCIIISE.
...SO I THOUGHT IT'D BE NICE TO HAVE ONE.
I'LL BRING IT UP AT THE MEETING.
HMM. SOUNDS PRETTY NICE.
...SO...

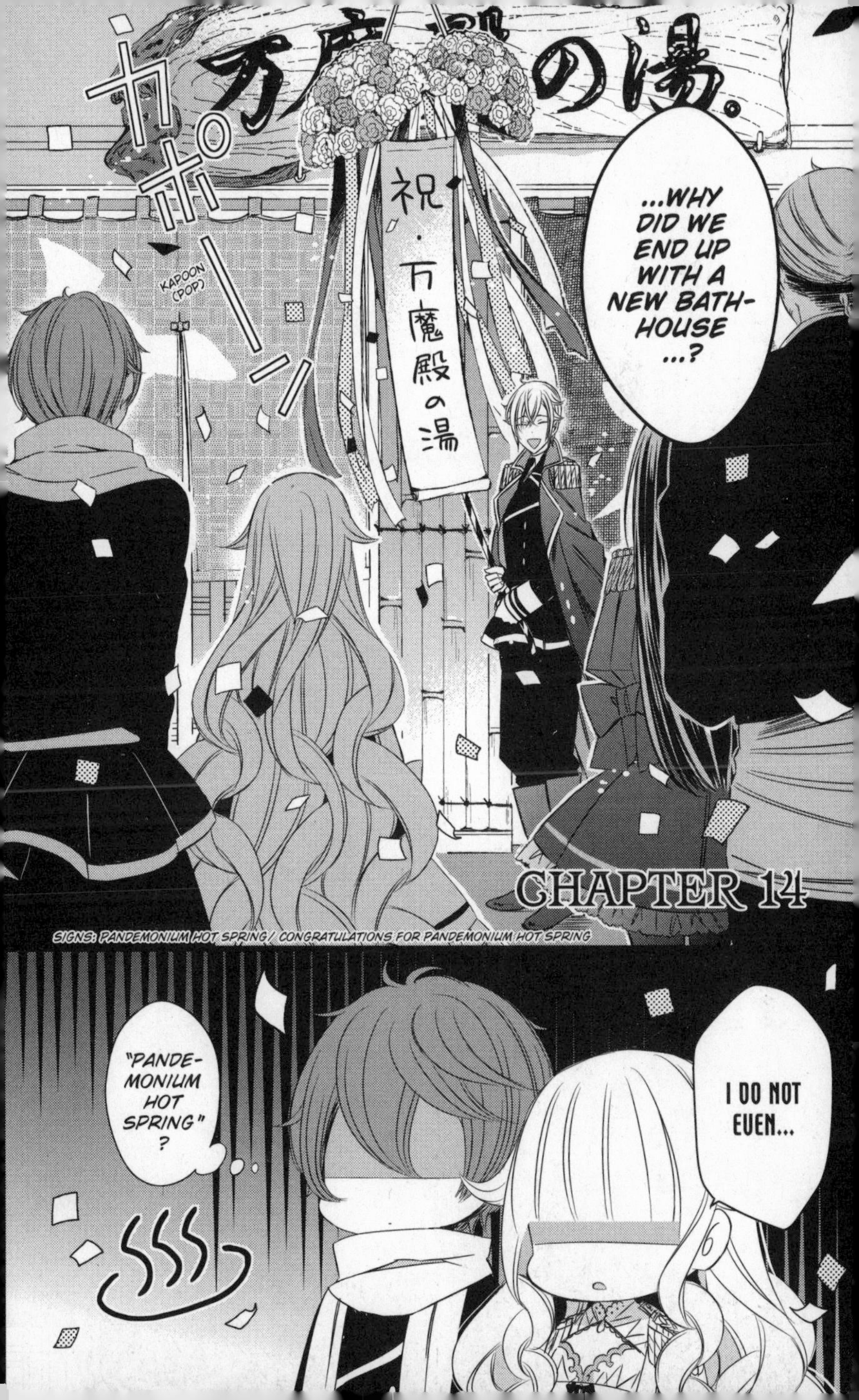
カポーン
KAPOON (POP)
祝・万魔殿の湯
...WHY DID WE END UP WITH A NEW BATH-HOUSE ...?
CHAPTER 14
SIGNS: PANDEMONIUM HOT SPRING / CONGRATULATIONS FOR PANDEMONIUM HOT SPRING
I DO NOT EVEN...
"PANDE-MONIUM HOT SPRING"?

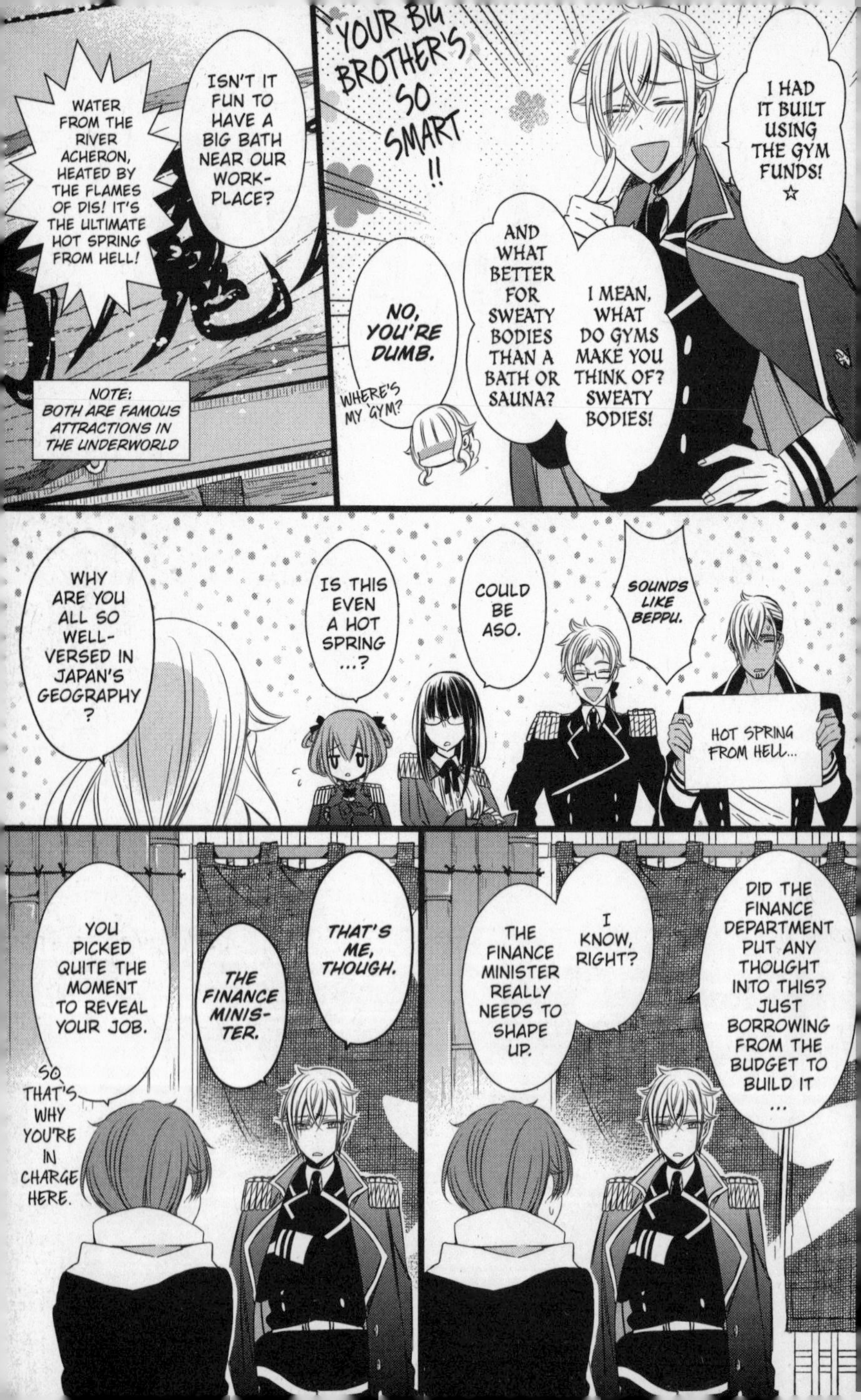
I HAD IT BUILT USING THE GYM FUNDS! ☆
YOUR BIG BROTHER'S SO SMART !!
I MEAN, WHAT DO GYMS MAKE YOU THINK OF? SWEATY BODIES!
AND WHAT BETTER FOR SWEATY BODIES THAN A BATH OR SAUNA?
NO, YOU'RE DUMB.
WHERE'S MY 'GYM?
ISN'T IT FUN TO HAVE A BIG BATH NEAR OUR WORK-PLACE?
WATER FROM THE RIVER ACHERON, HEATED BY THE FLAMES OF DIS! IT'S THE ULTIMATE HOT SPRING FROM HELL!
NOTE: BOTH ARE FAMOUS ATTRACTIONS IN THE UNDERWORLD
SOUNDS LIKE BEPPU.
HOT SPRING FROM HELL...
COULD BE ASO.
IS THIS EVEN A HOT SPRING ...?
WHY ARE YOU ALL SO WELL-VERSED IN JAPAN'S GEOGRAPHY ?
DID THE FINANCE DEPARTMENT PUT ANY THOUGHT INTO THIS? JUST BORROWING FROM THE BUDGET TO BUILD IT ...
I KNOW, RIGHT?
THE FINANCE MINISTER REALLY NEEDS TO SHAPE UP.
THAT'S ME, THOUGH.
THE FINANCE MINIS-TER.
YOU PICKED QUITE THE MOMENT TO REVEAL YOUR JOB.
SO THAT'S WHY YOU'RE IN CHARGE HERE.

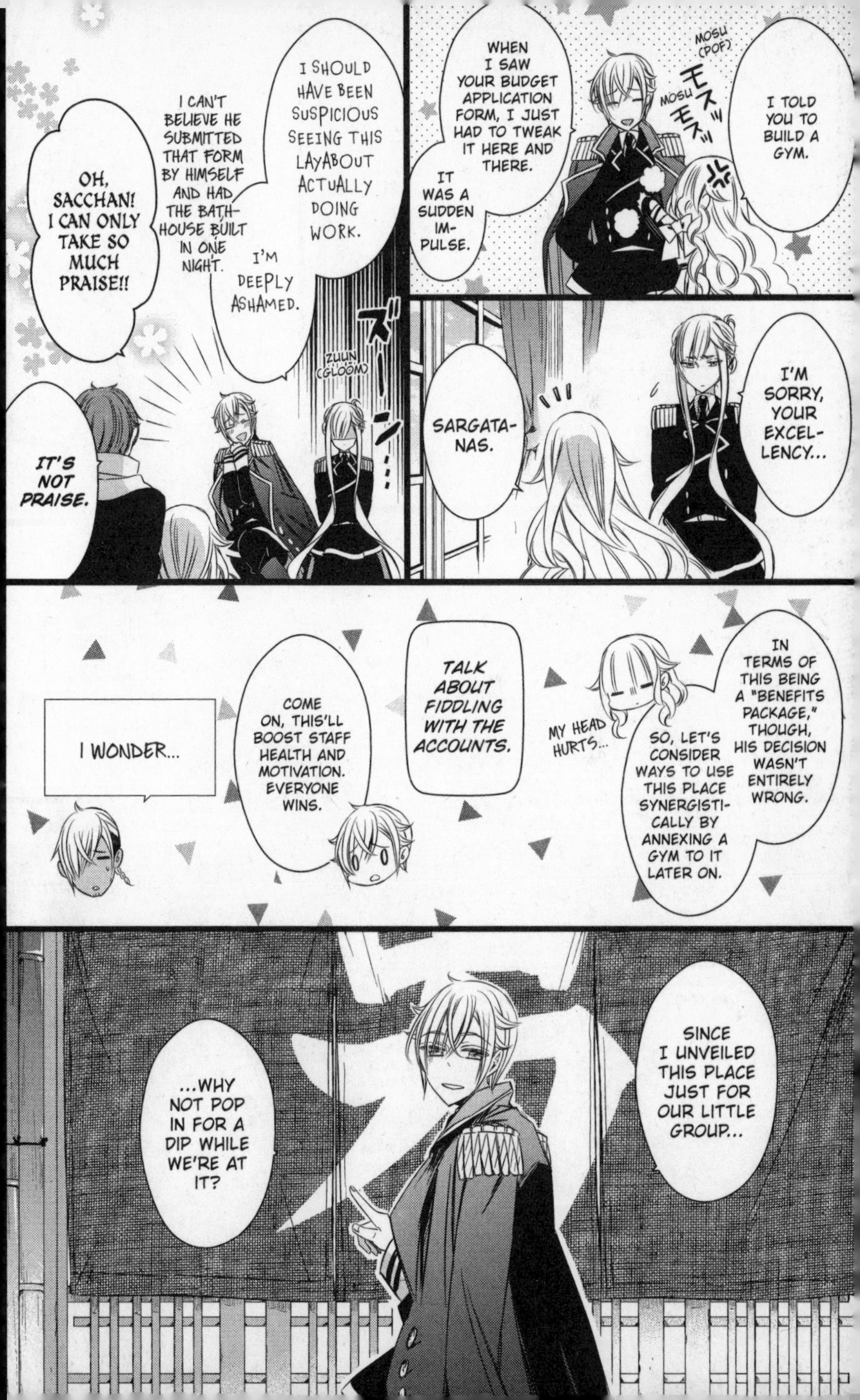
I TOLD YOU TO BUILD A GYM.
MOSU MOSU (POF)
WHEN I SAW YOUR BUDGET APPLICATION FORM, I JUST HAD TO TWEAK IT HERE AND THERE.
IT WAS A SUDDEN IMPULSE.
I'M SORRY, YOUR EXCELLENCY...
SARGATANAS.
I SHOULD HAVE BEEN SUSPICIOUS SEEING THIS LAYABOUT ACTUALLY DOING WORK.
I CAN'T BELIEVE HE SUBMITTED THAT FORM BY HIMSELF AND HAD THE BATHHOUSE BUILT IN ONE NIGHT.
I'M DEEPLY ASHAMED.
ZUUN (GLOOM)
OH, SACCHAN! I CAN ONLY TAKE SO MUCH PRAISE!!
IT'S NOT PRAISE.
IN TERMS OF THIS BEING A "BENEFITS PACKAGE," THOUGH, HIS DECISION WASN'T ENTIRELY WRONG.
SO, LET'S CONSIDER WAYS TO USE THIS PLACE SYNERGISTICALLY BY ANNEXING A GYM TO IT LATER ON.
MY HEAD HURTS...
TALK ABOUT FIDDLING WITH THE ACCOUNTS.
COME ON, THIS'LL BOOST STAFF HEALTH AND MOTIVATION. EVERYONE WINS.
I WONDER...
SINCE I UNVEILED THIS PLACE JUST FOR OUR LITTLE GROUP...
...WHY NOT POP IN FOR A DIP WHILE WE'RE AT IT?

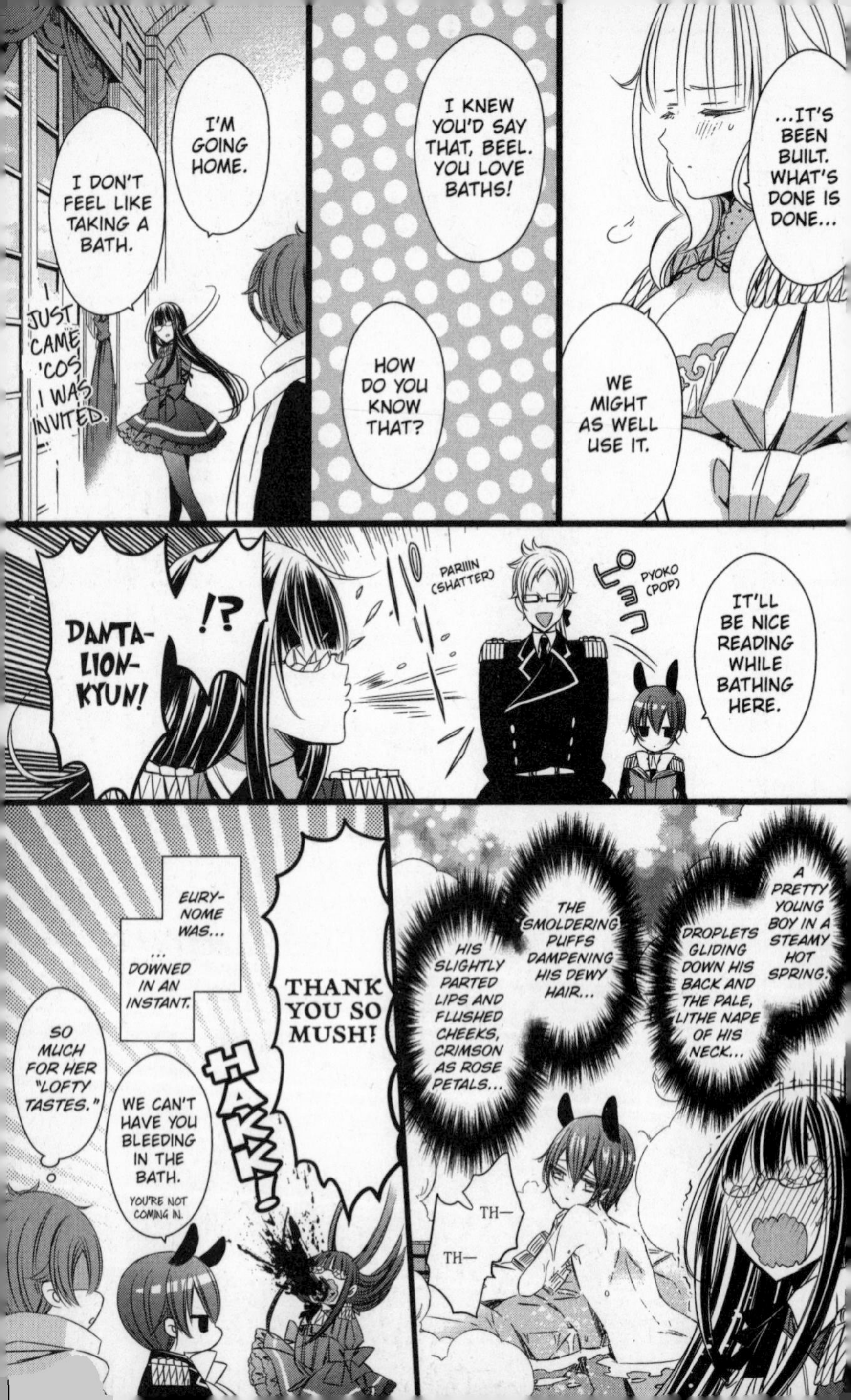
...IT'S BEEN BUILT. WHAT'S DONE IS DONE...
WE MIGHT AS WELL USE IT.
I KNEW YOU'D SAY THAT, BEEL. YOU LOVE BATHS!
HOW DO YOU KNOW THAT?
I'M GOING HOME.
I DON'T FEEL LIKE TAKING A BATH.
I JUST CAME 'COS I WAS INVITED.
IT'LL BE NICE READING WHILE BATHING HERE.
PYOKO (POP)
ピョコ
PARIIIN (SHATTER)
!?
DANTA-LION-KYUN!
A PRETTY YOUNG BOY IN A STEAMY HOT SPRING.
DROPLETS GLIDING DOWN HIS BACK AND THE PALE, LITHE NAPE OF HIS NECK...
THE SMOLDERING PUFFS DAMPENING HIS DEWY HAIR...
HIS SLIGHTLY PARTED LIPS AND FLUSHED CHEEKS, CRIMSON AS ROSE PETALS...
TH—
TH—
THANK YOU SO MUSH!
HAKK!
EURY-NOME WAS...
...DOWNED IN AN INSTANT.
WE CAN'T HAVE YOU BLEEDING IN THE BATH.
YOU'RE NOT COMING IN.
SO MUCH FOR HER "LOFTY TASTES."

TIED UP SINCE MORNING (OVER THE BATHHOUSE THING)

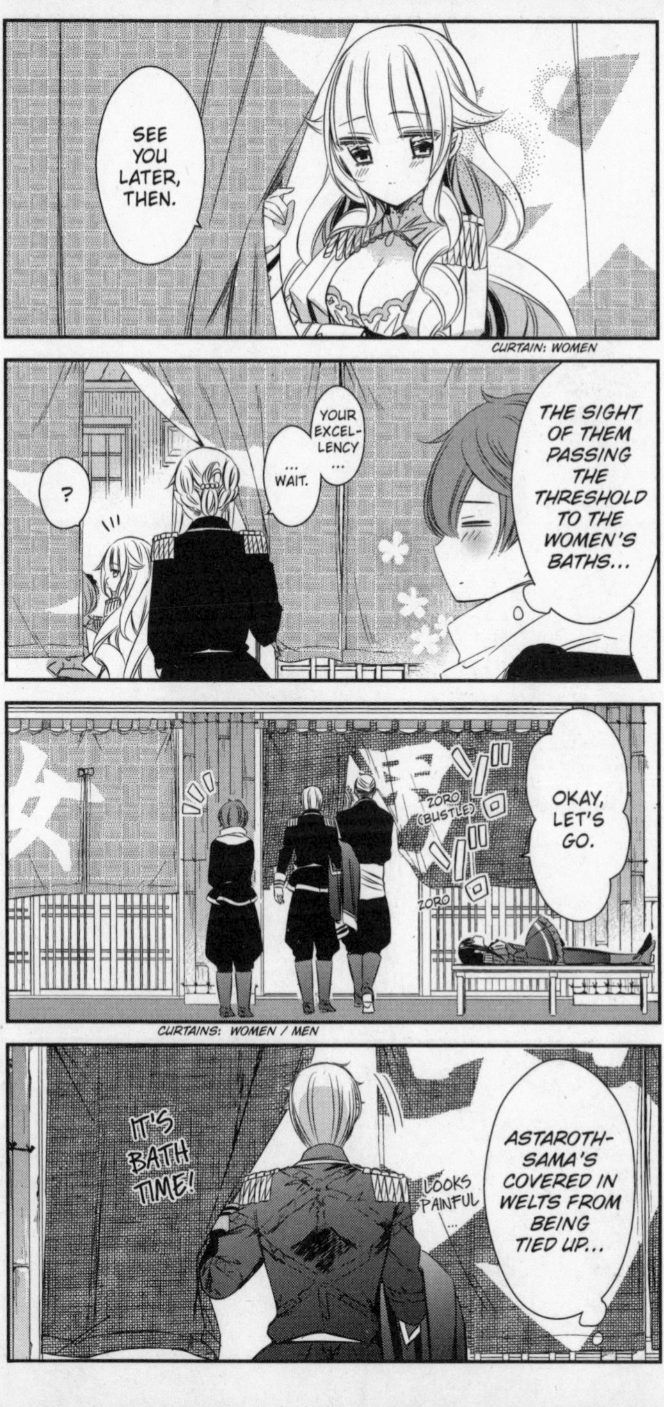
SEE YOU LATER, THEN.
CURTAIN: WOMEN
THE SIGHT OF THEM PASSING THE THRESHOLD TO THE WOMEN'S BATHS...
YOUR EXCEL-LENCY ...
... WAIT.
?
OKAY, LET'S GO.
ZORO (BUSTLE)
ZORO
CURTAINS: WOMEN / MEN
ASTAROTH-SAMA'S COVERED IN WELTS FROM BEING TIED UP...
LOOKS PAINFUL ...
IT'S BATH TIME!

WHEW!
I THOUGHT HE WAS AN IDIOT ...
...BUT I MIGHT LOVE THIS. SOAKING IN A BIG BATH ON THE WAY HOME FROM WORK...
FEELS AMAZING.
BASHA
BASHA (SPLASH)
YEAH.
BASHA
GABO (SPLOSH)
BASHA
...BRO, YOUR SIGN'S WATER-PROOF.
BISHA (SOAKED)
WAH HA HA HA!
YUP.
HOW DOES HE EVEN WRITE ON IT IN THE FIRST PLACE ...?

SHORTHAND OR SOME KINDA MAGIC?

ROMANTIC BATH-TIME ADVENTURE

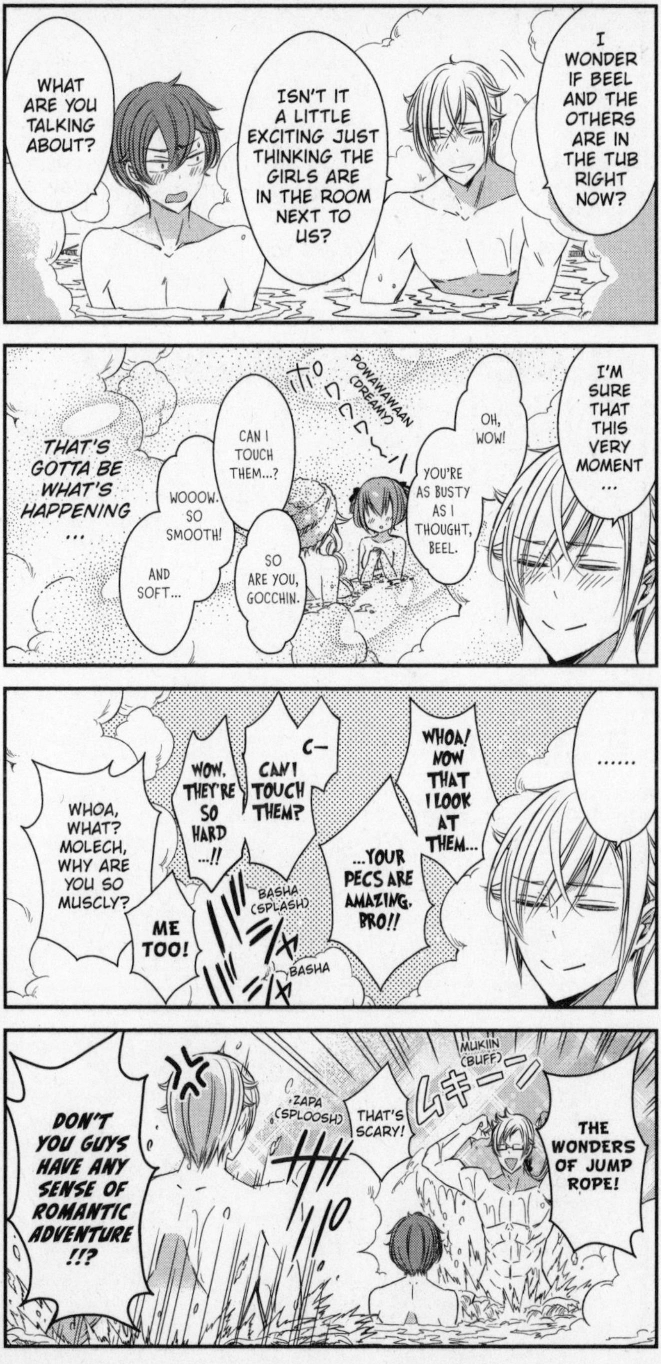
I WONDER IF BEEL AND THE OTHERS ARE IN THE TUB RIGHT NOW?
ISN'T IT A LITTLE EXCITING JUST THINKING THE GIRLS ARE IN THE ROOM NEXT TO US?
WHAT ARE YOU TALKING ABOUT?
I'M SURE THAT THIS VERY MOMENT...
POWAWAWAN (DREAMY)
OH, WOW!
YOU'RE AS BUSTY AS I THOUGHT, BEEL.
CAN I TOUCH THEM...?
SO ARE YOU, GOCCHIN.
WOOOW. SO SMOOTH!
AND SOFT...
THAT'S GOTTA BE WHAT'S HAPPENING...
......
WHOA! NOW THAT I LOOK AT THEM...
...YOUR PECS ARE AMAZING, BRO!!
C— CAN I TOUCH THEM?
WOW. THEY'RE SO HARD...!!
BASHA (SPLASH)
BASHA
ME TOO!
WHOA, WHAT? MOLECH, WHY ARE YOU SO MUSCLY?
MUKIIN (BUFF)
THE WONDERS OF JUMP ROPE!
THAT'S SCARY!
ZAPA (SPLOOSH)
DON'T YOU GUYS HAVE ANY SENSE OF ROMANTIC ADVENTURE!!?

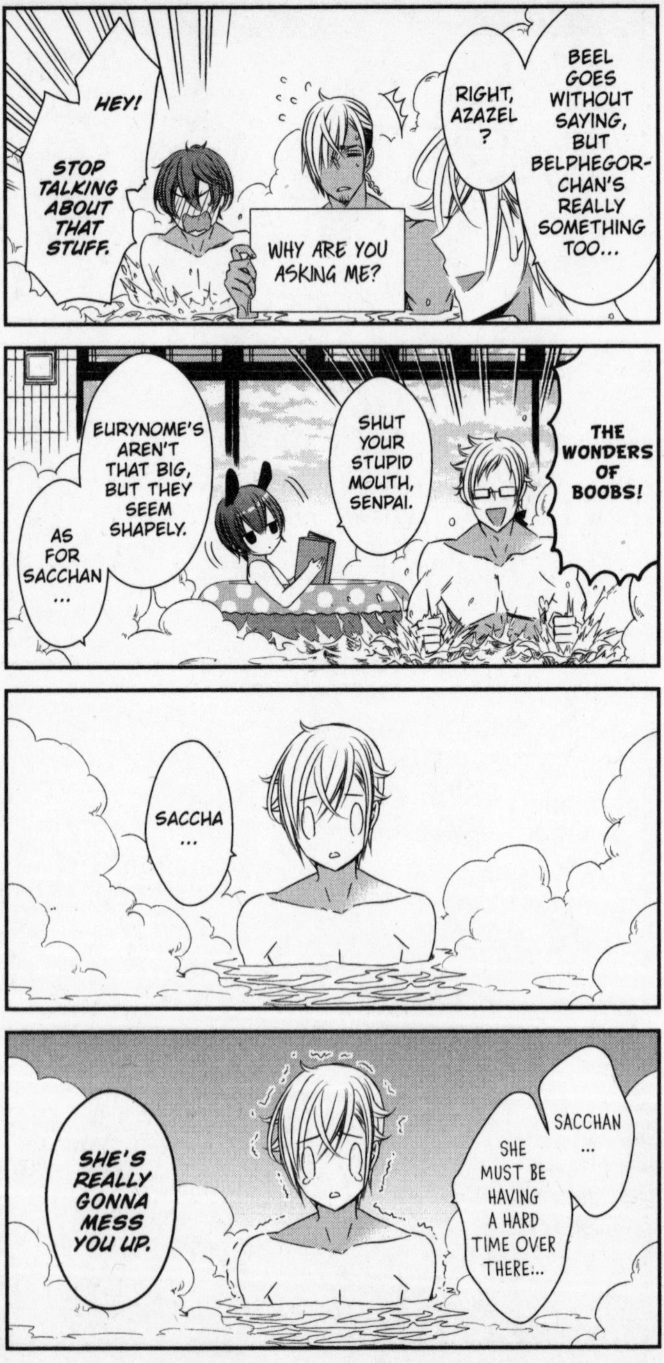
BEEL GOES WITHOUT SAYING, BUT BELPHEGOR-CHAN'S REALLY SOMETHING TOO...
RIGHT, AZAZEL?
WHY ARE YOU ASKING ME?
HEY!
STOP TALKING ABOUT THAT STUFF.
THE WONDERS OF BOOBS!
SHUT YOUR STUPID MOUTH, SENPAI.
EURYNOME'S AREN'T THAT BIG, BUT THEY SEEM SHAPELY.
AS FOR SACCHAN...
SACCHA...
SACCHAN...
SHE MUST BE HAVING A HARD TIME OVER THERE...
SHE'S REALLY GONNA MESS YOU UP.

NOW I'M SAD

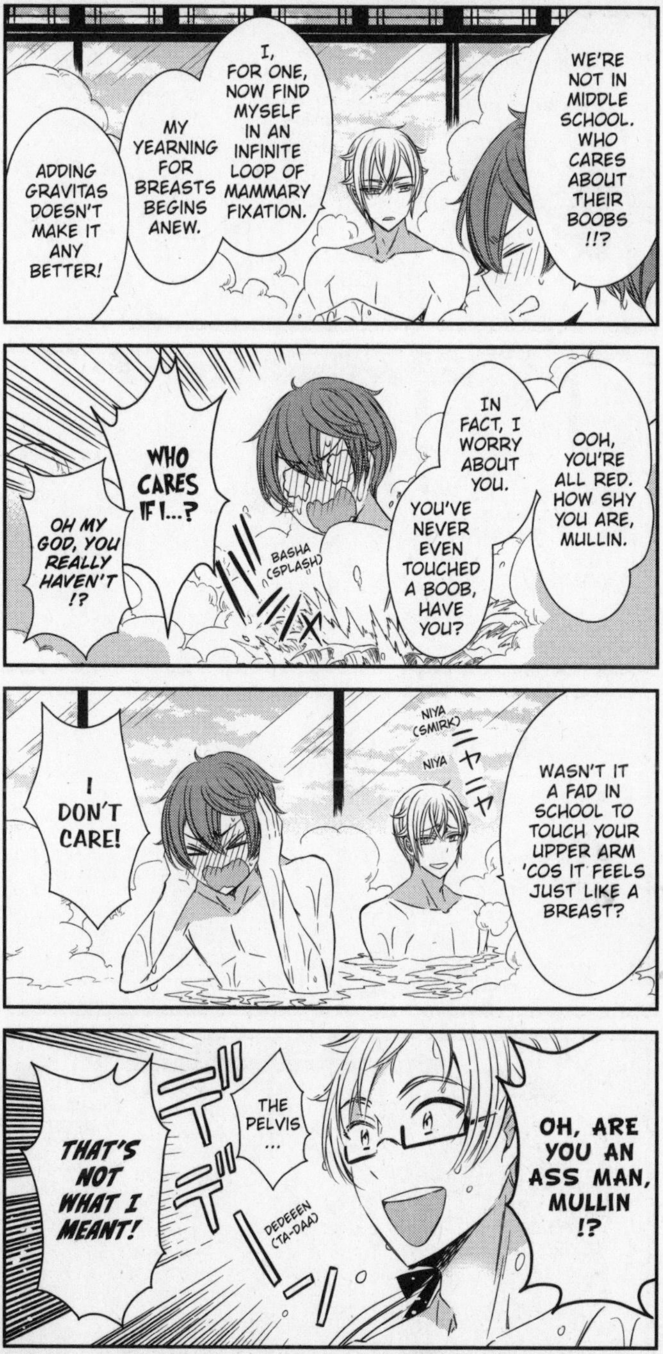
WE'RE NOT IN MIDDLE SCHOOL. WHO CARES ABOUT THEIR BOOBS !!?
I, FOR ONE, NOW FIND MYSELF IN AN INFINITE LOOP OF MAMMARY FIXATION.
MY YEARNING FOR BREASTS BEGINS ANEW.
ADDING GRAVITAS DOESN'T MAKE IT ANY BETTER!
OOH, YOU'RE ALL RED. HOW SHY YOU ARE, MULLIN.
IN FACT, I WORRY ABOUT YOU.
YOU'VE NEVER EVEN TOUCHED A BOOB, HAVE YOU?
BASHA (SPLASH)
WHO CARES IF I...?
OH MY GOD, YOU REALLY HAVEN'T !?
WASN'T IT A FAD IN SCHOOL TO TOUCH YOUR UPPER ARM 'COS IT FEELS JUST LIKE A BREAST?
NIYA (SMIRK)
NIYA
ニヤニヤ
I DON'T CARE!
OH, ARE YOU AN ASS MAN, MULLIN !?
DEDEEEN (TA-DAA)
THE PELVIS ...
THAT'S NOT WHAT I MEANT!

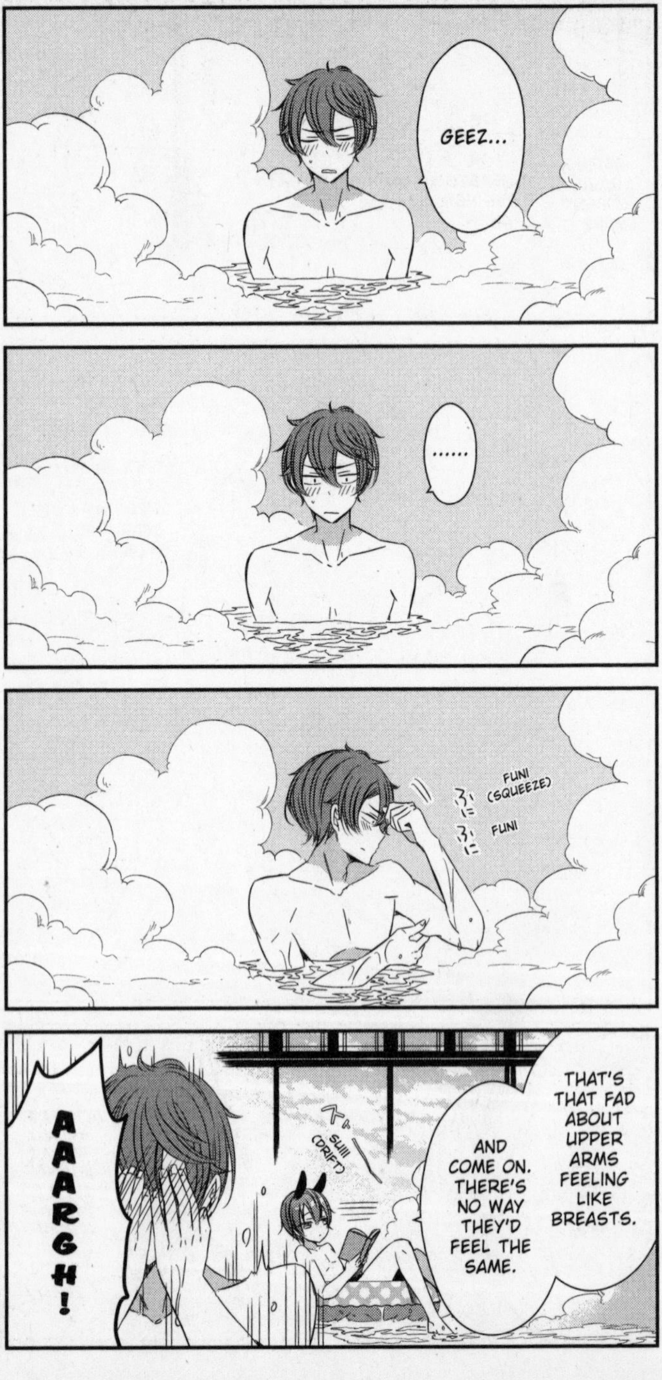
GEEZ...
......
ふに
FUNI (SQUEEZE)
ふに
FUNI
THAT'S THAT FAD ABOUT UPPER ARMS FEELING LIKE BREASTS.
AND COME ON. THERE'S NO WAY THEY'D FEEL THE SAME.
SUIII (DRIFT)
AAARGH!

IT'S AN URBAN LEGEND

I DON'T CHEAT

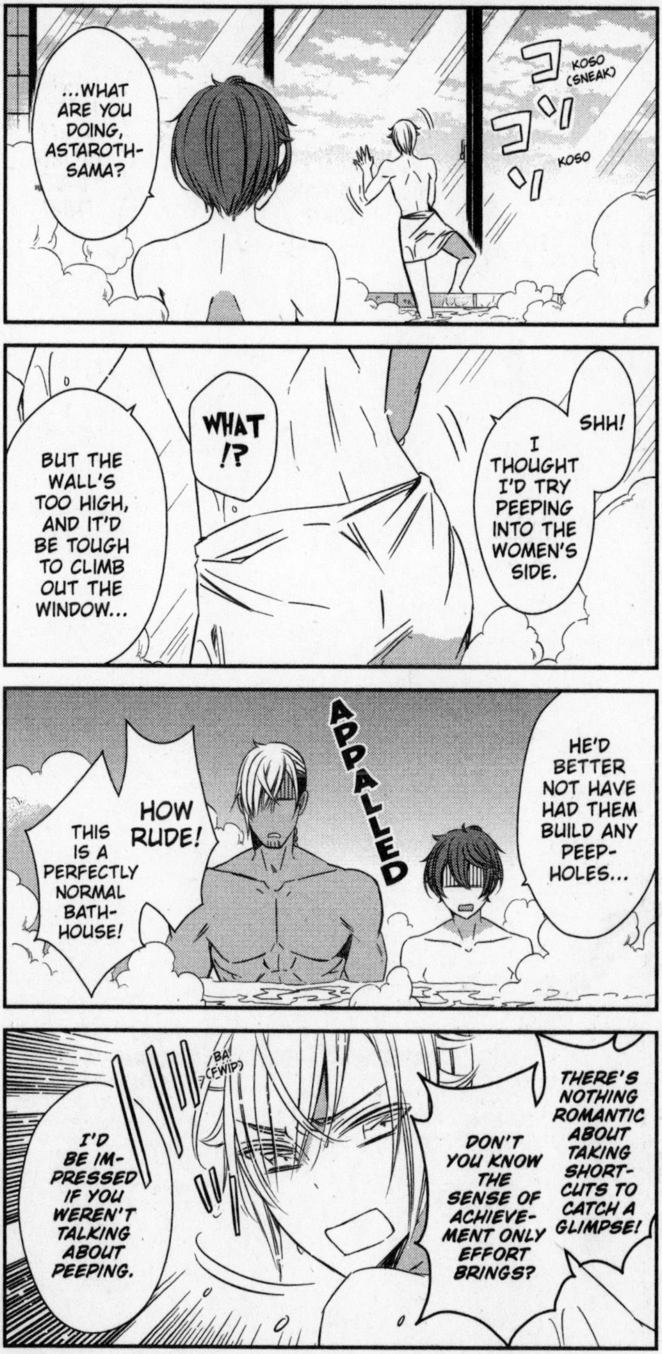
KOSO (SNEAK)
KOSO
...WHAT ARE YOU DOING, ASTAROTH-SAMA?
SHH! I THOUGHT I'D TRY PEEPING INTO THE WOMEN'S SIDE.
WHAT!?
BUT THE WALL'S TOO HIGH, AND IT'D BE TOUGH TO CLIMB OUT THE WINDOW...
HE'D BETTER NOT HAVE HAD THEM BUILD ANY PEEP-HOLES...
APPALLED
HOW RUDE!
THIS IS A PERFECTLY NORMAL BATH-HOUSE!
THERE'S NOTHING ROMANTIC ABOUT TAKING SHORT-CUTS TO CATCH A GLIMPSE!
DON'T YOU KNOW THE SENSE OF ACHIEVE-MENT ONLY EFFORT BRINGS?
BA (FWIP)
I'D BE IM-PRESSED IF YOU WEREN'T TALKING ABOUT PEEPING.

A MAIDEN'S PURE HEART AND SENSE OF SHAME

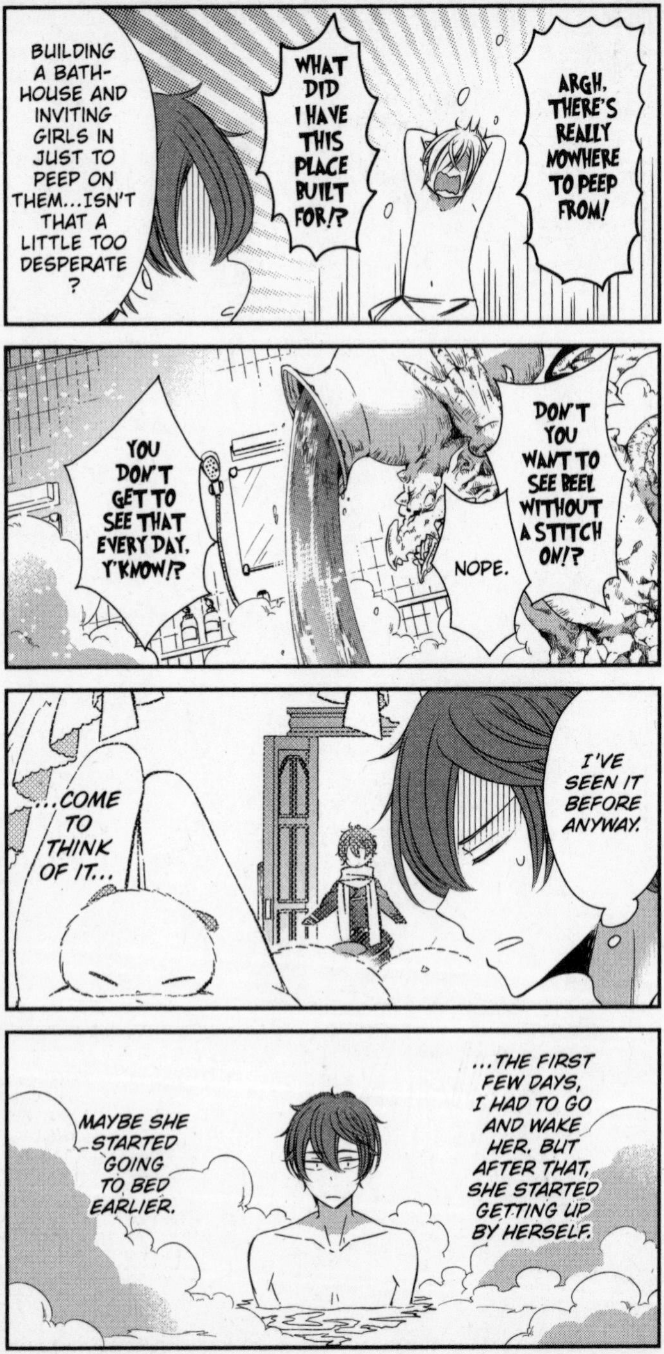
ARGH, THERE'S REALLY NOWHERE TO PEEP FROM!
WHAT DID I HAVE THIS PLACE BUILT FOR!?
BUILDING A BATH-HOUSE AND INVITING GIRLS IN JUST TO PEEP ON THEM...ISN'T THAT A LITTLE TOO DESPERATE?
DON'T YOU WANT TO SEE BEEL WITHOUT A STITCH ON!?
NOPE.
YOU DON'T GET TO SEE THAT EVERY DAY, Y'KNOW!?
I'VE SEEN IT BEFORE ANYWAY.
...COME TO THINK OF IT...
...THE FIRST FEW DAYS, I HAD TO GO AND WAKE HER. BUT AFTER THAT, SHE STARTED GETTING UP BY HERSELF.
MAYBE SHE STARTED GOING TO BED EARLIER.

WORRIES < HOT TUBS

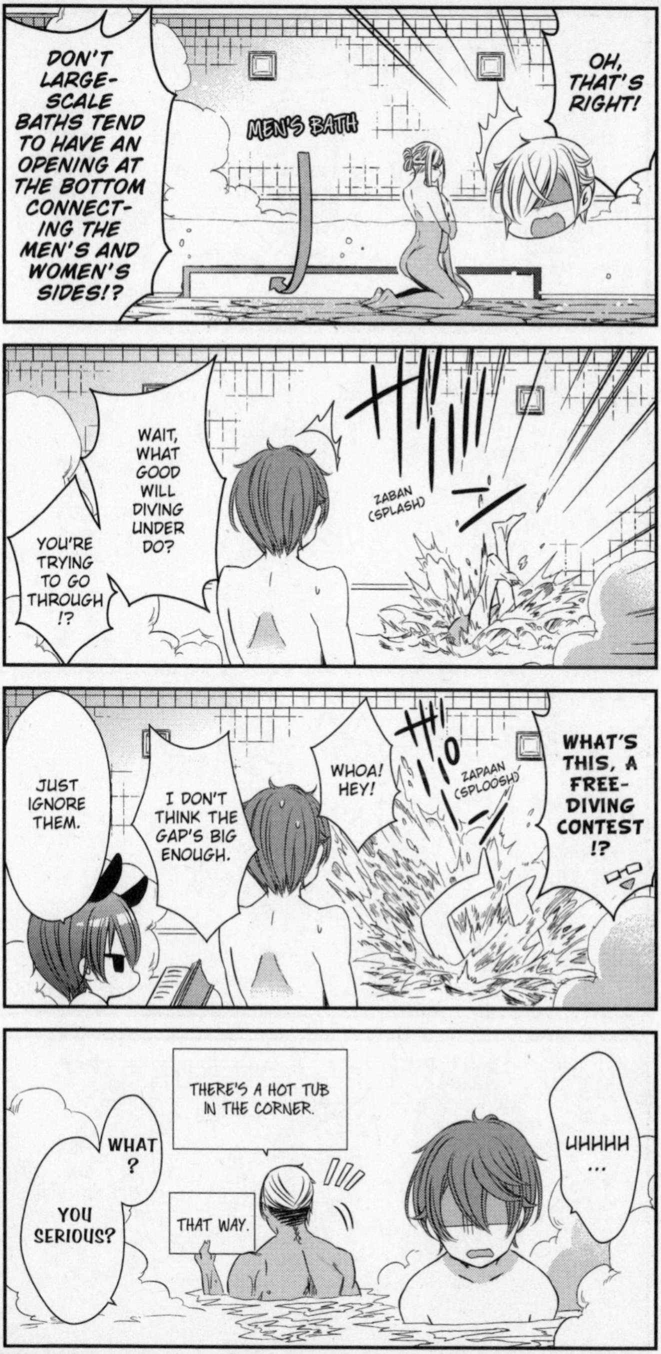
OH, THAT'S RIGHT!
MEN'S BATH
DON'T LARGE-SCALE BATHS TEND TO HAVE AN OPENING AT THE BOTTOM CONNECTING THE MEN'S AND WOMEN'S SIDES!?
ZABAN (SPLASH)
WAIT, WHAT GOOD WILL DIVING UNDER DO?
YOU'RE TRYING TO GO THROUGH!?
WHAT'S THIS, A FREE-DIVING CONTEST!?
ZAPAAN (SPLOOSH)
WHOA! HEY!
I DON'T THINK THE GAP'S BIG ENOUGH.
JUST IGNORE THEM.
UHHHH...
THERE'S A HOT TUB IN THE CORNER.
THAT WAY.
WHAT? YOU SERIOUS?

OUT OF BREATH

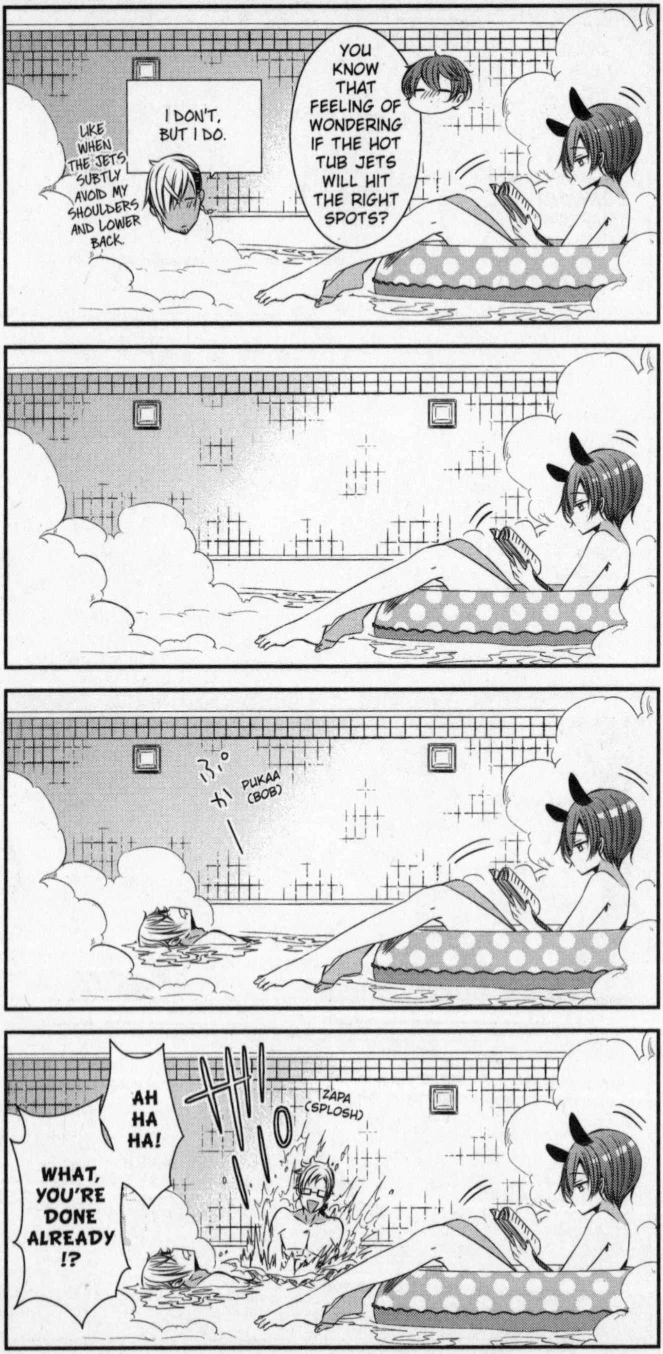

YOU KNOW THAT FEELING OF WONDERING IF THE HOT TUB JETS WILL HIT THE RIGHT SPOTS?
I DON'T, BUT I DO.
LIKE WHEN THE JETS SUBTLY AVOID MY SHOULDERS AND LOWER BACK.
ぷかー
PUKAA (BOB)
ZAPA (SPLOSH)
AH HA HA!
WHAT, YOU'RE DONE ALREADY!?

A FAMILIAR LINE OF REASONING

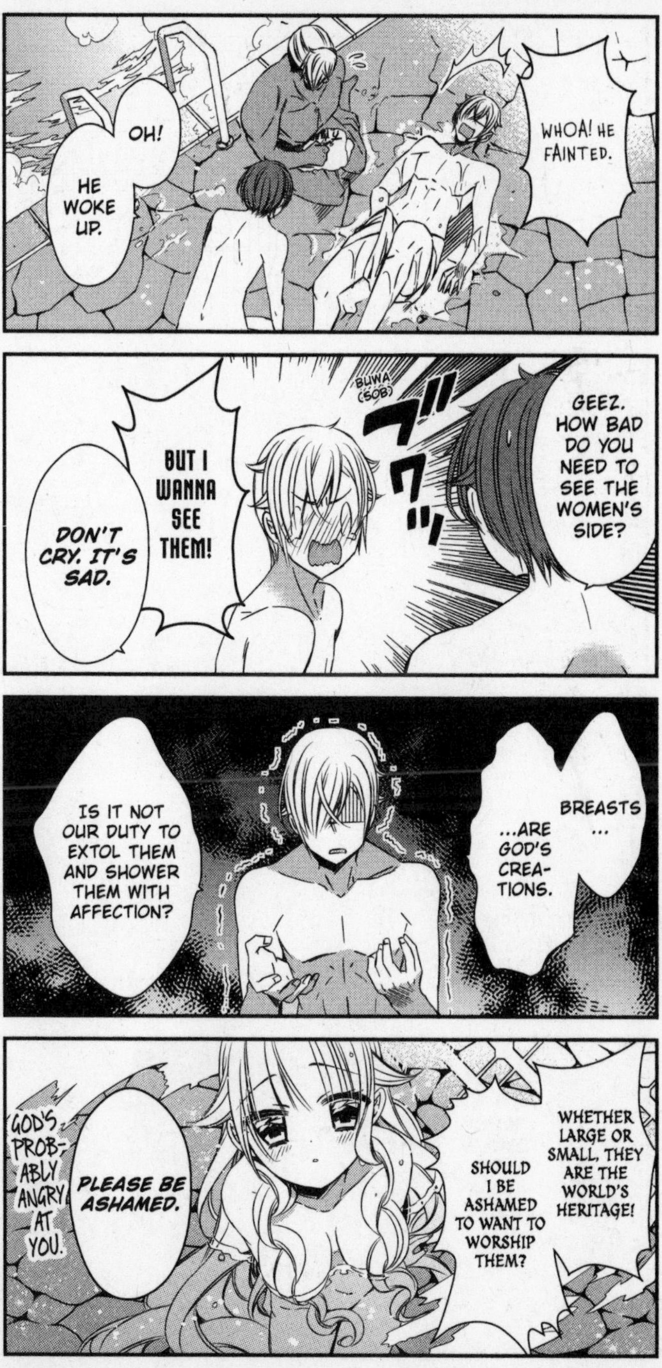

WHOA! HE FAINTED.
OH! HE WOKE UP.
GEEZ. HOW BAD DO YOU NEED TO SEE THE WOMEN'S SIDE?
BUWA (SOB)
BUT I WANNA SEE THEM!
DON'T CRY. IT'S SAD.
BREASTS ...
...ARE GOD'S CREATIONS.
IS IT NOT OUR DUTY TO EXTOL THEM AND SHOWER THEM WITH AFFECTION?
WHETHER LARGE OR SMALL, THEY ARE THE WORLD'S HERITAGE!
SHOULD I BE ASHAMED TO WANT TO WORSHIP THEM?
PLEASE BE ASHAMED.
GOD'S PROBABLY ANGRY AT YOU.

THE POLICE WILL COME

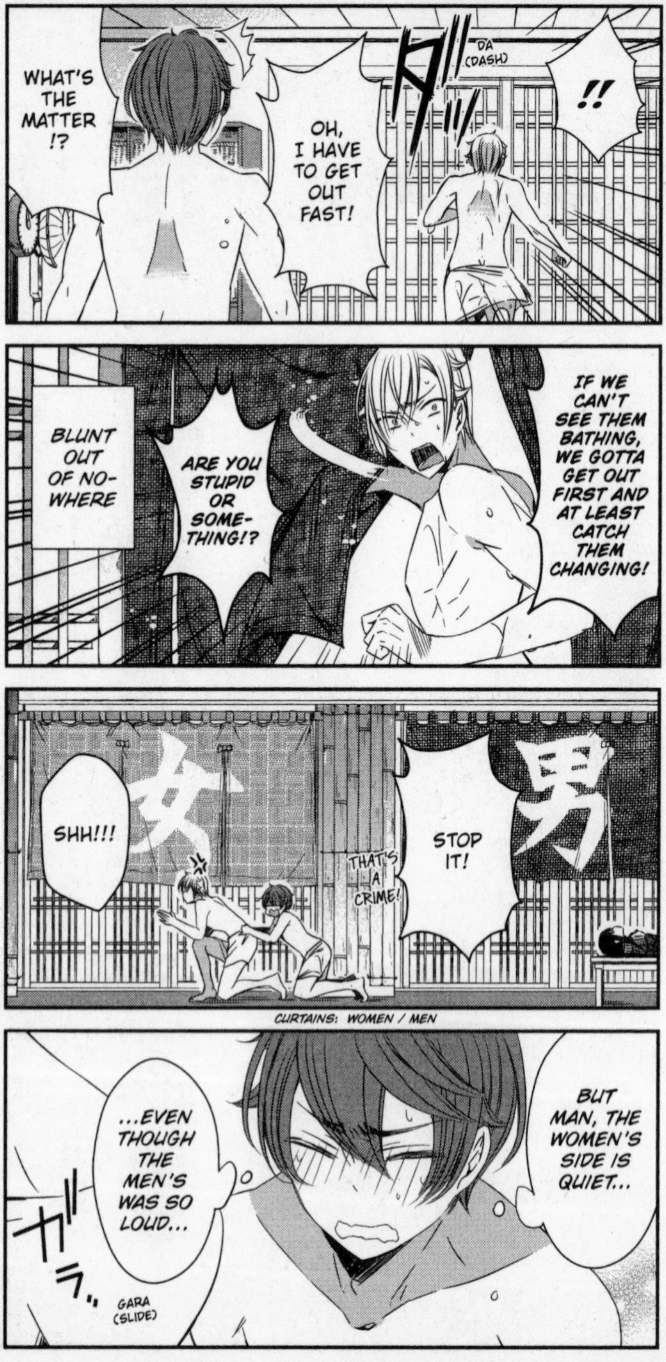
!!
DA (DASH)
OH, I HAVE TO GET OUT FAST!
WHAT'S THE MATTER !?
IF WE CAN'T SEE THEM BATHING, WE GOTTA GET OUT FIRST AND AT LEAST CATCH THEM CHANGING!
ARE YOU STUPID OR SOME-THING!?
BLUNT OUT OF NO-WHERE
男
STOP IT!
THAT'S A CRIME!
女
SHH!!!
BUT MAN, THE WOMEN'S SIDE IS QUIET...
...EVEN THOUGH THE MEN'S WAS SO LOUD...
GARA (SLIDE)

CURTAINS: WOMEN / MEN

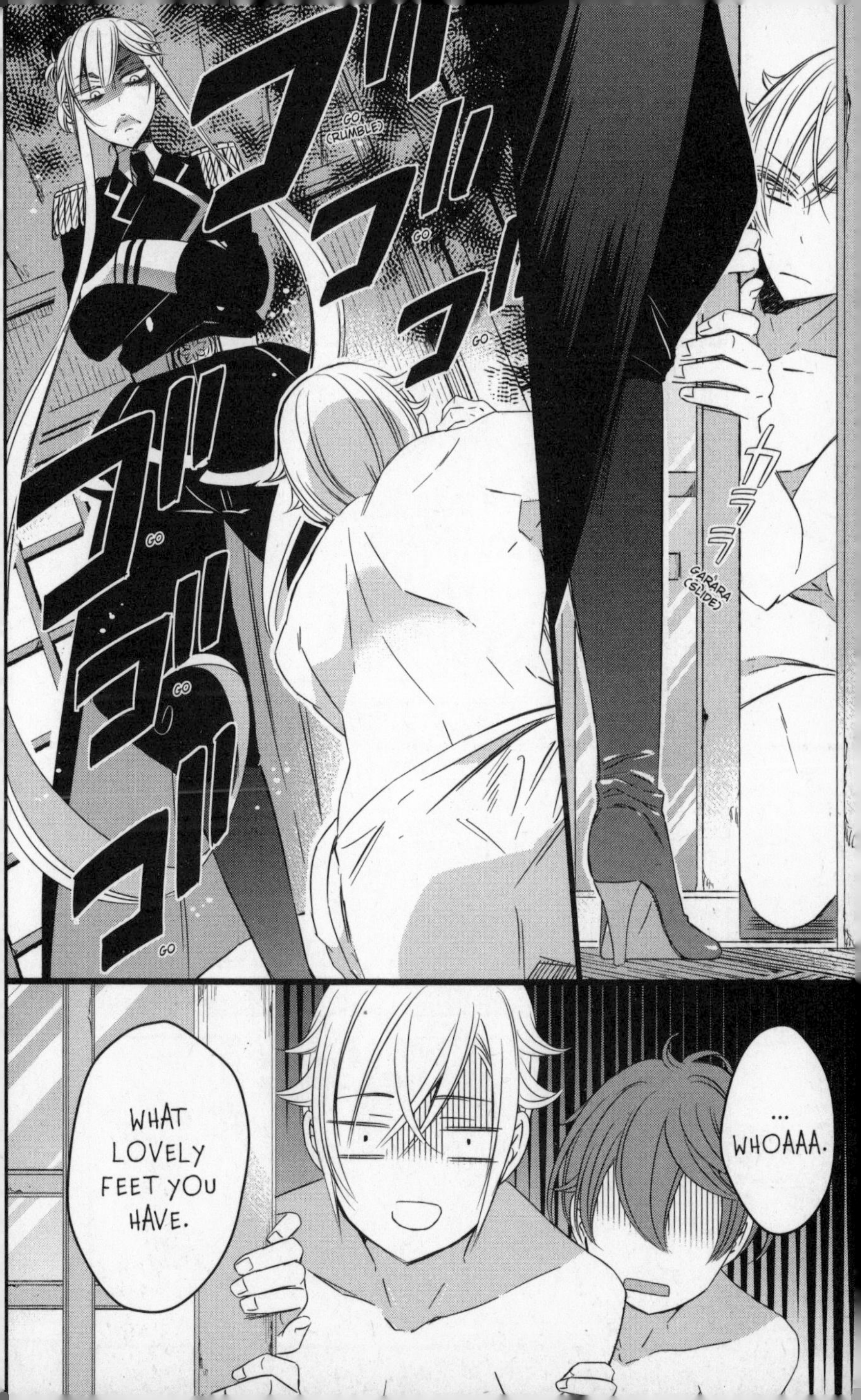
GARARA (SLIDE)
GO (RUMBLE)
GO
GO
GO
GO
GO
...WHOAAA.
WHAT LOVELY FEET YOU HAVE.

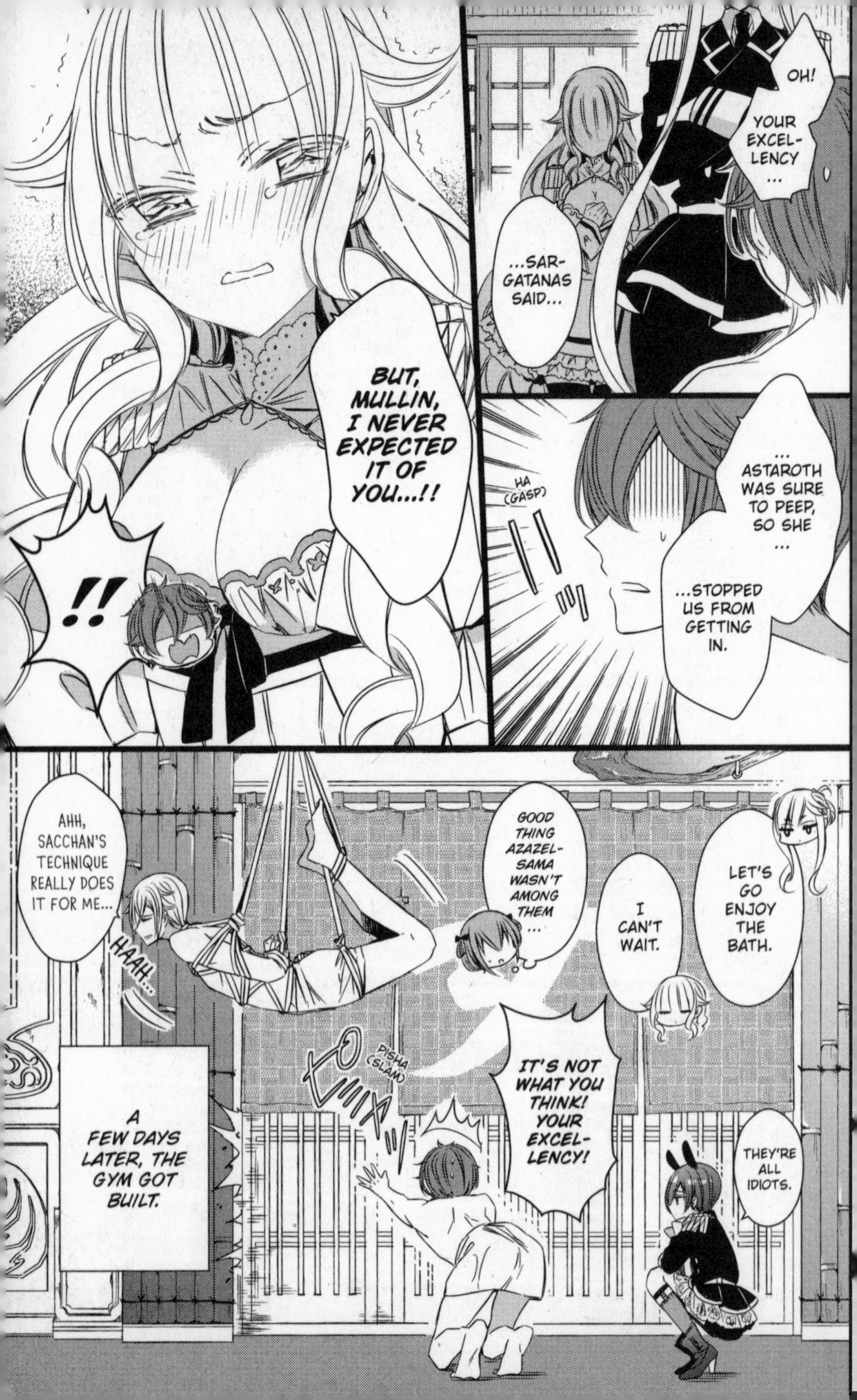
OH!
YOUR EXCEL-LENCY...
...SAR-GATANAS SAID...
HA (GASP)
...ASTAROTH WAS SURE TO PEEP, SO SHE...
...STOPPED US FROM GETTING IN.
BUT, MULLIN, I NEVER EXPECTED IT OF YOU...!!
!!
LET'S GO ENJOY THE BATH.
I CAN'T WAIT.
GOOD THING AZAZEL-SAMA WASN'T AMONG THEM...
THEY'RE ALL IDIOTS.
IT'S NOT WHAT YOU THINK! YOUR EXCEL-LENCY!
PISHA (SLAM)
AHH, SACCHAN'S TECHNIQUE REALLY DOES IT FOR ME...
HAAH...
A FEW DAYS LATER, THE GYM GOT BUILT.

CHAPTER 14 EXTRA

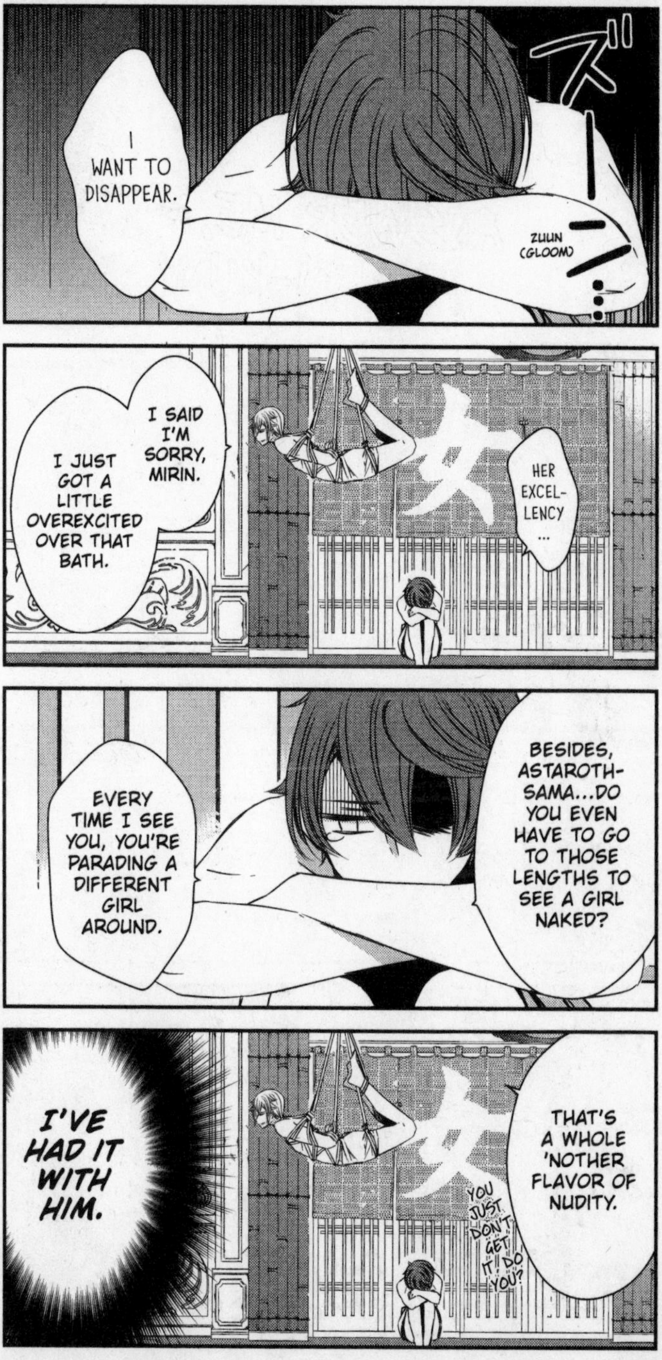
ズー…
ZUUN (GLOOM)
I WANT TO DISAPPEAR.
HER EXCEL-LENCY...
I SAID I'M SORRY, MIRIN.
I JUST GOT A LITTLE OVEREXCITED OVER THAT BATH.
女
BESIDES, ASTAROTH-SAMA...DO YOU EVEN HAVE TO GO TO THOSE LENGTHS TO SEE A GIRL NAKED?
EVERY TIME I SEE YOU, YOU'RE PARADING A DIFFERENT GIRL AROUND.
THAT'S A WHOLE 'NOTHER FLAVOR OF NUDITY.
YOU JUST DON'T GET IT, DO YOU?
I'VE HAD IT WITH HIM.

AS MISS BEELZEBUB LIKES VOLUME 2 END

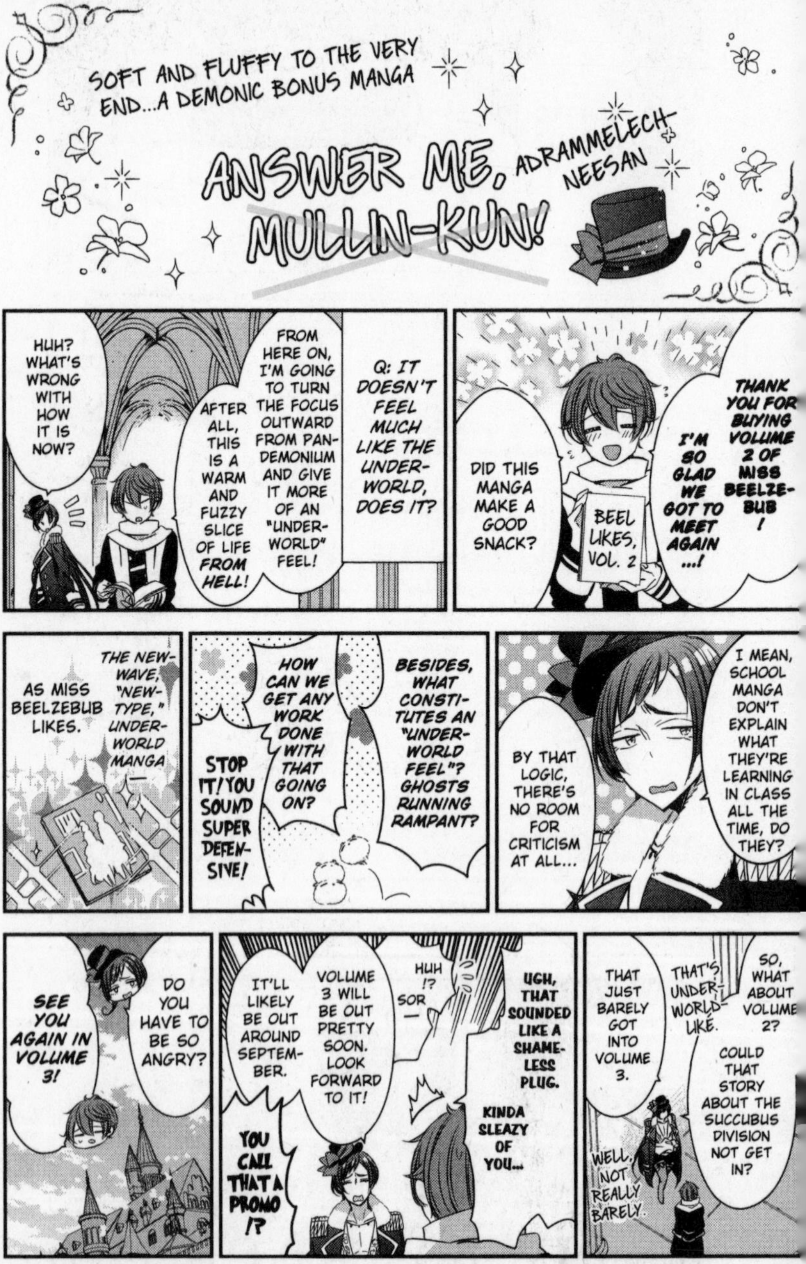
SOFT AND FLUFFY TO THE VERY END...A DEMONIC BONUS MANGA
ANSWER ME, ~~MULLIN-KUN!~~ ADRAMMELECH NEESAN
THANK YOU FOR BUYING VOLUME 2 OF MISS BEELZEBUB!
I'M SO GLAD WE GOT TO MEET AGAIN...!
BEEL LIKES, VOL. 2
DID THIS MANGA MAKE A GOOD SNACK?
Q: IT DOESN'T FEEL MUCH LIKE THE UNDERWORLD, DOES IT?
FROM HERE ON, I'M GOING TO TURN THE FOCUS OUTWARD FROM PANDEMONIUM AND GIVE IT MORE OF AN "UNDERWORLD" FEEL!
AFTER ALL, THIS IS A WARM AND FUZZY SLICE OF LIFE FROM HELL!
HUH? WHAT'S WRONG WITH HOW IT IS NOW?
I MEAN, SCHOOL MANGA DON'T EXPLAIN WHAT THEY'RE LEARNING IN CLASS ALL THE TIME, DO THEY?
BY THAT LOGIC, THERE'S NO ROOM FOR CRITICISM AT ALL...
BESIDES, WHAT CONSTITUTES AN "UNDERWORLD FEEL"? GHOSTS RUNNING RAMPANT?
HOW CAN WE GET ANY WORK DONE WITH THAT GOING ON?
STOP IT! YOU SOUND SUPER DEFENSIVE!
THE NEW-WAVE, "NEW-TYPE," UNDERWORLD MANGA—
AS MISS BEELZEBUB LIKES.
SO, WHAT ABOUT VOLUME 2?
COULD THAT STORY ABOUT THE SUCCUBUS DIVISION NOT GET IN?
THAT'S UNDERWORLD-LIKE.
THAT JUST BARELY GOT INTO VOLUME 3.
WELL, NOT REALLY BARELY.
UGH, THAT SOUNDED LIKE A SHAMELESS PLUG.
KINDA SLEAZY OF YOU...
HUH!?
SOR—
VOLUME 3 WILL BE OUT PRETTY SOON. LOOK FORWARD TO IT!
IT'LL LIKELY BE OUT AROUND SEPTEMBER.
YOU CALL THAT A PROMO!?
DO YOU HAVE TO BE SO ANGRY?
SEE YOU AGAIN IN VOLUME 3!

PREVIEW OF VOLUME 3 ☆

Who's this woman in the suspicious getup!? (Hint: She's flat as a board.)

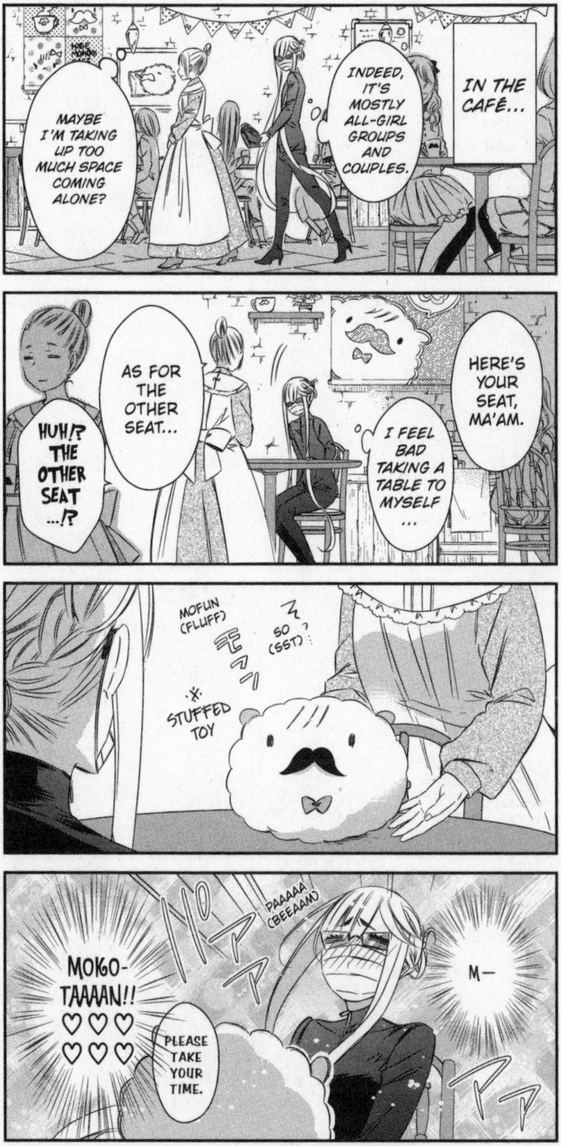
IN THE CAFÉ...
INDEED, IT'S MOSTLY ALL-GIRL GROUPS AND COUPLES.
MAYBE I'M TAKING UP TOO MUCH SPACE COMING ALONE?
HERE'S YOUR SEAT, MA'AM.
I FEEL BAD TAKING A TABLE TO MYSELF ...
AS FOR THE OTHER SEAT...
HUH!? THE OTHER SEAT ...!?
SO (SST)
MOFUN (FLUFF)
※ STUFFED TOY
M—
PAAAAA (BEEAAAM)
PLEASE TAKE YOUR TIME.
MOKO-TAAAAN!! ♡♡♡ ♡♡♡

SET FOR SEPTEMBER 2018!

...YOUR EXCELLENCY ...
UMM...
...IT'S FINE.
GO WHEREVER YOU WANT.
HEY! HOW SULKY DO YOU HAVE TO BE?
IT'S OBVIOUS I WAS JOKING!
IT'S NOT AS IF I'LL BE LONELY IF I NEVER GET TO SEE YOU, MULLIN ...
I'LL BE FINE.
LOOK, I'D NEVER APPLY FOR A TRANSFER...
...AND BESIDES, EVEN IF I WORKED ELSEWHERE, WE COULD STILL MEET UP!
LIKE, NORMALLY!
WHAT !?
WHAT !?

They're both too thick to get it! What fate lies in store for their budding romance...!?

AS MISS BEELZEBUB LIKES VOL. 3

As Miss Beelzebub Likes

matoba

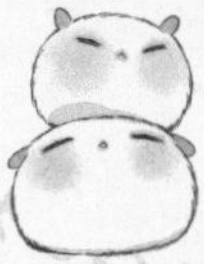

volume 2

Translation: Lisa Coffman
Lettering: Lorina Mapa

BEELZEBUB-JO NO OKINIMASU MAMA Vol. 2

First published in Japan in 2016 by SQUARE ENIX CO., LTD. English translation rights arranged with SQUARE ENIX CO., LTD. and Yen Press, LLC through Tuttle-Mori Agency, Inc., Tokyo.

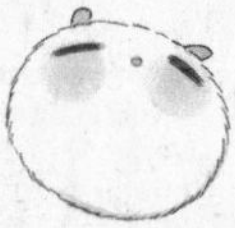

Yen Press
1290 Avenue of the Americas
New York, NY 10104

Visit us at yenpress.com

facebook.com/yenpress
twitter.com/yenpress
yenpress.tumblr.com
instagram.com/yenpress

First Yen Press Edition: June 2018

Yen Press is an imprint of Yen Press, LLC.
The Yen Press name and logo are trademarks of Yen Press, LLC.

The publisher is not responsible for websites (or their content) that are not owned by the publisher.

Library of Congress Control Number: 2017963582

ISBNs: 978-0-316-44771-3 (paperback)
978-0-316-44773-7 (ebook)

10 9 8 7 6 5 4 3 2 1

WOR

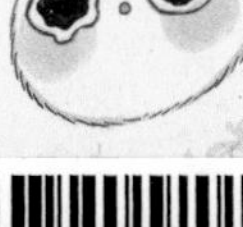

Printed in the United States of America